HOW WE DESTROY NIGERIA
HAVEN FOR FINANCIAL CRIMES AND CORRUPTION

JOHN WALKER ADETUNJI-ADEOYE

Facebook: Johnny JamJam

Instagram: Johnny JamJam - @JohnnyJamJam

Website: www.johnnyjamjam.com

Email: JohnnyJamJam@yahoo.com, contact@johnnyjamjam.com

ASCOLOGY LTD

Published By Ascology Limited

70 Allen Avenue

Ikeja, Lagos, Nigeria

ascology@yahoo.com, books@ascology.net

www.ascology.net

DEDICATION

To the memory of Junior, Adetayo, Kausarat, Zobodinar, Sylvester and all those I have lost untimely to the painful battle of death, mostly due to the Nigerian factor. May their souls rest in peace.

TABLE OF CONTENTS

ABBREVIATION & ACRONYMS

aka - Also known as
ANAN - Association of National Accountants of Nigeria
AP - Associated Press
APC - All Progressives Congress
ASUP - Academic Staff Union of Polytechnics
ASUU - Academic Staff Union of Universities
BBC - British Broadcasting Corporation
BCCI - Bank of Credit and Commerce International
BDCs - Bureau de Change
BRT - Bus Rapid Transit
BVN - Bank Verification Number
CBN - Central Bank of Nigeria
CCB - Code of Conduct Bureau
CID - Criminal Investigation Department
CNS - Chief of Naval Staff
DPO - Divisional Police Officer
DPR - Department of Petroleum Resources
DSP - Deputy Superintendent of Police
EFCC - The Economic and Financial Crimes Commission
FBI - Federal Bureau of Investigation
FCID - Force Criminal Investigation and Intelligence Department
FESTAC - Festival of Arts and Culture
FG - Federal Government
FGN - Federal Government of Nigeria
FMG - Federal Military Government
GDP - Gross domestic product
GIFMIS - Government Integrated Financial Management Information System
ICAN - Institute of Chartered Accountants of Nigeria

IDP - Internally Displaced Person/People

IG - Inspector General of Police

IIA - Institute of Internal Auditors

IPPIS - Integrated Payroll and Personnel information system

LGAs - Local Government Areas

MAMSER - Mass Mobilization for Self-Reliance, Zero Justice, and Economic Recovery

MDAs – Ministries, Departments and Agencies

MTN - Mobile Telecommunication Company

NAA - Nigerian Accounting Association

NAPTIP - The National Agency for the Prohibition of Trafficking in Persons

NBA - Nigerian Bar Association

NBS - National Bureau of Statistics

NDDC - Niger Delta Development Commission

NDIC - Nigeria Deposit Insurance Corporation

NFIU - Nigerian Financial Intelligence Unit

NIPOST - Nigerian Postal Service

NLC - Nigeria Labour Congress

NNPC - Nigerian National Petroleum Corporation

NITEL - Nigerian Telecommunications Limited

NYT - New York Times

OBT - Obtaining by Trick

ONSA - Office of The National Security Adviser

PENGASSAN - Petroleum and Natural Gas Senior Staff Association of Nigeria

RMAFC - Revenue Mobilisation Allocation and Fiscal Commission

SAN - Senior Advocate of Nigeria

SARS - Special Anti-Robbery Squad

TSA - Treasury Single Account

UN - United Nations

UNODC - United Nations Office on Drugs and Crime

UNILAG - University of Lagos

VOA - Voice of America

WHO - World Health Organisation

ACKNOWLEDGEMENTS

I have always believed that writers and historians must speak to people directly connected to the issues they address. I also believe that there must be no disconnection between the content of their books and life realities. In that regard, I must extend my profound gratitude to the several individuals who took me through the world of underground and criminal activities. That list includes politicians, racketeers, drug peddlers, pimps, "*yahoo*" boys, lawyers, military officials, private investigators, police officers, and some underground individuals who took me through the many life challenges in the Nigerian society. I commend these people who decided to help, as they were first-hand witnesses or actual perpetrators of activities that led Nigeria to the current state of anarchy we find ourselves in today. They spoke to me and supplied me with credible and vital information that has helped me understand the devastating effects of crime and corruption throughout different phases of our national history. I have decided not to mention a single name of these credible informants of mine; to keep them completely anonymous, as it should be.

I must acknowledge every book, media, publishing house and website whose works are cited and referenced in this book. Their contribution to the history of Nigeria, especially concerning its many challenges, is highly commendable. A special thanks to the late Stephen Ellis, whose book on the historical development of financial crimes in Nigeria is not just applauded by my humble self but vital to understanding crime in Nigeria.

I must also acknowledge my father, Mr LT Adeoye, whose constant words "an unacceptable proportion of Nigerians are criminally minded," however derogatory, resonated throughout my childhood and adulthood. Those words led me to a deep world of exploration to find out how accurate his opinions are and to uncover why many Nigerians share such a similar opinion.

The comment section of social media pages is one of the underestimated inventions of our time. It has allowed me to read people's minds, hear their opinions and know the individual, sectional and general perceptions of Nigerians. To the comment section pages and to every Nigerian whose opinions were used in the moulding of this book, I say thank you.

By the way, THE J IS CONSTANT!

AUTHOR'S NOTE: HOW TO READ THIS BOOK

This book, like its prequel, will not afford the reader a haven for grandstanding or political correctness to dwell. This will not be an attractive book to read, I assure you. It is a natural phenomenon of humans to be unimpressed by things that paint them negatively. This book is best read without the carriage of sentiments or emotional bias that have become partly responsible for the Nigerian situation. This book is best understood when read along with its prequel: *HOW WE DESTROY NIGERIA: PRECEDENCE OF DOOM.*

Truth hurts, and it hurts deeply. I do not know of any indigenous herbal medicine that works miraculously and superbly well but is not bitter to consume. In truth, this book is like such medicines. It has always been a universal human behaviour to suppress unfriendly ties to oneself or to one's family, ancestry, race, ethnicity, religion or other forms of association where possible. Non-Nigerians are not captured in the development of this book, and their activities relating to the Nigerian situation are not scrutinised. This book identifies only the citizens, including the author, as this country's problem. Also, every group, society, community and region has been identified as the originator of the woes and chaos of our nation.

To state clearly, the reader of this book should be mindful that the use of the word "we" in the title of this book was not accidental. "How We Destroy Nigeria" will show the roles played by every citizen of this country, both living and dead, in shaping present-day Nigeria.

This book is written in simplified Nigerian English. The author fully intends to ensure that the average Nigerian is able to comprehend this book in the simplest and most relatable way possible. It is a book on Nigeria, of Nigerians, by a Nigerian and for Nigerians. Lengthy titles and names of organisations and bodies have been abbreviated to make for better reading. Vital illustrations for this book can be found online at www.johnnyjamjam.com/books

Key moments, events and highlights of issues in the country's history have been marked in bold. Each chapter's end has a subchapter that defies the conventional style in book publishing. It is intentional and allows me to write, conclude and "speak" inelegantly, unedited and directly from my heart as a concerned Nigerian. If the reader were an enemy of raw truth, I might humbly advise that particular aspect of the book to be flipped over.

Topics in this book spill into the other since many of the country's problems are related and interwoven. Suppose the reader finds out that a particular topic or example has not been addressed in a particular chapter. In that case, I implore the reader to rest assured that the topic is in discourse in another chapter as a matter of relevance. For instance, matters relating to fraud and financial crimes have been spread into other associated areas. Also, political matters and issues relating to corruption are interwoven in other chapters, and so on.

1 : HOW WE SABOTAGE NIGERIA'S ECONOMY

A nation's economy is not independent of other factors, especially those that are socially and politically interwoven. The issues discussed in the prequel to this book are concomitant factors that have come to cause serious harm to our nation's economy. With such issues left unattended, there is no doubt that the economy will suffer considerably. Similarly, as you will read in this book, there are other accompanying factors that are sure to make a nation's economy comatose.

Contrary to the opinion of a large segment of people from the South, the North once differed from what it is today. Northern states encountered foreign traders as far back as the 16th century and blissfully traded various items and commodities that were exported to North Africa and other Arabian countries. As early as the 18th century, northern aristocrats and noblemen had established significant trade partnerships with foreign individuals. They successfully forged commercial relationships with foreigners throughout the region of West Africa and beyond. Kano, for instance, was a bustling city of commerce and one of West Africa's largest hubs for trade before the 21st century. Today, Kano has become a shadow of what it used to be. It has become plagued by various attendant drawbacks of social and economic progress; religious intolerance, rioting, violence, insurgency top the list.

Similarly, although some areas of the South could be argued to have developed geo-structurally, their people have not. For instance, it has become impossible to understand how the south-south region of Nigeria has remained impoverished to this very day. It was the first of the regions to encounter Western traders before any other did. When trade in commodities began, they benefitted immensely. When trade in humans began, they engaged in it and became the chief traders in the West African region. After palm oil and rubber replaced human exchange, the South-South emerged as the go-to region. Yet, foreigners who visited the south-south region before and during colonialism spoke of pervasive poverty and human neglect that was condemnable in every sense.[1] The region and its people remain impoverished despite the discovery of oil, which became the region and the country's major revenue source.

Since independence, Nigeria has suffered from economic downturns of all kinds. Nigeria has had its fair share of various economic systems, policies, planning, ideologies, and programs. Nevertheless, it is safe to assume that our economy set off on the wrong foot immediately after independence. Bribery, corruption, nepotism, political patronage, maladministration, and theft surreptitiously crept into the economic affairs of the new nation. Politicians and public office holders who took over the management of affairs from the colonialists and other foreign groups did not administer their roles to build an economically viable country. Instead, occupants of various economic seats saw their new-found positions as avenues to amass personal wealth.

When economists talk analytically about specific economic policies adjudged to be desirable, or not, to particular climes, they do so without paying attention to other prevailing factors that can impede or stimulate such policies. For instance, Western scholars were adamant that socialism and communism were bound-to-fail concepts and pushed resenting notions to the world. They championed the cause of capitalism and other esteemed allied ideologies without paying attention to their practicalities in different world climates. Today, Westerners have learnt to embrace some aspects of socialism, which were once arrogantly criticised by their leaders and scholars. Similarly, the global population have come to acknowledge that capitalism or socialism could succeed or fail, depending on the significant actors and players of the policies in focus.

Intentionally, this book does not entertain the various economic ideas and policies that carry counterfactual conditionals regarding their possible resultant effects. Instead, as you are about to read, many Nigerian leaders and managers lacked the credential, commitment, genuineness, credibility and initial dedication to steer the ship of the nation's economy in the right direction. What is also documented is the average citizen's ready-to-steal mentality and readiness to take full advantage of unconstrained economic loopholes.

It is also glaring that citizens' apathy and inability to demand concrete accountability from their leaders is also a significant reason for the economic collapse of our various entities. State and local government officials are not inclined to work progressively to improve their constituencies. Instead, they rely heavily on federal allocations to run their affairs. State and local government officials have turned public assets into their private affairs, making it difficult to distinguish public establishments from private ones at the lower tiers. As you will read, there seemed to be an agreement between state authorities and the citizens to send the country's economy into a perpetual state of comatose; an arrangement that both parties disingenuously continue to deny.

A "Water in a Basket" Economy

As early as 1970, Nigeria's economy proved to be one that was bound to fail. Different cataclysmic problems began to emerge immediately after the nationalisation of the petroleum sector in 1971. From that period, we systematically suffocated any hope of growth other sectors could have had. Even sadder was that we replaced other once thriving sectors with bribery, fraud and corruption as informal sectors of their own.

Suppose the oil and gas sector was the country's only source of revenue. Then the failure of leaders to ensure its optimal use and devoid of corruption is responsible for the woes that befell the sector and, by extension, the Nigerian economy. We are a country that permits the extraction of crude oil to be exported out of the country, only to spend huge sums of money to import its refined forms. At the initial stage, when the country was sending its oil out for refining, it did not occur to our leaders to work diligently on creating new refineries or protecting available ones from the ills of maladministration. Little did it occur to leaders that more refineries were needed for an unpredictable future? We have become a country where the oil and gas sector is unarguably the most corrupt, despite it being the major source of revenue for the country.

There was no point in time since independence that the economic situation of things could be said to be satisfactorily commendable. Nigeria's economy began to dwindle when its managers laid the groundwork for the systematic involvement of all things necessary to facilitate the collapse of any economy. Citizens, rather than disapprove of the brazen feasting on the national cake by their political and economic leaders, also took advantage of every backdoor left open to them.

Shortly after the creation of the regional governments and before the country attained independence, the regional and federal governments embarked on development plans to transform their respective economies. Since independence and to this day, several development plans have been put into gear by respective governments, both at the federal and state levels. Nevertheless, socio-economic policies such as the indigenisation and privatisation policies, SAP, and MAMSER, ended up ignominiously. They did not end up ruinously because they were terrible theoretically, but because the actors, players, participants or even the beneficiaries were themselves the catalysts for their failure.

Bad managers and actors are more capable of ruining perfect ideas than running them. On the other hand, bad ideas with excellent managers and

4

actors can provide excellent results. In a clime where blame games have become part of our national culture, it is necessary to understand that managers and actors of economic societies are essentially integral and inseparable aspects of each other. Economic managers include presidents, policymakers, ministers, governors, executives, directors, permanent secretaries, entrepreneurs, managers and supervisors. Actors include the people listed as managers and the general public, a list that includes civil servants, public workers, middlemen, contractors, private workers, consumers and, of course, the overall citizens.

Shortly after we became an oil economy, leaders began to spend money like drunken sailors. Stolen, wasted, misappropriated, missing, diverted or even untapped; Nigeria's money and resources have never been felt by the citizens but by an infinitesimal group of kleptocrats and their families and cronies. Areas such as steel, cocoa, palm oil, textiles, rubber, mining, coal, manufacturing, agriculture and others suffered devastatingly. According to the Nigerian High Commission in London:

> Nigeria used to be one of the largest producers of tin in the world, with production based around the highland district of Jos. Production collapsed from an average of 10,000 tonnes per year in the 1970's to 300 tonnes in 1995. Tin reserves are estimated at 16,000 tonnes. Independent estimates place iron ore reserves at 800 million tonnes, averaging 37 % metal content. Iron ore mining began in 1984 and 1989 reported a stockpile of over 500,000 tonnes. By 1997, it was unlikely that iron output was more than 50,000 tonnes per year.[2]

It is evident that Nigeria does not lack the resources to cater for its people; it lacks adequate planning, proper management, credible socio-economic leadership, and political governance. Many Nigerian political and economic leaders are intellectually lazy. They do not think about the future and are concerned with securing what is available for them to steal throughout their tenure in office. It is a scary challenge for them to invest in what the future holds: a future they are frightened that when the benefits come, they may not be in office to partake in the profits that come with such ideas. As we know, the country has abundant human and natural resources, yet leaders and citizens alike are only interested in the immediate gains. Although the world has evolved, Nigerians have not. An unacceptable portion of Nigerian youths carries the notorious mentality of entitlement to social media spaces. They would rather be spoon-fed and given "giveaways" of $10 than $1000 worth of business orientation and industrial acquisition skills. The youth population, as studied on social media, have shown that the future is very bleak as regards commerce and industry in the country.

An economy that hopes to fetch water in a basket is one that is bound to fail. A former minister once said that the Nigerian economy was exporting cassava but importing *garri*.[3] For reasons bordering on unfavourable factors of production, most entrepreneurs would prefer to look towards imports than produce locally. Bad roads, insecurity, lack of infrastructure, inaccessible loans, corruption, indiscipline, depreciated currency, epileptic power supply, unpredictable socio-economic and political climate, and many other factors are responsible for why genuine businesses and industries cannot function adequately. These setbacks continue to put Nigerian businesses, entrepreneurs and even public establishments at extreme disadvantages and where they cannot compete favourably.

Outside of oil, Nigeria produces next to nothing and imports everything. Federal, states and local governments have refused to encourage the production of material goods outside the oil and gas industry. Today, the majority of the 36 states of the country are unproductive and are a liability to their people and the country's purse. The LGs under them are even worse. The "Abuja" money, as it is called, has become all they have to execute their regional projects. They have become ineffectual regarding income and revenue generation. It has been reported that some states have been borrowing to pay salaries for years. In general, some states have been debt-ridden for far too long than necessary.

Nigeria's loss continues to be the gain of more organised countries. The global world of manufacturing, tourism, sports, food, trade, entertainment, and technology enjoys substantial progress because of the overwhelming patronage of Nigerians who consume their products in absurdly high proportion. The Nigeria of today, or our dreams, has no business importing foods or raw materials that we have handy. That makes a paradoxical description and mockery of our national flag and emblems, which symbolises agriculture and abundant natural resources. It is foolhardy to expect our economy to experience relative growth as much as we continue to abandon our economies for international competitors.

Today, we suffer the effects of the devastating policies and misconduct of previous generations. Their failure to facilitate adequate electricity supply has continued to haunt the country's overall growth. No country can expect progress with unstable and unreliable electricity distribution. Skyscrapers are unable to be built. Farmlands, manufacturing, production, etc., cannot function optimally; rather, they rely on highly expensive self-generated power supply systems. Yet, Nigerians in need of a stable power supply ironically pamper unscrupulous citizens who continue to sabotage the little efforts made by the government to provide stable power. Vandals sabotage our power cables, electric transformers and other necessary materials. The stolen items are sold to crooked businessmen who know quite well the adverse effect their activities would cause to communities and the entire nation.

Nigeria is a land of many missed opportunities. In fact, the argument that the country has degenerated worse than it was, has some attached facts, even if I were not inclined to accept the generality of that statement. The movement of goods and raw materials from one region of the country to another was through rail as far back as the colonial era. Today, the country's rail industry is in a severe state of neglect. Lorries, trucks and other articulated vehicles spend strenuous time on perilous and laborious roads to deliver goods from one region to another. A functioning rail system is all the country needs to ensure that such unproductive means of transportation have no place in modern Nigeria.

At the three tiers of governance, revenue generation in the country seems like rocket science to the country's administrators. Despite their fanciful and eloquent electioneering speeches, most come into offices to find archaic and malfunctioning systems for which they have no idea how to make corrections or gear for effective running. For instance, they get into office to find out that only a meagre population pays their taxes. Tax evasion is prevalent among the same population of citizens and businesses who demand the growth and progress of a country that they deprive of its appropriate contributions. A large population of the country's adults have never paid tax throughout their existence as income earners. So notorious is the issue of tax evasion that a former finance minister said just 214 people pay taxes above N20 million or above despite the country being home to so many multimillionaires and billionaires.[4] Tax evasion itself is something that has the connivance of officials of federal, state and LG revenue officials. Along with the connivance of such government agencies, individuals and businesses would prefer to offer kickbacks than pay their fair share into the government's coffers. Nevertheless, that is just one out of several means of revenue generation that inefficient political and economic administrators in the country are incapable of utilising.

What kind of country expects to function economically when 90% of government expenditure is recurrent? What kind of country expects to function when at a point, an alarming 100% of government's revenue was said to be used for debt servicing? In fact, recurrent expenditure as a percentage of total expenditure is as high as 115% on average in the last 10 years.[5] What kind of country expects economic growth when its capital expenditure is often neglected, and even when budgeted for, such funds find their way into private pockets? According to the former finance minister Kemi Adeosun, in 2015, it was discovered that the amount budgeted for travel expenses was N64 billion. At the same time, the amount spent on roads was N19 billion for the whole country. What kind of country expects to grow with such impracticable disproportionate spending? How do we empower our young ones to be economically productive when we spend public funds on pilgrimages and personal fulfilments of people rather than investing in commerce, business education, creativity and talent management? A lot of the relevant answers and issues will be discussed in due course.

In truth, we are a wasteful country. We rely on impracticable economic systems that encourage leakages, waste and economic fruitlessness. As should have been realised, we must conclude that our economy is like fetching water in a leaking bucket; but how long shall we expect the fetched water to hold?

Ruins: The Sad Story of the Nigeria Airways

Many Nigerians usually wonder what happened to some of the country's once efficient MDAs and government-owned establishments. The appropriate answers to feed their curiosity correlates with the problems associated with the country's economy. The personnel of affected establishments had no business in the running of affairs of such high-profile entities. They have top executives and employees who never had any genuine intention of promoting or engineering the success of the organisations they are employed to administer. The same could be said of most staff and personnel below them in the pecking order.

The sad and scandalous case of the defunct Nigeria Airways should illustrate everything that went wrong, and is still wrong, with non-functional corporations and MDAs in the country. How did a corporation like Nigeria Airways, which was once the pride of the nation, allowed getting to a debt-ridden state and becoming an eventually dead entity? Understanding the factors that hindered the organisation should give the reader an accurate knowledge of what took place in other similar government establishments.

The appointment of unqualified and corrupt managers to manage the affairs of Nigeria Airways was not the only explosive problem that eventually buried the corporation into the ground. Societal leaders from all walks of life manoeuvred their ways and bypassed procedures without paying applicable flight fees. They would often pack their entourage of travellers, mostly family members, into NA flights with the connivance of airline and aviation officials without making appropriate payments. It is also on record that some elite citizens accorded themselves special privileges such as ordering flights to be delayed until they are ready to board, much to the chagrin of other passengers. Ticketing officers and agents took advantage of an inefficient and archaic system to issue duplicated tickets that were attached to the same seat numbers to multiple customers. Overbooking caused by corruption and fraud meant that airports became disorderly as passengers jostled for seats on overbooked commercial planes, with each person claiming the right to seat ownership.

Manifest lists were tampered with at the last minute of a flight departure for devious reasons. It was done to replace rightful passengers with others (especially VIPs, "big men", or those who could bribe their way to have their itinerary treated with some degree of urgency). In addition, it was done to extort genuine but naive flight passengers before their names could be included on the final manifest. Passengers marked for extortion but failed to do the "needful" were frustrated or even prevented from embarking on the particular flight and possibly subsequent ones unless they did the needful. In fact, officials would rather have a plane take-off with numerous empty seats than cave in to intransigent authentic customers who refused to pay bribes.

Missing passenger items and broken luggage became commonplace. Thieves and saboteurs infiltrated the Nigeria Airways cargo division and looted cargoes and customer items. Harassment and unruly behaviour towards passengers and customers by staff and airport handlers became a way of life. While these narrated events were customary noticeable features that infringed upon the rights of customers and passengers, some other catastrophic events similarly happened behind closed doors. Some of which were:

- Senior public officials diverted the salaries of junior officials and personnel.
- Private contractors who were denied their entitlements for reasons bordering on corruption stopped providing essential services and engagements.
- For mostly selfish or political reasons, officials were hiring more personnel than necessary to such an extent that overstaffing became a significant financial burden on the airline and an eventual alleyway to its debt and collapse.
- Unpaid staff, especially NA mechanics and engineers, started to rip and sell off aircraft materials to make up for their unpaid salaries.
- Civil litigations and judgement debts against the NA continued to pile up and eventually took a devastating toll on the company.
- Incomes generated by the NA were manipulated and diverted by corrupt officials to short-change the government.
- Despite its moribund stage, the government's appropriated funds to heal the financial wounds of the NA were diverted for personal use.
- Aircraft and valuable spare parts were acquired at significantly overvalued figures or, in some cases, not bought at all despite funds allocation for their purposes.
- Foreign organisations sanctioned Nigeria Airways for failing to comply with applicable safety protocols, some of which included hefty fines or suspensions.

As those continued, the organisation concurrently bled profusely, and several ill-treated passengers and customers started to seek alternatives. The simultaneous introduction and emergence of more private airlines and aviation companies were sufficient for even the most ardent customers of the Nigeria Airways to look elsewhere for patronage. Some unforgiving customers blacklisted the Nigeria Airways and its services as a result of the traumatic experiences that they had suffered. Short on financial revenue and customers, yet simultaneously suffocated by persistent corruption and fraud, the company was unable to continue its operations and was forced to shut down. Today, Nigeria Airways is dead, and the rest is history.

I have to say again that the reader of this book can use the story of Nigeria Airways as an illustration of all that went wrong, perhaps still ongoing, with other MDAs at federal and state levels.

In 2001, President Olusegun Obasanjo set up an inquiry to investigate Nigeria Airways' activities between 1983 and 1999; the reports were shocking. It revealed that an estimated $400 million (as of 2003) were stolen by officials and their cohorts. It was gathered that a former minister sold off aeroplanes without proper authorisation. It was also discovered that properties of the company were sold for half the estimated values for reasons that border on corruption, fraud and economic sabotage.[6]

The Nigeria Airways was not the only sufferer in the aviation industry. Other airlines and businesses in the aviation sector suffered damaging losses. The syndrome of fraud and corruption started to find their way into foreign airline companies, who began to view Nigerian travellers with deep suspicions. Foreign airlines lost money because of counterfeited travelling tickets. They also lost money due to fines incurred anytime foreign authorities detected Nigerian travellers made use of fake entry visas or travel documents to board their commercial flights. Crooked individuals used

12

stolen credit/debit cards to book flight tickets for passengers only for the airlines or ticketing agencies to experience an electronic chargeback later on. Fraud became prevalent that some airlines had to open offices in the country for strictly cash-based transactions, and only people whose names were compiled from the offices were allowed to fly.

Generally, trust in the aviation industry declined. Stakeholders started withdrawing their investments and interest from the country's aviation industry. Local and foreign passengers who used the country's airports recollected how airports became flooded by all manners of people, some with ill intents. The country's airports could not be differentiated from traditional markets with hawkers, thugs, touts, racketeers, and the needy taking refuge in them.

As the aviation industry was met with severe setbacks, its sister industries, such as tourism, travel, shipping, transport, maritime, and the railway, also got their dosage of the Nigerian "down" syndrome. The story of the Nigeria Railways Corporation is another sad story that is not any different from the events that ran the Nigeria Airways to the ground. Ticket racketeering has become an identifiable feature at railway stations. Ticketing officials do issue dud tickets or at inflated prices. Traders, hawkers, marketers, swindlers, beggars, destitute and others have taken up refuge at various rail stations, making life uneasy for actual passengers. Despicable individuals sabotage rail lines by breaking up the rails and their components for eventual sales on the black market.

In modern-day tourism, a country's rail transport system is vital and inseparable from its tourism industry. It is the cheapest means of transport for citizens and foreigners to unique and fanciful destinations. A rail transport system that makes life unbearable for passengers will affect tourism and the economy. Of relevance and about to be explained, we can further understand the collapse of the Nigerian economy through an analysis of what went wrong with the tourism sector.

The Collapse of Culture and Tourism

Unlike the aviation industry that still enjoys some form of patronage today, the ruin of the culture and tourism industry was rapid. In fact, the decline in the country's tourism industry preceded the usual concomitant factors that are natural killers of tourism in any country, such as insurgency, terrorism and general insecurity. Although those factors became the nail in the coffin of tourism in Nigeria, terrible economic management and the dependency on oil had done enough damage. Tourist attractions across the country that once enjoyed local and global patronage have become an eyesore. A visit to any present-day zoo or other conservative centres with a careful study of how animals kept there are treated will introduce a reality that symbolises the state of the nation; hunger, starvation and bad management. As top officials divert public funds meant to discharge their duties, junior officials equally divert animal foodstuff and items for sale on the black market. People who had no business being in the business of tourism or its sub-divisions were hired to draw wages for reasons that border on nepotism or political patronage.

Some government administrators who tried to improve tourism had their plans thwarted by successive administrations for reasons bordering on negligence, incompetence, maladministration or corruption. Private practitioners and experts who lobbied governments to take drastic action regarding the state of the country's tourism sector were ignored. Those who took it upon themselves to create private tourist attractions had their business severely impacted by the inseparable negative socio-economic and political chaos.

Former governor of Cross Rivers, Donald Duke, built an applaudable recognition for himself as an ardent champion of tourism in the country. Before his tenure ended in 2007, he had turned the ancient city of Calabar into the country's tourism capital, including creating the Tinapa Free Trade Zone and Resort Centre. However, by 2020, the much-celebrated, renowned, and heavily invested Tinapa tourist attraction had been severely hit by the Nigerian disease of maladministration and political inconsistency. By estimate, the failure of Tinapa to kick fully into existence (at least continuously) cost taxpayers and private investors an estimated $2 billion in financial investments; a monumental loss in an already bleeding economy for both the state and the federal government.

Sports, which could have helped cushion the economy of states in the country suffered its own woes. Stadiums are abandoned and left to rot. Equipment and facilities are plundered and looted by everyone who could. People without passion for sports are appointed as administrators and managers.

Decades before now, some countries have used similar issues detrimental to our growth to their advantage. For instance, religion as a tool to cause bloodshed has become a source of revenue for countries globally. Britain, through Anglicanism, has ensured that some of its finest cathedrals are open to tourists from around the globe. The Vatican and the Italian government have ensured that religious sites are protected and used to bring tourists to ancient sites for revenue purposes. Germany, Iran, Portugal, Sri Lanka, India, Nepal, Greece and Turkey have ensured that their tourist destinations, especially those connected to religion and spirituality, are well protected and enhanced to attract global visitors. Hindus, Buddhists, Muslims, Christians and Jews, among others, carefully select their favourite destinations annually to fulfil their personal and religious satisfactions. Some may argue that pilgrimages and tourism are slightly different, yet they are conjoined twins in the world of commercial travelling and economics.

Saudi Arabia is said to welcome an average of 2.5 million tourists to the country, thereby recouping estimated revenue of $12 billion annually from the hajj alone.[7] According to the National Portal of India, religious pilgrimages in India contribute $40 billion annually to the country's economy.[8] The figure could be much higher when we consider other pilgrimage-induced forms of tourism. Some aspects of religious tourism are connected to archaeological tourism and heritage tourism. That is because some sites cited in Abrahamic and other religious books are of interest to global visitors. Yet, Nigerians have decided to shed the blood of one another, cause divisions and inflict pain on their fellow citizens over religious matters that have become beneficial to the actual importers of the religion they claim to hold dear.

Religious tourism in Nigeria is not adequately harnessed and not taken seriously by the country's citizens. Ironically, such a statement contradicts how citizens take matters such as religious crusades, conventions, outreach programs and other religious programs that are primarily associated with Pentecostal churches. The adverse effects of the place of religion in our nation seemed to overshadow the positive influence. For instance, religiously occasioned forms of violence and bloodshed have been responsible for why foreign tourists and religious visitors prefer other destinations than geographical Nigeria. We continue to be our own enemies even in areas and matters that demand piety that we claim to have in abundance when we possess it in the least quantifiable measure.

Federal and state governments sanction pilgrimage programs abroad to the detriment of the country's tourism sector, thereby creating devastating effects on the national currency and economy. The death of Nigeria's tourism was sure to be certain with the practice of going on holy pilgrimages using state resources. Religious pilgrimages are not of concern to me as an author, and it is furthest from my intention to question individuals' intention to fulfil their spiritual obligations. However, it amounts to contempt for reality and fairness when people of religious faith find it convenient to embark on pilgrimages through public funds. It is inappropriate to divert public funds to fulfil the religious wishes of a few citizens in a country where almost all necessities of daily life are absent and where citizens are in dire need of infrastructural developments. In the 2021 federal appropriation budget, the FG appropriated a total of N2.6 billion to finance the pilgrimages of private citizens to the Holy Lands. The figure becomes much

16

higher when funds from states and other public institutions are summed. Public officials have used their positions to siphon funds to fulfil citizens' religious yearnings. As the country continues to witness rapid debt increase, such gross illogicality does not indict authorities but also the beneficiaries. In all of these, it is sad that debt-ridden states that should naturally promote local and regional tourism have become the facilitators of foreign tourism.

Expecting political leaders and their cronies-in-chief to help grow the country's culture and tourism industry might be foolhardy. Incidentally, the country's leaders do not seem to believe in its ability to flourish or in building and maintaining infrastructural amenities. On the other hand, they have agreed with opinions from a certain segment of the population that the country was doomed. Recent events involving the country's political leaders are appropriate to cite as examples. The wife of former President Chief Olusegun Obasanjo, Stella Obasanjo, died in a foreign clinic while Obasanjo was in power. The country's former president, Umaru Musa Yar'Adua, died in a foreign hospital while serving his term in office. The incumbent president notoriously spent enormous time seeing his doctors abroad for a sizeable period of his term in office. Most of the country's governors, ministers, commissioners and other political and public office holders have children all over the world for educational purposes.

Curiously, one is left to wonder what kind of humans we have been so unfortunate to have running our social and economic affairs. Leaders and citizens jointly lost hope in the country. Rather than attempt to revive the country's sectors, they jointly orchestrated its downfall further. For instance, federal and state governments, MDAs, NGOs and private citizens started to embark on "educational tourism" abroad. Leaders abandoned the country's educational institutions and sponsored indigenes abroad for reasons bordering on sycophancy, the patronage system, self-embellishments or outright fraud. Shamefully, some of such foreign sponsorships were to neighbouring countries of Benin and Ghana.

Nigerian citizens, like their political leaders, are part of the culture of shame that sent the tourism sector comatose. For all they care, it is a badge of honour to travel abroad, talk fancifully about foreign destinations and ensure to promote those places at no cost. Having noticed that many Nigerian social media influencers, celebrities and famous figures post notable destinations abroad and urge their followers and fans to travel to those places, I decided to find out the reasons behind their actions. Perhaps it could relate to the nature of commercial relationships between those Nigerians and the management of those foreign entities they promote. From conversations I had with some of the country's famous figures, I found out they do not get paid but rather do so for "packaging" reasons and to ensure that their persona as showbiz personalities remains polished. What kind of people sabotages their own country, even at personal economic and social cost? I was curious to find out what was responsible for the low patronage of Nigeria's tourist destinations and why relationship between them and the country's famous figures and influencers was not cordial. A confidential source who is a top-level manager at the popular Obudu Mountain Resort answered my question even further in an email response to my request:

> The issue is that many of these people are selfish, most especially members of the media and your so-called celebrities. (They are) very selfish people, I can tell you. We have cases where the media would demand an enormous amount of money to advertise for us, which is not a problem, but then we hear they have travelled abroad and spent huge sums of money to cover those places for free. So, you are telling us you will pay to cover foreign places abroad but want us to pay you enormous amounts to give us media coverage? The celebrities are not any different. I understand they have to get paid as popular figures and all that. But do they get paid when they go to Dubai, London and all those places and post them all over their social media account? I can tell you they do not. We have a package

18

for popular celebrities and always tell them to come here for free. We offered them hotels and stipends for travel to ensure they do not have to spend from their pockets just because we want them to help us advertise our resort to the world. Still, they would rather spend their money to fly abroad to foreign locations, take pictures and advertise those places for free. This is very sad. And we are wondering why our ranch and others cannot compete with foreign ones. We are doing our best to revive these places, but Nigerians are not helping matters. You will agree that it is a waste of resources to continue to spend enormously without revenue or patronage. The tourism industry in Nigeria bleeds for support, but we Nigerians are our problems.

As the tour manager lamented above, our collective mentality towards patriotism, national growth and development are shocking. Yet, we wonder how we are in today's situation when obviously we jointly set out to kill all sectors of our economy by day and lament bitterly at night. Tourist centres in Nigeria have become a gathering of ruffians and misfits who sell drugs, and molest visitors. The famous Lagos beaches like the Bar Beach, Elegushi, Oniru and Atican beaches have become notoriously crowded by disturbing elements that should typically have no business with tourism and cultural lifestyle. As I said in the preamble to this subchapter, the country's tourism sector has been further nailed to the coffin by the presence of insecurity and needs no further analysis. It is foolhardy to expect foreign visitors to tour a country where they fear they could be kidnapped, maimed or even killed. Many Nigerians continue to lament the unemployment rate in the country, yet insecurity is a killer of any hope that the country has to revive employment and job creation.

Our wildlife is threatened by the continuous killings and destructions of animals and other natural species. Illiteracy, poverty and ignorance are not excuses for a man to kill and eat what is available today to the detriment of what would fetch him and his community food for a lifetime. It is common to see people engage in the butchering and consumption of wildlife animals that they come across when such animals could be fed, preserved, managed and controlled for tourism purposes.

Traditional and cultural items are stolen from their various places of keep and shipped abroad to collectors. State-owned museums across the country are silently pilfered and emptied by nefarious individuals who prefer to collapse the country's tourism industry to the merit of their account balance. Nigeria is not working because every one of us has made it a mission to destroy, sabotage, steal and send our economy into comatose.

Indeed, Nigeria has had its fair share of opportunities to display and sell the aspects of its cultural values to the rest of the world. We have had opportunities to cement our place as a global hub of tourism and cultural commerce; but we failed woefully. Nigerians colossally stifled such opportunities as they came. One such opportunity was the Festival of Arts and Culture in 1977 (FESTAC' 77). FESTAC '77 was one missed opportunity to sell our cultural images (collectively as a nation or heterogeneously) to the rest of the world and cement our place as a hub for Pan-Africanism and Black culture. Tourism would have been a strong contender for a place in the country's source of revenue at the time of the event when Nigeria was coping with a severe economic crisis. Some years before the event, Nigeria had witnessed a period of a massive boom in oil revenue, only to be faced with an economic recession shortly before the event got started as the global price of oil stabilised. The columnist, Levi Obijiofor, had this to say about FESTAC '77.

> FESTAC was marked with so much flourish and excitement. Lagos and other major cities experienced massive flood of overseas visitors. Streets were decorated with FESTAC emblems. Special vehicles, in particular buses were imported to ease transport problems. The airwaves were jammed with radio jingles about FESTAC '77. The

government constructed a FESTAC village in Lagos. Decades after the event, that part of Lagos is still known as FESTAC Town. Experienced and promising entertainers comprising actors, dancers, musicians, singers, comedians and high-profile scholars celebrated and rejoiced with Nigeria. No one remembered that Nigeria was under the oppressive rule of military dictators.[9]

On the road to the FESTAC event, Nigeria's FMG budgeted more than enough for the cultural event and was eager to host a successful outing. But as the FMG took an unprecedented step in affording Nigerians a chance to showcase their beautiful culture to the world, and with lots of money to go around, a heightened culture of theft, embezzlement, and corruption crafted its way into FESTAC '77. The successful and widely applauded event became an avenue for avaricious individuals to display their culture of destructiveness and sabotage.

A retired arts officer stationed at FESTAC '77 and an avid art collector told me how the event became an avenue for embezzlement and theft. He explained how civil servants and public office holders jettisoned their initial positions for transfers to FESTAC-related activities. He described how citizens connived with foreign expatriates to dupe the Nigerian government through grossly inflated prices and contract frauds. Nigerian contingents at FESTAC '77 were short-changed by those who should have catered for them and resource officers diverted funds and resources meant for their upkeep.

I reliably gathered from numerous sources that FESTAC '77 was the silver platter that was given to art thieves who carted away some of the country's most prized historical artefacts with the connivance of crooked collaborators in the country. Their activities further contributed to the death of the Nigerian tourist industry.

Rather than sell positive images of Black arts and culture as intended, Nigerians sold an impudent culture of theft, embezzlement, fraud, indiscipline and corruption to the rest of the world. Immediately after the event, civil servants and private collaborators plundered the facilities, items, equipment and remnant of funds for the event. Today's housing district known as the FESTAC area of Lagos was hurriedly maladministered into the hands of public officials and their cronies. For a fact, nothing better illustrates the charade of shame called FESTAC '77 than the FESTAC area of Lagos. The area has become tainted with filth, hooliganism, cultism, robberies, violence, crime and every other embodiment of societal decay. **Festival, Arts, and Culture indeed!**

Although FESTAC '77 was a missed opportunity despite costing the country billions of naira, Nigerians later encountered other sociocultural events that cost them monumental figures despite lacking tangibility, feasibility or even accountability. Cultural and social events in Nigeria would later become an avenue for people to steal whatever they could. The African Nations Cup football tournaments, the FIFA-U21 World Cup in 1999, and the Commonwealth Heads of Government Meeting (CHOGM) in 2003, among other cultural, political and sports events were all accompanied by so much wastage and corruption. Facilities and equipment used during the events became individuals' private properties, and subsequent similar events faced the challenges of budgeting for newer items and equipment. Sports events in Nigeria, such as the Nigerian University Games Association (NUGA), the Nigeria Professional Football League (NPFL), and the National Sports Festival, have become riddled with bribery and corruption.

Fraud and corruption in sports and their umbrella organisations have gone on to affect the participation of our sportspersons in global events such as the Olympics, the World Athletics, the Africa Cup of Nations, and the FIFA World Cup tournaments. From a country that terrified fellow African countries and, to an extent, the global world of football in the 1980s and 1990s, we have become an experimental joke of a nation. Our recent performances at continental tournaments have not echoed our "Giant of Africa" status. With an estimated population range of 130-210 million people over the last few decades, the country has only been able to escape with a consolation of three (3) gold medals, eleven (11) silver medals and thirteen (13) bronze medals in the history of the Olympic Games despite billions of naira that had been appropriated for participation at the events. The country has failed to make it past the Second Round of the FIFA World Cup despite boasting a prideful population of young footballers that are scattered all over the country.

It has been reported that Nigerian athletes go on self-sponsored training and appearances at international games to boost their performance, recognition and professional career. Sports events are some of the recognised and standardised ways of highlighting a country's prowess and to display the skills and intellectual dexterity of its citizens. And when Nigeria and Nigerians are found lagging at such events, it shows that our so-called "beautiful cultures" that we so flamboyantly love to talk about, are nothing other than patriotic fabrications and very different from reality.

Outside sports, one is forced to ask the significance of some relevant MDAs in charge of cultural promotions in the country. For instance, the National Arts Theatre has been in abject condition for decades and cannot compete against the rise of modern cultural inventions. The National Arts Theatre, the Nigerian Television Authority and others have proven incapable of competing with modern sociocultural developments like social media, Video on Demands, YouTube, Netflix, and other streaming/new age inventions in cultural and information dispensation. We could strongly argue that our thriving entertainment industry is an autopilot one that does not enjoy the support of any relevant government organisation. Funds that have been disbursed to act as relief or provide grants to industry experts by development banks or other agencies have been diverted by a few or shared to unqualified persons.

While it is true that socio-economic disruptions typically ensure the relegation of conventional apparatuses to the backstage of affairs, the failure of a national monument like the National Arts Theatre to live up to its reputation is critically due to maladministration and inefficiency. A similar publicly owned entertainment centre like the O2 Arena in London, UK, still stands strong and serves profitably. Sitting not far from the O2 Arena is the prestigious Wembley Stadium in London, which has served the English people, and, by extension, the global community of sports and entertainment. Yet, our stadiums and other monuments have been nothing but graveyards, characterising our usual culture of wastage and redundancy.

Nigerians are aggressively unpredictable in areas of social consumption or acceptability of innovative indigenous practices. Despite being home to a large pool of rich cultural heritages, cultural flamboyance and traditional practices, which have been abandoned at home, the Nigerian contingents at foreign carnivals (such as the Notting Hill Carnival in London) are large and noticeable. One could also ask how and why foreign cultural practices such as Halloween, school proms, and thanksgiving, among other Western celebrations, have been accepted by many youths. Generally, Nigerian youths are largely unpatriotic and are quick to turn their back on anything that carries indigenous or national symbols, no matter how competitive or innovative it is in nature. As we have realised, the instruments for cultural exports are limited or non-existent in Nigeria. Yet, the imports of foreign cultures directly for our consumption are made available to us. By our hands, we have defiled cultural and traditional activities that should have been good for us. We have made mockeries of practices that should have become industrialised into economic and commercial vitalities.

The once-celebrated Eyo Festival in Lagos is a prime example of how we used our hand to kill our cultural prospects. The Eyo festival is a celebration of Yoruba cultural heritage that is exclusively performed in Lagos (the Lagos Island specifically) through exquisite dancing and acrobatic displays by masquerades in typical white robes and attires. It became so celebrated that residents are known to empty the entire streets of Lagos mainland and the hinterlands to witness the beautiful culture and a celebration of history and tradition on its Island. Again, the Nigerian factor set in. The decline of the festival started with the unhelpful attitude and character of the festival actors and players. The festival became known for sporadic gangster violence and rival cult clashes than the actual display of the rich cultural heritage of Lagos.

There is a darker side to the shameful display of events that often overshadows the brilliant festival. Lagos Island, the traditional home of the festival, had secretly become a breeding ground for cultism, gangsterism, hoodlumism, drug peddling and usage, and other criminal activities. As far as I could tell and had witnessed in person, the festival became an opportunity for rival gangs to take advantage of the "unknown man behind the mask" feature of the Eyo masquerade to attack one another to the detriment of onlookers, tourists, and entire citizens. These acts are sufficient to destroy the reputation of what ought to have been a glorious celebration of cultural heritage, avenue for tourism, provision of jobs and other accompanying benefits of similar festivals around the world. The Eyo Festival, therefore, became a lost opportunity that should have enabled us to document and package the beautiful city of Lagos and its people to the rest of the world. Yet again, Nigerians became the architects of sociocultural collapse. Some of the problems facing the Eyo Festival are similar to other cultural practices like the New Yam Festival, Argungu Fishing Festival, and Osun Osogbo Festival, to name a few.

Hostile receptiveness or disinterest in matters concerning their native cultures and traditions also play a vital role in our cultural degradation. For some not-so-friendly reasons or those affiliated with pure taste, trend or fashion, we have become a people who would readily desecrate our indigenous ideas and creativities. In truth, there are affiliated reasons why many Nigerians view their cultural practices with resentment. Much of such has been discussed in the relevant chapter of this book's prequel. For many others, their dislike for anything Nigerian is out of pure ignorance and lack of patriotism. They have concluded that nothing good could ever come from their traditional practices or Nigeria. Nigeria's Minister of Information and Culture, Lai Mohammed, once learnt a bitter lesson as he got ridiculed over a harmless suggestion he had made to promote a vital part of the country's cultural heritage and create jobs for most youths. Here are his words:

> Most states today have more than one festival a year, but the packaging and lack of capacity have not enabled them to make the most out of these festivals. If this masquerade is well-packaged, it can provide employment in one week for more than 1000 young men. These are some of the untapped potentials. I worked in the airport for 10 years, and I know that if you want your passport stamped as a foreigner, you slip $100 into your passport. No tourist would come back to a country where he has to bribe immigration to enter. No tourist would come to a country where, when he leaves immigration, he enters a 'one-chance' taxi or 'one-chance' bus. It's a holistic problem and these are all contained in the national tourism master plan, which I would make available to the house. We must make a difference between tourist sites and tourist attractions; what we have in Nigeria are tourist sites. They are not tourist attractions. You need infrastructure to convert a tourist site to a tourist attraction. If you don't have infrastructure, it would always remain a tourist site.[10]

A well-thought analysis of the above statement by Lai Mohammed should typically embolden concerned stakeholders to find ways to industrialise the tourism sector by following the laid down suggestions of the minister or finding other ways around it. But then, Nigeria happened again. A bandwagon of social media hooligans lambasted the minister's opinions. Today, some new hoodlums exist in their own right and have become more destructive than the conventional weapon-wielding ones; they are the inflammatory boys and girls of Twitter and other social media sites. In addition, there are always trendsetters for every topic regarding national discourse, such as the one that emanated from the minister's desk. This time, they were the political bulldogs of opposition political parties and people whose survival on social media streets thrives on disorder and anarchy. Sadly, Nigerians fell for the unpatriotic gimmicks of those elements that launched riotous and contemptuous attacks on such an innocuous proposition. One of such disreputable social media personality is a man called Reno Omokri, who had this to say on his Twitter handle:

> First it was manufacturing pencil in 2 years by Onu, now Lai Mohammed wants our youths to become professional masquerade dressers. Issorai!.. No problem Lai. If APC's idea of job creation is dressing up masquerades, why don't we give your kids that job.[11]

Firstly, it is disingenuous to highlight and focus on "masquerade dressers" out of all the issues the minister raised. Omokri and his cohorts were uninterested in educating fellow citizens on the catastrophic consequences of corruption at our airports. They also failed to use the medium to galvanise support for the facilitation of tourism by creating tourist sites and attraction centres, as opined by the minister. All that mattered to them was how they could make a mockery of a man who, despite his countless mistakes on several issues, actually got that one right.

A popular but erroneous perception that precipitated their attack is that natural resources and conventional business buildings are the solitary routes to building a vibrant economy. Of course, they thought wrong. Today, it is an unfathomable truth that some football clubs in Europe are richer than some states in the country. Without Nigeria in the equation of comparison, tech giants Google, Microsoft, Apple and Facebook are, independently, mathematically richer than the West African nations combined.

As regards festivals, I feel compelled to bring to the reader's attention something about the lackadaisical attitudes of Nigerians towards improving their cultural exports. Even worse, we have become accustomed to having an unpatriotic syndrome to matters bordering on improvements in our social and economic lives. The Notting Hill Carnival in London best illustrates the failure of African countries to take massive advantage of their cultural heritage and profiteer from its display to the outer world. The Notting Hill Carnival is an annual festival event that has taken place in London since 1966 and currently boasts an estimated 2.5 million attendees.[12] The overall economic impact of £93 million as far back as 2002, and 3,000 full-time equivalent jobs and even larger part-time jobs per year were enough for the London government to grant organisers an annual contributory fund of £710,000.[13]

In a country like Nigeria, where corruption stinks and where officials are quick to use opportunities that should serve the public interest for their upliftment, the British government taught us another lesson on how to deal with economic saboteurs. When the carnival organisation's former finance director stole £800,000 after making 530 transfers into her private bank account, disguising them as payments to carnival suppliers and others, she was sentenced to six years in prison.[14] The Notting Hill Carnival is just one out of many numerous carnivals or festivals that are held in several regions across the world.

Nigeria is a grossly overpopulated country with an equally matched number of those without jobs. The economy is bleeding and we must explore every avenue to create jobs for the teeming population of unemployed youths. When I converse with Nigerians, they talk fancifully about our abundance of natural resources and believe it is all the country needs to move forward. Modern-day reality disagrees with their perception, at least partially; and the fact that some European football clubs are richer than some state governments, at least in mathematical terms, is enough to understand that the abandonment of culture and tourism in Nigeria is a collective woe that we cannot afford to permit any longer.

The Sad Tale of Agriculture in Nigeria

I must reiterate that this subchapter, like other aspects of this book, will try not to delve into the various agricultural policies that should have worked or not. It will also not focus on theories, policies or programs. Rather it will focus on the intentional human factors that affected the agricultural sector.

At the time of British departure in 1960, agriculture accounted for well over half of our GDP. It was also the main source of export earnings and public revenue. The share of agricultural products in total exports was above 70% in 1960. Today, the country's agriculture exports to total exports remain below 2%. Agricultural raw materials exports (% of merchandise exports) in 1963 stood at 18%, but today it is shamefully less than 1%.[15] Before independence, Nigeria was the world's major exporter of palm oil products. As far back as the 1950s, the Food and Agriculture Organization was commending palm oil exports from Nigeria for "remarkable improvement in quality".[16] Today, palm oil has become unaffordable to Nigerian citizens, much more sufficient for exports. To further understand the collective shame, here is a recent analysis from the audit firm PricewaterhouseCoopers:

> Between 2016 and 2018, the country's total agriculture exports was driven by export of sesame seeds, fermented cocoa beans, cashew nuts, ginger, crude palm kernel oil, soya beans, frozen shrimps and prawns, among other commodities. Cumulatively, the country earned N0.53 trillion from agriculture export between 2016 and 2018. In contrast, Nigeria's total agriculture import bill over the same period stood at N2.39 trillion. As a result, agriculture trade deficit stood at N1.86 trillion. Thus, the country is a net food importer.[17]

The rapid change from an agriculture-based economy to an oil-based economy did more harm than good. The ruinous condition of the agricultural sector started when the country's political leaders embarked on an oil-only driven economy. It continued when citizens started to see agriculture as a "for the poor only" sector. In their mass numbers, citizens began to abandon agriculture to seek white-collar jobs in urban areas. Although it could be argued that Westernization, globalisation and urbanisation were killer effects of agriculture, the human catalysts for such effects must shoulder the blame. Initially, at least as far back as the 1960s and early 1970s, the importations of food items were not seen as a problem since the country had so much money to spend at that time and "money was not a problem", as a former head of state had stated. So much money, like never experienced or imagined, was coming in from oil, which had replaced agriculture as the country's source of revenue. Unknown to many Nigerians then, they were nowhere as rich as they thought, and futuristic problems were looming with their abandonment of farmlands and over-reliance on food importations.

As citizens (especially educated, elite and middle-class) abandoned farmlands and the agricultural sector, they also imbibed attitudes and beliefs that became detrimental to the sector and the overall economy. Importation and consumption of foreign food items were seen as a pride badge and one that carried status embellishments. Citizens no longer saw the need to consume locally produced food items for reasons that border on taste, fashion, trend, satisfaction, health, preference or mere aggrandisement. Consumers were not alone. They had simultaneous support from retailers, wholesalers and importers, who all jumped on the economic nature of demand and supply to make quick profits through the sales of foreign agricultural produces. The results of such mental constructs are what we suffer today, especially because such practices have become a cultural phenomenon among today's Nigerians. In fact, I could say affirmatively that some Nigerians began to see the consumption of locally grown items as one of impoverishment and a badge of poverty.

The most relevant question on the lips of concerned foreigners is how we lack amid plenty and how a country with abundant arable lands has become afflicted with the problem of food scarcity. With a devastatingly high population of impoverished people, how do we expect to feed them when we rely on imports? How did we become a people who mock our national symbol, which carries agricultural characterisations, by importing items and commodities that could be easily produced on our national soil and even distributed beyond our shores at no inconvenience to our population? All things being equal, the nation itself can feed the whole of West Africa with its abundant supply of agricultural resources, yet we are a severely underfed nation.

The agriculture sector itself is heavily reliant on other sectors. For instance, 21st-century agriculture cannot be carried out significantly using crude items such as hoes, cutlasses and axes. The uses of such crude equipment are only viable to feed individual families but are unsustainable to feed a community, let alone a grossly overpopulated nation. Apart from feeding the population, mechanised involvement using modern-day equipment is compulsory to cope with the competitive global market. Sadly, modern farming has been left in the hands of rural farmers who rely on crude methodologies to make ends meet. They cannot optimise productivity enough to feed their community, let alone the nation or for export purposes.

The driving factors of agriculture became inefficient or even non-existent to move the sector forward. Such factors include transportation, infrastructure, road networks, credit facility, and government support. It is inconceivable to expect inefficient trucks to convey food items from far distant areas of the North to the South and vice-versa. As times evolved and the country failed to improve on electricity and other important aspects of sophistication, it was sure to hamper the efforts of the agricultural sector. Banks in Nigeria do not offer adequate loans to those in the agricultural sector. When they do, they offer flawed and unfriendly interest rates to farmers. Those banks would rather have their loans and credit schemes handed over to top politicians during electioneering due to the illicit returns that come with potential victories for their supported candidates. The Bank

31

of Agriculture and other similar institutions meant to cater to agriculturalists in the country have challenges of all kinds that make their presence more of a cosmetic than an actual financial support sector.

Despite their penchant for rebuking their political leaders, Nigerians must learn to take some forms of responsibility for their own recalcitrant and unpatriotic acts, a bulk of which has led to today's problems. The former head of state, General Olusegun Obasanjo, during his stint as military head of state, introduced a major policy to encourage citizens to go back to the farm. The Operation Feed the Nation (OFN) policy aimed to take the country back to its historical economic root of agriculture. Despite the enormous plans made by Obasanjo and the FMG to reactivate the agricultural sector, the obdurate citizens were not going to have any of it. When the new civilian administration of Shehu Shagari introduced the Green Revolution to replace the OFN, citizens equally ignored it. Rightly or wrongly, people had gotten used to white-collar jobs and the accompanying benefits, and it was widely acknowledged such jobs were the sole ladder to attaining prosperous heights. In 1979, to curtail the growing infiltration of agricultural imports into the country, the government banned items such as fresh milk, vegetables, roots and tubers, fruits, and poultry. To ensure the country had an enormous supply of food items to cater for its people, items like milk, sugar, flour, hides and skins were banned from exportation. Recently, the President Muhammadu Buhari government put several restrictions on the importation of rice and other commodities that could be easily grown in the country. Regardless, in all of the examples given so far, Nigerians' astute characterisation of back-door inventions saw them use every loophole to beat the government's barriers. Rather than shun the illegally imported items, Nigerian consumers embraced them in full despite the high cost.

In education, agriculture became a no-go course of study for students. Suddenly, everyone wanted to become a doctor, a lawyer, an engineer or a banker; some even dared to become astronauts and scientists in a country that affords them zero or little chance of such dreams becoming a reality. When neo-cultural changes emerged, and the younger population started to seek other professions in artistry, music, entertainment, and social media influencing, among others, agriculture was still not considered a go-to area. Ironically, the same youths who despise agriculture and have abandoned it to peasant farmers, the aged, and the largely uneducated rural farmers could be seen on social media lamenting the cost of items they had abandoned.

Up to this present day, the "get-rich-quick" syndrome waged its battle against agriculture through the rural-urban migration and acted as a pivotal killer of the sector. Young men from rural areas of the North could be seen trooping down to urban centres of Lagos, Abuja and Port Harcourt for engagements in the *okada* transportation business. It has been widely reported that young men from rural areas sold their farmlands and other agro business to enable them to set up *okada* and other similar business ventures in urban areas. Notably, such awkward engagement in crude activities serves little or no economic value to modern nations. The abandonment of farmlands for engagements in activities such as *okada* is a "penny wise pound foolish" move and one that typifies the prevalent "get-rich-quick" syndrome. As of December 2021, an *okada* was sold for N500, 000. It comes with the risk of accidents, possible theft, mutilation, and even loss of life. Yet, for that same amount, a viable poultry business could be set up, which according to analysts, could bring in future profits than the *okada* business. But then again, Nigerian youths, through a warped "get-rich-quick" mentality, have been informed that any business that cannot fetch immediate returns is a business not to be engaged in.

Still, the problems of the agricultural sector are deeper than the surface problems that most know. The sector continues to face a series of attacks due to the attendant effects of dishonesty, crime and corruption that have become an alarming part of our culture. The Nigerian agricultural sector is replete with diverse opportunities. Effectively harnessing these opportunities will drive agricultural development, expand agricultural export, create job opportunities and give Nigeria's economy skyrocket gains. However, human impediments continue to catalyse setbacks for the country.

Firstly, dirty politics became the order of the day. The usual ugly factor of regionalism, tribalism and prejudice also played a factor in the scheme of things. I feel compelled to bring attention to concurring words of a former Minister of Agriculture, Audu Ogbeh, that best describe the narrative of tribalism and prejudice and its effect on agriculture:

In 2016, six months after I became the minister, I raised a warning that there could be trouble emanating from herders and farmers and that the problem would escalate if we did nothing. And I wrote a letter to every governor in the country, asking if they would allow us to create ranches within their territories. Only 16 of them replied. Of the others, some said they were not interested and others did not respond at all. But I saw it coming. And people forget that a herdsman is also a farmer. If we are helping rice, cassava, beans and cocoa farmers, we should also help the herders. But the attitude is 'no, this is a private business. Why should the government be involved?' The cassava farmer is a private farmer; he does not grow cassava for the ministry. Cocoa and rice farmers are not growing them for the government, but we help them. The elite are like saying, "when it comes to cattle, don't talk about them. Why cannot they build their own ranches?" Building ranches are not cheap. People forget that we all need beef and that Lagos consumes 7,000 cattle per day. The cattle are grown somewhere else. The cattle are not the best; they are not properly grown and they walk too much. Some of them are infected, poorly fed, drink less water, and we produce the lowest quantity of milk, about one litre per cow daily....... (On importation of varieties of grass to feed livestock) One tragic thing in Nigeria is that whatever topic you bring up, there are some commentators who know next to nothing about the subject, but would be the first to criticise. I do not mean to be rude to them, but how many of them know about livestock? Clergymen were on the air attacking from the pulpits. People say all kinds of things. But Saudi Arabia imports grass from South America to feed cattle because they cannot grow grass. Qatar just brought 10,000 milk-producing cattle to their country because they have been isolated by their neighbours. They flew in the cattle and they are (sic) shipping in the grasses to feed them. I met a minister of Saudi Arabia in Germany, who said if we were serious about growing grasses, they would buy from us…. They cannot grow the grass, and so they must buy. A cow eats up to 10 kilogrammes of grass daily. Most of the attacks on our ideas are not based on logic. I keep some cattle, but I am not a Fulani. A son of the Minister of Health, Professor Isaac Adewole, was here last week to see me. He has a ranch in Osun State with 198 cattle. He has 18,000 chickens. He is not a Fulani. There are many Nigerians who keep cattle who are not Fulanis. But it is still talked about that anything cattle business is Fulani. It is not…. Of course, I do not like the idea of herdsmen wandering around and eating farmers' crops. I am a victim too. I cultivate yam and cassava. I do not want any herdsman to carry a riffle, enter a farm, kill a farmer and rape a woman because he wants his cattle to feed. That is condemnable. And I saw the danger. When I wanted to work on it, I did not have access to funds immediately, and the reaction from society was, by and large, repulsive. So, I had to take my time and now, many more are convinced that we need to take drastic actions, if not, the conflicts may not stop. Once the rains stop in the far North, Chad and the Republic of Niger, in their desperation, they will start coming down…I once met with herdsmen at the palace of the Lamido of Adamawa, who is a Fulani. He told me that that was the first time any highly placed government official would do something on the business of herdsmen. When I met with him, he got an interpreter, and I sat with about 300 herdsmen interacting for nearly two hours.... I asked them why they were carrying guns and killing farmers. They bought these guns from ex-fighters from Libya. They said they bought the guns to tame the activities of cattle rustlers. They accused rustlers of attacking them, killing their wives and carting away their cattle. But I told them they were using the guns against farmers, and they admitted that some of them did, not everyone, saying most of the violent ones came from Chad and Niger Republic.[18]

The lengthy words from the former minister are intentionally cited to show several factors I agree with that impede agricultural development in the country. The former minister is, although not a man I hold in high esteem for reasons immaterial to this discourse; however, his words corroborate my long-held perception as regards the mentality and behaviour of some of the country's so-called patriots. Reactionary activism damages the country's efforts to make progress. People are quick to condemn and lambast every decision taken by even the best of the country's policymakers, especially on issues that border on ethnicity, religion or tribe. Nigeria's present challenges with food security and agriculture have an imprint on every one of us, and we must take responsibility and blame the past, present and glaring futuristic dangers.

Furthermore, political and public officers in charge of agricultural developments became looters and criminals, like their counterparts in other sectors. Funds budgeted for the sector is diverted into private pockets for personal use. To talk about misappropriation, theft, and diversion of public funds will amount to a tautology, as such practices need no reminder or analysis to the author or reader. Even sadder is that the remnant of funds that are eventually released in the form of credit schemes and grants to farmers often end up in the hands of policymakers, associates, saboteurs and their cronies. Citizens are known to open fictitious agricultural businesses to get such financial support and then elope into thin air, leaving the actual farmers with nothing. Donations and grants in the forms of cash or modern equipment, fertilisers and pesticides do not end up in the hands of intended micro-farmers. Rather, scheme administrators connive to divert them for sale on the black market or to their own established and unqualified farmlands. In public-owned agricultural establishments, senior officeholders often request for farm produce to be given to them without payments, only for such items to be sold to black marketers, given to family members, or distributed for electioneering purposes. Such behaviours effectively short-changed state-owned businesses and resulted in eventual loss and collapse.

The problem of greed, indiscipline and corruption also affected Nigeria's exports and was partly responsible for why some Nigerians abandoned indigenous farm produce. I reliably gathered that exports such as cashew, groundnuts, cocoa, fruits, and palm oil were adulterated to short-change consumers. For instance, fruits such as bananas and mangos were treacherously ripened, packaged and exported, but rejected by foreign Customs. Neighbouring countries such as Benin, Ghana, and Togo had designated officers who found out that Nigerian agricultural products were hastily made to look ripe for harvest and were delicate for consumption. Nuts were soaked in water to gain weight to short-change the market but were eventually detected by eventual retailers, buyers, consumers or even foreign authorities. Crooked Nigerian Customs personnel and other relevant officers connived with such exporters to approve sub-standard items unsuitable for exports. Eventually, foreign buyers and authorities not only red-flagged Nigerian products but also warned their citizens to desist from them.

In communities where integrated farming was practised, it was reported that community members would often pilfer farm produce. Stories were told of how people set fire on large farmlands in their communities to loot farm produce, leaving the owners to rue the cost of both the fire outbreak and the thefts that had taken place. Former farm owners in the Middle Belt confirmed such practices contributed to reasons for the closure of their businesses. It was shocking to them that the arsonists did not care about the consequences of their actions. They did not just rue their financial loss but also the fact that hundreds of community members also lost jobs after the eventual close of their agro businesses.

Communal clashes, such as the infamous farmer-herder clashes, were also responsible for the abandonment of farmlands and an eventual shortage of food supply. Farmlands, pastures, cattle, animal herds, and other agricultural communities are razed to the ground by indigenes during violent outbreaks between people or communities. States of the North that once traded and soared in agricultural products have been plagued by terrorism, insurgency, banditry, and kidnapping. States of the South that once revelled in their ability to forge alliances with foreign traders have today become plagued by militancy, cultism and urbanisation. Up to this day, these problems have served as compounding factors for food scarcity, inflation, unemployment and other economic woes in the country.

One sad reality of the present Nigerian situation is that the solution to one problem does not immediately eradicate the entirety of the agricultural problems of the country. Terrorism in the North, farmer-herder clashes that are predominant in the Middle-Belt, militancy crisis in the Niger Delta and the high spate of insecurity in the country will continue to kill any hope of reviving agriculture in the country. The bulk of discussed problems seem interwoven. And if we were to go by the popular proverbial saying that "a hungry man is an angry man", it is sadly evident that Nigerians might be heading for greater problems regarding food insecurity and perhaps an eventual economic collapse.

Economic Fraud, Waste and Sabotage

Nigeria claims to operate a mixed economy. However, the government's over-reliance on funding activities for which it should have no business is partly responsible for the country's economic woes. Nigerians have become aggressively entitled to the public purse to the extent that they pay limited attention, or none, to the economic viabilities of some viable sectors that should have contributed significantly to the nation's economy. Attempts to redundant and inefficient privatise public establishments are often met by staunch adversaries of the free market system. Public corporations and MDAs became the ultimate casualties of misconduct in our socialist systems.

The decline of Nigeria's public corporations started when our political, societal, and economic leaders saw national wealth as an extension of their private wealth. Public establishments began to deteriorate because public servants at all tiers of government started to orchestrate unpatriotic activities to enrich themselves without a duty of care to the consequences of their actions. Establishments and industries that have become "cash cows" in other countries have become debt-ridden or wholly obliterated in Nigeria.

Moreover, while some of our public establishments have survived the bricks and stones of theft, embezzlement, corruption, and inefficiency thrown at them, others have not been that lucky. Establishments like the Nigeria Airways, Nigeria Railways, Ajaokuta Steel Company, NIPOST, NEPA/PHCN, NNPC and others have become either comatose or a bane of our public purse. Leaders, administrators, public servants, middlemen, contractors, and agents, to name a few, all took turns to profiteer from a broken and malfunctioning system that activates and supports economic sabotage. Everyone with access, no matter how little, to render service to the public on behalf of the government used their hand to destroy the institutions they were meant to represent. We became a united people, not in peace, stability, or progress, but in theft, corruption, fraud, and national sabotage.

In addition to the already explained reasons that led to the collapse of Nigeria Airways and the Nigeria Railways Corporation, other reasons are responsible for the moribund state of other government establishments. Top on the list of reasons includes lack of operational facilities and equipment, non-availability of essential amenities, obsolete means of revenue generation, poor capital base, lack of financial support and investment, an inadequate workforce, lack of maintenance culture, corruption, indiscipline, unruly staff, crooked contractors, citizenship sabotage, and poor organisational and leadership problems to mention but a few.

Establishments like ECN/NEPA/PHCN, NIPOST and NITEL depict citizens' role in sabotaging the country's national assets. Private citizens and corporate organisations paid miserly amounts as bribes and kickbacks to corrupt officials rather than pay for their actual usage. They took advantage of an unaccountable system to short-change public corporations, the government and the general society. Today, individuals and businesses owe monies to electricity distribution companies for services rendered and are in no hurry to make payments. Incidentally, the same corrupt citizens often wonder why such corporations are inefficient and are quick to lament the state of the nation's economy; the same economy they sabotage and destroy.

Globally, government-owned enterprises are established to provide cheap services to the people using public funds, support tools, mechanisms, and subsidies, among others. Sometimes, they are created to operate as a monopoly or compete favourably against the private sector. In Nigeria, the innocuous acts of thrusting government funds into these establishments have resulted in the criminal act of sabotage by citizens who see such funds as personal entitlements. Corporations such as the NNPC, Nigerian Ports Authority and Nigerian Coal Corporation continue to suffer setbacks of various proportions due to widespread inefficiency, lack of accountability, fraud and corruption that their managers and actors perpetrate.

We can also understand the failures of Nigeria's corporations and establishments through comparative analysis. For instance, where private companies like MTN, Globacom, Airtel, and 9Mobile have recorded tremendous successes, the heavily financed publicly owned telephone service provider NITEL failed woefully. It is also relevant to mention that when the country's telecommunications industry received a boost in 2001 with the introduction of the GSM, among the three companies that initially started operations,[19] the government-owned MTEL was the only one that gave up the ghost and got buried, both in rapid succession. Similarly, while the government-owned postal corporation NIPOST struggles, foreign-owned businesses like UPS, DHL and FedEx have dusted off socio-economic challenges to enjoy commercial operations in the country.

Nigerian public corporations are home to one of the world's most unruly and nonchalant personnel. Poor services from civil servants in our public sector are commonplace. The use of public services has become the last resort for many who would instead consider every other opportunity available for use. Wilful absenteeism and lateness to work by public officials are rife and continue to affect productivity and revenue generation. Acts of indiscipline and other behaviours such as alcoholism, overstaffing, wrong organisational structure, undue external influence, understaffing, workplace harassment and bureaucracy are reasons why our public establishments have been pegged back. Many public servants hired into various government establishments lack modern and updated knowledge of the operations and practices of commercial businesses in today's era.

In a fast-changing world where technology continues to evolve, outdo and outdate itself, it is inconceivable to find that public establishments that enjoy massive government budgetary allocations still use archaic tools and resources in communication and general services. A private research I carried out in September 2021 regarding the communication tools used by public establishments returned a shocking revelation. It shows how the surveyed establishments lag in organisation and managerial affairs. For instance, many federal, states and LG establishments still rely heavily on outdated communication tools such as PO Boxes, PMBs and fax machines. Obsolete or unreachable phone numbers are common in such public establishments. Even when updated, the affected changes are hardly relayed to the public. Modern communication tools like emails and websites are unavailable or conspicuously absent from listing and publicity agencies.

The results of an "enquiry email" (test) I sent out to 20 public establishments (corporations, institutions and MDAs) in Nigeria and did the same abroad expose a troubling result. From the 20 test emails I sent to public establishments in the country, 7 recorded a failed delivery response (basically due to expired domain names and inexistent/closed email accounts). Of the 13 that seemingly delivered, only 2 responded appropriately. That meant that a shocking response rate of 10% was achieved with the "enquiry email" test I carried out. Using a similar pattern, I recorded a percentile of 85% in Canada, 60% in Kenya, 75% in Australia, 90% in the United States and 36% in Ghana. Oddly, my investigative analyses contradict the fact that Nigeria reportedly had, and still has, the highest number of Internet users in Africa. Undeniably, this shows that Nigerians are represented by the wrong people in our public service institutions.

Other areas that peg back the operational conducts of public establishments and our overall economy are archaic practicalities in accounting, security, networking, auditing, revenue generation, budgeting, science and technology, administration, human resources, training, and management. With archaic methods of handling organisational affairs in a heavily digitalised and modern world, we should not be alarmed as to why our public establishments fail. We should also be unsurprised that local and foreign investors continue to look elsewhere for investments rather than geographical Nigeria.

Many Nigerians who grew up during the "good old days" erroneously believed the country was rich. At the time, they fell for the fraudulent campaign gimmicks of their federal, regional/state and local politicians. They failed to ask the viability of the promises that were ditched out to them. They were promised free education, free housing, free healthcare, employment, free transportation and other deceitful campaign promises. They did not care about the shattering social consequences and economic impact of the "freebies". They did not care about the long-term implications of the things that they thought were free, adequate or infinite. A wrong mental approach set in. Citizens who found their way into public offices did so with an erroneous mental understanding to take what belongs to them - an elegant definition of theft - after all, there is more from where what they took came from. At least, so they thought. Nigerians continued their acts of impunity despite the intermittent recessions and the country plunging into debt. Even after public corporations and MDAs bled profusely, Nigerians refused to learn their lessons and continued their acts of fraud and economic sabotage.

Today, the Nigerian economy has plunged into chaos. Everyone who participated in the fall of our economy refused to agree that they took part in the country's economic collapse. Some of their offspring, sadly, are benefiting from the woes their fore-generations have brought unto our present generation.

Let me relate to the reader an encounter I had with an Octogenarian friend, Baba Jerry. Baba Jerry once recalled how as a director in the country's civil service, he was given two official cars and an official residence. As we shared opinions on the historical and current state of the nation, he recollected how the Yakubu Gowon administration was "kind" to him and how things began to dwindle from the middle of the 1980s. I sharply but respectfully told him there was nothing genuinely brilliant about the Gowon administration or the leaders before or after him. I respectfully told him that events elsewhere, such as the politics of the Cold War, OPEC's influence, and the then ever-persistent Middle East crises, were responsible for soaring high prices of oil.

Albeit unintentionally and unexpected, our country benefited immensely from the woes, afflictions and turmoil that had befallen other regions. Yet, our country never prepared for the engulfing fire right under our roof. The Niger Delta region, for instance, was an impoverished region that suffered greatly despite its oil being plundered to serve the entire nation. I reminded Baba Jerry that the blood, sweat and misery of the Niger Delta people and the chaos in the Middle East were responsible for the freebies he thought he enjoyed and not a result of Gowon's magnanimity or that of any political leader for that matter. As global demand and consumption of oil began to reduce despite increased production, Nigeria started to face its turn of economic hardships; something the political and economic leaders of Nigeria were never prepared for. They had lived in the false delusion that things were working and great when they had limited bearings in the financial growth that occurred. I explained all these to Baba Jerry, who is not the only one that needs to be respectfully corrected. A large percentage of the elderly also thought things were good during their time. They were wrong and mistaken, and their perception only fuelled the danger that has come to befall us today.

When people talk down on particular leaders while praising their preferred ones, they superficially forget the roles played by the latter in the state of decay. The proverb "a spoiling banana is not a ripening banana" best illustrates the case where people seem to misconstrue the relative dividends they enjoy as the barometer for performance regardless of awaiting dangerous implications. Political and societal leaders are often quick to engage in a scavenger-type attitude regarding sharing the nation's wealth when they should be saving for rainy days.

An issue of important relevance was the hostile campaign against the Yar'Adua-Jonathan administration by some state governors who persistently pushed against the federal government from withholding funds for savings in the Excess Crude Account, the Sovereign Wealth Fund and other related savings devices. Incidentally, some of the governors who insisted that the savings mechanisms of the Jonathan administration be halted and the available monies shared were members of the opposition party, the APC. After the APC won the 2015 presidential election, some governors who later became ministers and top executives in the new administration bickered around the country, telling the citizens that nothing was left in the national treasury. Although they were correct, they must have taken the intelligence of Nigerians for granted. A few months prior, they were the same propagators of the idea that the entirety of the nation's wealth must be shared rather than saved.

Citizens' rough perception and hostility towards innocuous ideas by the government are among the factors responsible for our economic collapse. On the one hand, they become hostile to plans that could bring about positive socio-economic changes for reasons bordering on selfishness and discomfort. On the other hand, citizens quickly embrace wasteful economic cultures even if they impede sustainable growth and development. As such, political demagogues engage in unnecessary infrastructural spending and wastefulness, much to the delight of a susceptible portion of their people.

Furthermore, citizens lack accurate information on economic issues and are sometimes left to choose between genuine knowledge and those from a hostile and biased section of the population. For instance, part of the failure of the much-maligned Structural Adjustment Program (SAP), aside from the usual corruption syndrome, was that it was given a bad name and heavily criticised by the intransigent public, thanks to prejudiced pressmen and two-faced activists. People erroneously believed in socialist ideologies and heavy government spending as the only means of socio-economic survival. It became (and still) politically suicidal for any public administrator to tell them otherwise. A policy like the Structural Adjustment Program was heavily frowned upon in a clime like ours where previous leaders and policymakers misleadingly engaged in acts of overstaffing and overspending. Therefore, it became strange and considered taboo for anyone to attempt policies such as downsizing extremely overstaffed organisations, rationalising administrative spending or eliminating MDAs of government that were ineffective or unproductive.

Across the three tiers of government, the public sector is known to be overstaffed with people who offer nothing economically or socially to the public besides debt. Attempts by well-meaning leaders to shut down unproductive segments of the country have been met with unbending confrontation from certain dogmatic labour groups and shadowy oppositions. We are a wasteful nation, a profligate society and one where impunity and wastage of resources play elegantly in the mind of the average public servant. Government officials embark on a spending spree beyond the comprehension of logicality or pragmatism. Incumbent governments abandon projects flagged off by their predecessors for politically motivated reasons or for that associated with ego and character warfare. Public officials are known to approve procurements of items and expenditures that are not needed or by excessively procuring items for their convenience, to the detriment of the state's purse.

Speaking at an event organised by the Covenant Christian Centre in Lagos in 2016, former Anambra state governor Peter Obi lamented the waste culture that has become a syndrome of political governance in Nigeria. Similarly, in what could only be construed only as an act of socio-economic lunacy, an abandoned aircraft that belonged to the Rivers State government was discovered at a German hangar after ten years of neglect. According to Rivers Governor Nyesom Wike, there was no documentation to show that such an aircraft was missing in the first place or why it departed the country for eventual abandonment in Germany.

According to the World Bank, Nigeria remained among the Top 7 countries notoriously renowned for gas flaring activities for 9 years.[20] It has been estimated that most of our natural gas is flared off. In 2020 alone, gas flaring resulted in an annual loss of $717.8 million in the nine covered states by Nigerian Gas Flare Tracker.[21] Nevertheless, successive governments did not see the need to declare gas flaring as a national emergency that requires an urgent solution, even when our nation needs a constant power supply that the availability of gas can tackle.

A wasteful culture is why state governors, whose states are heavily reliant on loans and have become debt-ridden, find it incumbent and economically tolerant to hand out cars, lands, houses and other extravagant gifts to selected individuals when areas such as healthcare, education and security bleed of financial assistance. Political executives would use state resources to award luxurious gifts to civil servants, traditional rulers, religious and societal leaders, labour leaders or other private persons for reasons that border on political patronage or nepotism. Regardless, the beneficiaries of wasteful systems never deemed it necessary to reject extravagantly wasteful items or openly criticise such acts. We receive such items when it benefits us, forgetting that the cost of economic wastage and social injustice is often greater than the accompanying benefits.

The mentality of the average Nigerian is shocking and sadly not something he does in secret or finds repugnant. We pillage oil resources for decades without putting elongating and futuristic plans in order. The forester falls trees and engages in deforestation while moving from place to place without planting new ones for a better, productive tomorrow. The commercial driver you employ does not care about putting your vehicle in good condition. Rather he has turned the vehicle into a disfigured and unprofitable item. Roads and motorways that could have been patched are left to deteriorate further before appropriate authorities wade into action, resulting in unimaginable but preventable spending. The average Nigerian allows a machine to reach a dying stage before calling it in for repair, at which point he has to spend enormously to repair it or perhaps call for replacement. Many government officials treat public utilities at their disposal with recklessness and utmost lack of care. Public buses, offices, stations, washrooms, labs and other public utilities have deteriorated due to the absence of a maintenance culture. As I have said repeatedly, some people alarmingly think the country is doomed, a decision they solely arrive at through financial and economic measurements. However, the social causes of national regress are mostly not talked about and never taken seriously by the Nigerian populace.

Corrupt officials and criminal elements have taken over industries and establishments that the government should typically control to help generate revenue for their respective tiers. Illegal mining and exploration of valuable resources are ongoing in most parts of the country. Some public officials, such as commissioners, local government executives and worst of all, governors, have multiple "special" assistants and advisers to fill in sinecure positions for the sole purposes of drawing salaries and fund disbursements. A survey by the News Agency of Nigeria revealed that governors in each state of the federation had an average of 100 political appointees; even worrisome was that some of them were debt-ridden. In fact, some governors were said to have over 300 political appointees who carried out similar functions or were even redundant. Such is the level we have sunk so low as a people that low-level officials fly first-class tickets along with their own entourage to the demerit of the public purse.

It has been reported that political and public office holders factor five-star hotels, expensive meal tickets and unnecessary costs into the overall cost of meetings and gatherings. I once came across an expense bill where a state government funded-symposium budgeted N50, 000 per meal for attendants for each day. The public event lasted seven days and was attended by middle-level civil servants. The reader does not need a reminder of the true picture of things underneath the surface of the actual receipts and official documentation. Abroad, Nigerian officials shamefully live lavish and expensive lifestyles far above the moderate standards of their host and leaders of other advanced countries. An NBC report in New York once exposed the flagrant and abusive lifestyle of African countries' representatives at a UN summit; of course, Nigeria featured. The report said, "Nigeria's delegation is keeping five vehicles parked outside the Pierre Hotel where the cheapest room is about $800 a night – or roughly what most Nigerians earn in two years."[22]

Our culture of waste and economic sabotage is often conveyed during civil discontents, such as protests and riots, where we find it convenient to destroy public and private properties. During the *End SARS* protests that took the country by storm in late 2020, violent protesters took over cities across the country to perpetuate their forms of mayhem. Lagos, the city with the most recorded cases of destruction and damage, claimed that no less than 80 BRT buses were damaged.[23] City properties such as public buildings, police stations, monuments, traffic lights, halls and courts were burnt to the ground or partially destroyed. Private businesses were not spared as superstores and business offices were looted. Arsonists and burglars took advantage of the lack of security presence to perpetrate thefts and vandalisation. By the time calm was restored, losses incurred through damages, destructions and thefts were valued above N1trillion.[24]

During riots and violent clashes, churches, mosques, schools and other public buildings and infrastructure are targeted by those who take it upon themselves to destroy such properties at an alarming level of impunity. Various concomitant factors have ensured that the Nigerian economy was bound to fail. Proverbially, we are like the farmer who takes a broken basket to his farm for harvest, an unwise decision that could see the escape of harvested produce before he gets to his destination. As long as we continue to engage in economic waste and sabotage, the prices that lay waiting are predictably disastrous for our future generations and us.

The Fall of the Naira

Many economically learned citizens have reserved opinions concerning the issue of the naira's downfall and that of the country's economy. Some believe that the problems started with the devaluation of the naira. A quarter of experts argue that it was the SAP; some said it was deregulation and others claimed it was industrialisation policies by past administrators. Some insist that foreign influences on our economy are to be blamed, and others believe that some economic theories could have saved the country from the current shambles. Personally, some or all the arguments could be valid if only Nigerian leaders and citizens had not set out to destroy their country through crooked and sometimes unintentional acts of sabotage.

Generally, we can agree that the various actions of past and present economic and political leaders were enough to send the country's currency into a lethargic state. Nigeria has operated an economy that pretends all is well for most of its existence. In actuality, the country's economy has required emergency surgeries and treatments. Despite not being a socialist country, Nigeria still heaps more debts through needless public expenditures. A grossly overpopulated citizenry that continues to expect the government to micromanage and grant them things that should never have been free, rising spates of insecurity, insurgency, terrorism, and political instability, among others, create problems of their own for the economy. Nigeria's public debt totalled N39.56 trillion ($95.78 billion) due to hefty expenditures and comparatively lowers revenues.[25] As of the time of publishing this book, the naira currently exchanges for the dollar at the rate of N420 at the official market and N575 at the parallel market (where most transactions occur). Therefore, it is pertinent to delve into our national history regarding the currency, the economy and where it all went wrong.

In January 1973, the country's government took a transitioning step concerning its currency and economy. The government replaced the Nigerian pound with the naira. The elder statesman and former federal finance commissioner, Chief Obafemi Awolowo, coined the name for the nation's currency. Since its creation, citizens have embarked on a mission to inflict injurious wounds on it and the country's economy. Where a loophole does not exist, one was created and made wide open to feast joyously, to the detriment of the entire nation. The economic sabotage of the country as regards its currency preceded the launch of the naira itself. Currency smugglers took advantage of the civil war to help traffic currency notes in and out of Biafra. Even after the war, they felt reluctant to give up their new-found lucrative dealings. They smuggled currency notes in and out of the country, especially in neighbouring West African countries where the CFA Francs were used.

The sad state of the naira has become so as a result of the manipulation of the currency, fraud, corruption, theft, self-deceit, hypocrisy, and dare I say, illusory conditioning of the totality of Nigerians. The naira has become a symbol of the country's true state; a symbol of depreciation and collapse. Nigeria is a country where the economic factors that typically affect things such as the currency are eventually outweighed by external non-economic factors that should never be at play in the first instance. These non-economic factors have become the pivotal killer influencers of the naira and our economy.

The reader should be tired of my constant reminder that it is intentional for this book not to play into the hands of economic theorists or their arguments. Intentionally, I am omitting factors outside human behaviours used to destroy the country's currency and the overall economy. Nevertheless, it is instructive to understand that the determining factors of the value of a country's currency are inflation, the balance of trade, political stability, public debt, currency speculation, current account balance/deficit, unpatriotic behaviours, dollarization, economic and political leadership among other things. For clarification, the entireties of what has been documented in this book are associated factors of a nation's currency and economy. Now, concerning the naira, when precisely could it be said that the national currency, the naira, began its state of decline?

As Nigeria descended into one of indiscipline and corruption in the 1970s, the country's production and manufacturing industry began to suffer, albeit for reasons that were partly the fault of practitioners in the manufacturing industry. Locally made goods no longer carry the hallmark of originality and quality. People started churning counterfeit and pirated materials into markets. Local producers engaged in short-changing consumers by manipulating the quantity or quality of items sold. Rather than practitioners and industry stakeholders clean up the mess and ensure that manufacturers and firms are held accountable, they worsen their actions. Oversight and supervisory organisations like the Standards Organisation of Nigeria and Manufacturers Association of Nigeria, both created in 1971, watched as bribery, corruption, and inefficiency became the order of the day. Manufacturers and producers, knowing they could easily bribe their way through whatever logjam they encountered with regulatory agencies, carried on their activities with reckless abandonment and careless disregard for logic and consequences. Then again, they were foolhardy to believe that the repercussions would not come back to haunt them like a wrecking ball.

The first lessons they learnt came from foreigners and foreign countries. Nigerian consumers hoping to benefit from the cheap but counterfeit products from manufacturers might have embraced such fraudulent activities through a "penny wise pound foolish" producer-consumer unwritten accord. Foreign entities were not that kind. Producers of massive counterfeit products burnt their fingers with their assumption that the corruption that allowed them to engage in the flagrant introduction of their products into Nigerian markets would be applicable in foreign countries. Foreign Customs and administrative/control agencies rejected export commodities from Nigeria in their numbers and impounded them for their failure to meet standards. One manufacturer and exporter of timber products once told me that because of the greed of a few, exports coming from Nigerian markets were flagged for further stringent checks. That put them at a competitive disadvantage against other exporters from other countries. That was not all.

Knowing that locally made goods and items fell short of their expectations, the section of Nigerian consumers who needed quality and value began to look elsewhere for optimum satisfaction. Naturally, their demands got met. Importers brought competitive products that Nigerians deemed better and flooded them in the open markets. The "Made in Nigeria" slogan that was once an embodiment of our national pride soon became a near-taboo for consumers, retailers and everyone else. We moved from one of the major exporters of various commodities in the West African region and got relegated to the role of a chief importer. Soon after that, the country not only became Africa's principal importer of foreign goods and even services, but it also eventually became a dumping ground for inferior and ulterior goods as well. There you have it, one of many stories of how Nigerians used their hands to crash their currency and the economy, especially regarding the trade balance issue.

Also, knowing that they could benefit greedily from import licenses, several individuals and businesses applied for import licenses, which were recklessly granted to them by, corrupt leaders. Importers opened letters of credit with foreign banks, not for commercial purposes but to benefit from illicit profit involved in their acts. Many underhand dealings went behind the curtains that were unknown to the public at the time. During the infamous Johnson Matthey Bankers scandal of 1984 in London, which led to the near-collapse of one of Britain's leading financial institutions, numerous letters of credit fraud were discovered that aimed to rip off the Nigerian Treasury.[26] Brian Sedgemore, a British Member of Parliament at the time, wrote:

> The problems for JMB became serious when early in 1984 the coup took place in Nigeria. Then, the letters of credit were no longer honoured. When Mr. Fraser (the former loan manager of JMB) went to the customers and asked for his money back, they bluntly told him to "sod off", because he knew about the frauds that were taking place at the time. I believe that the Foreign Secretary has been having some difficulty in sorting out affairs with Nigeria in relation to the matter.[27]

53

At the time Nigerians thought their currency was stronger than the dollar (as it indeed looked on paper), it was a currency bleeding profusely and facing attacks of all sorts under the watch of apathetic authorities. The naira was simply valuable on paper, absurdly over-valued at the exchange rate market, and near-worthless in reality. The former head of state, General Ibrahim Babangida, decried how corrupt private persons sabotaged his government. He said:

> Everybody, especially in our country, tries to put the problem at the doorsteps of the government, but I think, and I said it before (that) it is the responsibility of every Nigerian..the best we could do is to go to the source of corruption in our system and to try to see what we can do about that system. For example, we knew that one of the sources of corruption when we came in was the issue of import license, and we put it off. We cancelled it.[28]

Ironically, after Babangida got to power, the door of corruption got opened to citizens, wider than ever. If Babangida had thought, as he opined, that his blockage of the import license was enough to crown him as an anti-corruption hero, he is greatly mistaken. Citizens took massive advantage of Babangida's carelessness to launch attacks of various kinds against the nation's economy. As it later happened, the second-tier foreign exchange market, which Babangida replaced the import license system with, became even more disastrous than what he initially thought was a problem. By the time the import license system got restored, more currency criminals had gotten wind of how best to attack the naira. I must remind again that some of our beloved parents, uncles and those we worship today were part of a gang of criminals who brought the country to its knees. Mansions, luxury cars, businesses, expensive items and luxury lifestyles were profiteered from the country's woes. It has become instructive to agree that most of our rich and powerful are not truthful to their children and generation about how they made their "hard-earned" wealth. Similarly, many who superstitiously believed their parents to be angels and innocent of the country's horror of shame are either blind or intentionally disingenuous not to investigate their parents deeper.

The usual suspects, the political and public office holders, also drew out their attack swords and launched warfare that bordered on greed, fraud and treason against the naira. Firstly, they thought it wise to start receiving their salaries in dollars. Public officials made contract payments, disbursements and other government expenditures in foreign currencies. Secondly, till today, large volumes of dollar notes are laundered, hidden, and stored for use during electioneering and political campaigns. Their ever-ready civilian counterparts followed suit. Local businesses, schools, embassies, and other organisations/institutions demanded that they be paid in dollars or other foreign currencies. Momentarily, the possession and spending of the dollar became a VIP card and a badge of flamboyance within social and political circles. As the country's economy crumbled in the 1980s and more Nigerians began to look abroad for greener pastures, coupled with the previously mentioned problems that faced the country's economy, more trouble began to surface.

Trouble loomed after Nigerians started to see a compulsive need for the dollar, some for genuine reasons, others for reasons bordering on fraud. As a result of the demand and overdependence on the dollar (termed dollarization), unpatriotic individuals saw an opportunity to feast upon the currency exchange system. For instance, by the time the General Sani Abacha government (which had the pegged official exchange rate at N22 to $1 while selling at ₦80 at the parallel market) and its colossal rent-seeking group of depraved personalities left office, a selected few people had begun to profiteer from the colossal loss attributed to dollar trading. They were commercial bankers and bureaux de change operators. Unmonitored and unchallenged, they carried out destructive and explosive activities on the nation's currency and economy. The illicit gains were so mouth-watering that by 2021, the country had seen BDC operators rise from 74 in 2005 to 5,500 in 2021. Although officially stated, these numbers could be incorrect as the actual numbers of illegitimate/unofficial operators are far larger than officially known numbers.

The naira depreciation due to the government's incompetence and citizen sabotage culture alarmed the CBN governor, Godwin Emefiele. The CBN governor lamented at a press briefing in July 2021 that an unprecedented 500 fresh applications were being received monthly by intending BDC operators in the country, a trend he claimed was extraordinarily suspicious and worrisome. At a separate briefing on September 17, 2021, the CBN governor told an audience of a study highlighting the repulsive behaviours of fraudulent people who played grave parts in the naira sabotage. He said:

> We conducted a study (at) one of the banks. In one day, they sold to fifty-two people who said they wanted to travel. After two weeks, they (authorities) went to check, forty out of the fifty-two persons have cancelled their travel tickets...Banks sold to them, they then turned back and went to sell it at the black markets because they wanted to enjoy the arbitrage.

The CBN itself played a major role in the fall of the naira. For decades, the CBN and various governments had allowed economic saboteurs and vultures to dictate the gameplay of the currency market. By the middle of 2021, everyone had brought out their tableware to the table of national economic sabotage. Military administrators, political appointees, public officials, bankers, regulators, legislators, traditional rulers and private citizens became owners of BDCs in the country. Their intents were far from patriotic or nobility. Fraud, theft, greed, treason and economic sabotage automatically became key features of the currency exchange service in the country. Intransigent and fraudulent network of individuals matched each step taken by the CBN and other authoritative bodies to prevent the dollar from getting into underserved hands. For instance, the CBN innocuously ordered banks to provide citizens' dollars or other foreign currencies, provided they had necessary documents (for purposes such as travels, international trading, foreign education etc.) to such effect. The CBN directive, however, backfired.

Bank officials readily turned down people with legitimate intentions to pave the way for their cronies. Round tripping is rampant, as bankers cunningly shipped off foreign currencies given to them by the CBN to their privately owned BDCs or those owned by their cronies. Citizens, sometimes working in connivance with bank officials, presented fraudulent travel or import documents to secure high volumes of dollars only to resell them at the parallel market. All these lead to devaluation and depreciation of the naira. They were able to cause artificial scarcities of currencies, only to sell to those desperately in need but for legitimate reasons at artificially inflated prices, thereby sabotaging the economy.

Rent-seeking operators quickly stood by and continuously took advantage of open doors made available to them by the CBN. International organisations, foreign embassies and their representatives, and development finance institutions (DFIs) bypassed existing laws to purchase currencies from black markets to fund their operations. As the country's chief monetary guardian, the CBN itself should be embarrassed for allowing people to use backdoor mechanisms to inflict wounds on the country's economy. Chidiebere Nwobodo, in a July 2021 column in Vanguard newspaper, fittingly had this to say:

> The CBN sells estimated $5.7billion annually to over 5000 BDCs. This figure is not only outrageous but highly unsustainable. Imagine selling most of the forex to BDCs on official rate while manufacturers—the people that really need the forex struggles to access forex needed to import raw materials. It is like starving one's

asset portfolio and funding his liability portfolio; bankruptcy is in the offing. And yet we wonder why naira is depreciating and unemployment rate is skyrocketing. It is not only self-harming but self-defeatist.[29]

The CBN ought to have realised that it is up against a significant set of unpatriotic yet arrogantly unrepentant citizens who will do anything to make a fortune at the expense of the national economy. The CBN should have known that it is up against intransigent forces who will continue to move against every decision it takes for their benefit, not minding if the economy collapses. The reader might wonder why I have turned this particular segment of the book into one of lamentation and castigation of Nigerian citizens (actually, there are more of such to come). This is because no country can survive the onslaught that our fellow citizens launch against their country yet still expect the same country to survive miraculously. Suppose both the reader and the CBN doubt the repercussions of currency manipulation on a nation's economy. In that case, I should be permitted to bring as a reminder an infamous incident that occurred in one of the world's most powerful nations.

On September 16 1992 (also called Black Wednesday), the United Kingdom was forced to withdraw its currency (the pound sterling) from the European Exchange Rate Mechanism after a failed attempt to keep it above the lower currency exchange limit as mandated.[30] The UK's loss was estimated at around £3.3 billion, although previous estimates placed the loss between £13 billion and £27 billion.[31] The loss of the British government favoured a Hungarian-born American businessman, George Soros. Soros short sale of $10 billion worth of pounds sterling was enough to make him a profit of $1 billion in just one day. Several people like George Soros exist in Nigeria, and the Nigerian government and its citizens cannot allow them to carry on their activities freely. In fact, while Soros action was deemed to be legal, the activities of his counterparts in Nigeria are purely illegal, criminal and treasonable. Many are people's fathers, uncles, sisters, brothers, mothers, aunts, friends, family members and associates. I repeat, Nigeria cannot afford to self-destruct because of the activities of currency speculators, fraudsters and economic saboteurs.

A staggering proportion of our elites and educated citizenry are responsible for the attack on the naira and the country's economy, regardless of the patriotic persona and lamentations they misleadingly sell to the public. Some reasons for the dwindling state of the naira could be attributed to unthinkable factors that could not feature in the research analysis of the world's best economists. Egotism, greed, inferiority complex, lack of confidence in the naira, cynicism, doom prophesies, sabotage mentality, doom-to-fail public nuances, panic trading, and erratic perception of the naira are just a few examples. These non-economic factors are a noticeable trend among the country's young and elite population.

Many fellow citizens believe the country is doomed, and they think it is doomed beyond possible repairs. It has almost become a national culture for everyone who could afford foreign education to embark overseas for the furtherance of their education or to send them overseas for the same purpose. It has also become the dream of the average Nigerian youth to not just travel outside the country but to engineer a permanent move that involves the repatriation of his local assets to foreign climes. The average Nigerian has been urged to abandon the local economies for foreign vacations, tourism, weddings, celebrations, travels and tours. Of course, these activities are understandable and within the fundamental right of people to spend their hard-earned money as they please. However, such people should not be surprised when they find the naira in a sorry state they cultivated. Citizens who use every opportunity to earn locally but then buy foreign-made goods should not pretend to be ignorant about the consequences of their actions.

There is also the rankly unpatriotic set of citizens who continue to launder the near-treasonable chants of telling their fellow compatriots to "save in dollars" to encourage illicit profits. They let you know that the country's currency is in danger and will be ruined. However, their actions are forged out of recklessness to encourage the panic buying of foreign currencies, resulting in unwarranted scarcity and chaos. Those economic traitors scare people into withdrawing their naira to save dollars and to make profits should their "prophecies" come to pass. They are bent on destroying the country at every opportunity. They are not economists or prophets and are not intelligent analysts in any way or form. They are purely treasonous persons who have told you to destroy your national currency and sabotage the economy. They want you to think you are making profits when you will be responsible for inflation, bad economy, regression, recession, unemployment, market collapse and all the economic ills you can think of. What manner of citizens intentionally set out to destroy their currency and economy with unfathomable degeneracy? Where do Nigerians get their audacity? The audacity to set ablaze the same house they know they will spend the rest of the night with their family and loved ones.

Our currency is in trouble, and our economy is in ruins. We cannot afford to be that country that produces nothing yet consumes everything. Other factors that impede the strength of the naira, such as currency smuggling, illicit trading, forex manipulation, and crypto currency fraud, will be discussed in due course. Most of us are grown enough to remember that there was a point when the Ghanaian currency GH₵ was a lot worse than the naira. Unpatriotic acts connected with treason and sabotage against the naira can no longer be tolerated. The CBN and other regulatory bodies must wake up to enforce adequate laws and put regulations and policies in place. They must also ensure that backdoor mechanisms are no longer granted to recalcitrant personalities who are hell-bent on destroying the country for personal gains.

Phoney and Parochial Economic Beliefs

Nigerians have lived in a perpetual state of ridiculous and phoney beliefs. Persistent problems were allowed degenerate further. And for every generation, developed and developing problems seemed too tough to handle. Hence, ensuing chaos is further postponed for future generations to manage.

How were Nigerians able to believe that their national currency's equality to that of the dollar indicated a robust economy? How on earth did we believe that our economy was at one point stronger than some European and Asian nations even though we could only boast of a few multinational firms? On what ground was the country declared the "Giant of Africa"? I must say emphatically, again, that any notion that Nigeria's economy was ever strong - after the departure of the colonialists in 1960 - was a farce. From a purely economic angle, Nigeria has never had its "glory days", as erroneously opined by a segment of the elderly population; at least, not at any point since the country's independence. As noted throughout this book, since independence, the country has been thrown into the muddled waters of financial fraud, corruption and ineffectual economic systems and policies. Also, the country, as a result of many inexplicable factors, did not allow its citizens to know the true state of the economy.

Our general belief system was so doctored to make us erroneously believe that, at a point in history, our economy was strong enough to compare itself with other top economies. We acted on the fallacies sold to us by economic and political leaders and their "intellectual" cronies. Thus, we could not comprehend the enormous task that needed to be carried out. We got lackadaisical, short-sighted and ineffectual. We have carried on with that dirty illusion up to this day. We mistakenly, perhaps gullibly, neglected the laborious and intellectually demanding art of nation-building, especially as regards the national economy. We remained behind as the world moved ahead in science, technology, research and development, and modern financial and economic practices. We believed that jobs such as hawking, street begging, crude artisanship, *okada* and *danfo* transportation and other outdated aspects of the low-income generation were sustainable. Many woke up to the sudden reality of the modern changing world to find out that they could no longer cope with the new world order. Suddenly, they could no longer afford to send their children to school, feed their families or afford the necessities that are required in the modern world they found themselves in.

We must say a thing as they are because phoney statements based purely on jingoism contradicts stark reality and statistics. For instance, at the time the dollar was said to be equal to the naira on paper; most Nigerians during the same period lacked all the necessities and amenities of everyday life (access to potable water, stable power supply, basic education, good clothing, and shelter among other). As of 1985 - the last year, the dollar was said to be of lesser value than the naira - a shameful 0.24% of Nigerians had access to fixed telephone subscriptions compared to a very disproportionate comparative percentage of 49% in the United States, 40% in France, 7% in South Africa and 2% in Egypt. [32] To analysis this in simple mathematical and logical terms, the implication is that if 90% of Nigerians today now have access to telephones and other digital device, items which are not produced locally but imported, the country's currency is sure to take a beating from such aspect of progress that was in fact inexistent prior to now. The consequence of such figures can easily be understood analytically in simple mathematical and logical terms. With 90% of Nigerians having access to telephones and other communication devices today, the implication is that such items, which are not produced locally but imported, are sure to affect the country's currency negatively. Logically, that is because such aspects of socio-economic progress were inexistent before now, not even at the period when many claim the country was abundantly rich.

It is shameful for anyone to suggest, especially in comparative terms, that Nigerians enjoyed the "good old days" when a paltry 0.24% of its population had access to telephone subscriptions as of 1985; not 1900, not 1930 and not even 1960 but 1985! Furthermore, in the same period (1985), Nigeria's GDP stood at a mere $74 billion compared to the US, which stood at $4.34 trillion. Suppose comparisons, as often done by political demagogues, are what we have to show that our country once fared better. In that case, we could extend such comparative figures and data analysis, as it relates to other aspects of our social and economic lives, to some other viable economies across the globe.

Most Nigerians, especially lay thinkers and disingenuously opinionated people, think that inflation rates and a depreciated currency are the only determinants of a country's economy. This idea could be valid on one part, yet in reality, a half-baked truth. I intend to explain further, not in economic terms but from a social angle that should help the reader comprehend the country's true picture and economic problems and how impoverished life in Nigeria was pre-2000.

An individual owned a car in an entire community of tens of thousands of people during the period that some Nigerians fancifully thought things were great. An *otunba* was the sole owner of a telephone device in his town of over 100,000 people. Travelling abroad was an extraordinary feat, and parents frantically warned their children never to announce their plans to anyone for fear of such plans being thwarted by jealous evil-wishers. It is a well-known fact that some youths at a point in time (even into the 1990s) were the first barrier breakers (to either travel overseas or graduate from tertiary institutions) in their respective villages and communities. Just a measly number of citizens were able to purchase cars and houses; they were adult pensioners or corrupt individuals.

Today, we have seen that an unacceptable percentage of Nigerians who grew up in those "glory days" lacked basic education, with women being the major casualties of a faulty social and economic culture. They also lived without basic amenities, some of which they thought were not a problem then, but their absence has created significant problems for today's generations. So fancifully, they reminisced about when they could do several things with N1, yet are not so inclined to accept that the equivalent of $1, €1 or £1 means nothing to the relevant nations of those same currencies. In their misrepresented feeling of reminiscence, they think the country is badly damaged and wonder why they cannot purchase a car or a house for N1,000 like they could at a point. Yet, such people would not agree that inflation is part of the universal nature of money and economics.

Nigerians must understand that phoney and parochial beliefs impede economic growth as it sells a lie to generations. For reasons bordering on ethnic prejudice, some believe their region is richer and economically buoyant than the rest. In a country where debate on ethnicity and tribal affiliations overshadow moral discourses, such parochial beliefs often come into play by people who desperately want to see their regions secede or gain some form of autonomy. As I have said repeatedly, this book is not a platform to concur with secessionist ideologies. However, I must conclude that apart from the fanciful remarks and phoney attributions of abundant resources that political demagogues often sell to their people, many states in Nigeria are mostly impeded by the maladministration and ineptitude of their own state governors and regional administrators. The opinion that others are holding back their regions is purely illogical. It is another parochial belief that their indigenous leaders have sold to escape accountability and activate their blame-game machinery. Then again, such parochial beliefs have become a compulsive weapon in the armoury of political demagogues for propaganda reasons.

Inelegant Conclusion

In the scheme of economics, when we talk about growth, productivity, labour and investments, we talk about them by including everything necessary and mandatory that permits such. Inelegantly, as it has been shown, the Nigerian state is not ready to grow economically. The leaders are ever docile, incapable and too corrupt to make things work. The citizens, on their part, have proven that aside from their daily lamentations, they are not ready to see their economy grow. Many of our activities and behaviours create infertile grounds for local investment opportunities.

Nigerians should forget any hope of having investment opportunities in their country, at least anytime soon. To speak prophetically, in relativeness with the ongoing situation, I am inclined to say that jobs are not coming anytime soon. Unemployment rates are going to get worse. Things will get even worse than in years to come. In a country where citizens pride themselves on religious and spiritual beliefs, my doom prophecies should not be the focus. Rather, leaders and citizens who are guilty of the ongoing shame must be the ones to ensure that prophecies of doom by myself or those of experts around the world do not come to pass. Why do I believe things will worsen and investment opportunities are not coming?

Some Nigerians have never stepped foot in their ancestral hometowns and villages. Others who have done that are not any better at marketing their places of origin in a positive light. Real or not, merely superstitious or not, a joke taken too far or an outright reality, it is crucial to understand that the popular "village people" parlance is an existential feature that many people have come to see as an impediment to their productive existence or success. Likewise, so many Nigerians in the diaspora have ignoble memories of their home country and have sworn never to set foot in the country. Of relevance, job creation and economic growth are strongly attributed to foreign investments and how they can convince foreigners that their clime is worth investing in.

Therefore, it is imprudent to expect foreigners to treat our territories, nation and people with reverence when in actuality, all we do is treat the same with derision. Citizens that do not regard their own country would be foolhardy to expect foreigners to invest financial and material resources in the same region. It is very foolhardy for violence, insurgency, terrorism, secessionist threats, economic sabotage, fraud, corruption and crime to be allowed to gain fertile ground on our soil and simultaneously expect foreign investors to troop in. Inelegantly repeating, investments are not coming. Many who lament the country's high unemployment situation are mistaken to presume that foreign investors in their millionaire and billionaire status are stupid. For many investors, it is common for them to carry out their due diligence regarding the terrains they wish to invest their hard-earned money in, and thanks to our new digitalized world, research has been made easier. They see the comment section of youths who perceive financial fraud as a norm. They see you worship corrupt individuals and see how abnormalities have become a norm in your geographical clime.

No government can successfully micromanage the citizens or determine their tastes, addictions and interests. We are stubbornly obsessed with foreign products. Such obsessions come with grave consequences like unemployment and economic downturns. The ignorant yet obstinate "slay queen" on social media who is obsessed with Apple products is unaware that she and millions like her are responsible for the country's state of unemployment, the attack on our currency and the overall economy. The yahoo boys, whose obsession with Mercedes Benz cars and other foreign brands despite no reasonable ground for such other than their warped mentality, do not know that they have declared war on the Nigerian economy. The obsession of this group of people is the primary weapon, and their warped mentality is the armoury, all of which are necessary to continue launching attacks of various kinds on our economy.

I particularly signalled those two brands (Apple and Mercedes-Benz) for intentional and analytical purposes. In the last decade, they have enjoyed billions of dollars of purchases from the Nigerian market alone. Yet, it has not occurred to them to see Nigeria as an investment opportunity. Arrogantly, they do not bother to impact our economy, especially in advertising, promotional, education or other corporate social responsibility areas. Why should they? The Nigerian consumer is fanatically obsessed with those brands and their products, not necessarily for the quality their products present but as a bragging right to those set of misguided people. Why should other brands and manufacturing firms that have remained loyal to the country and invested a significant amount of money continue to operate when Nigerians have turned them down, even before their arrival? This pattern ensures that locally made products and their producers lack a competitive advantage against foreign counterparts.

Disastrous consequences have followed such unpatriotic acts of overreliance and obsession with imported goods. Apple and Mercedes-Benz are not the only profiteers of our economic woes; citizens have stubbornly decided to align with many products and brands, even in areas where the case should never be. As one of the country's chief economists once said, "If we do not kill unnecessary imports, imports will kill us all. Without jobs, we promote crime, kidnapping and terrorism."

Our obsession is in almost every area of our economy. In Sports, we ardently follow European football leagues, allowing our local and grassroots football to rot. Yet, we are foolhardy to expect a miraculous win at global competitions such as the World Cup. We expect wins in the same areas that we have abandoned. There is patriotism, and there is extravagant foolishness. The rot in our local league systems has not allowed for support. Regardless, that would be taking excuses too far. The excuse factory itself is one that I am not inclined to open for Nigerians to dwell in; when afforded to them, they dwell in it proudly. We have excuses for everything, and our excuses have come to copulate with our self-sabotage culture to produce a vicious and crushing result.

2: FINANCIAL CRIMES AND CORRUPTION

The Oxford English dictionary defines corruption as "dishonest or illegal behaviour, especially of people in authority."[1] Over the years, public and private officials have audaciously engaged in securing ill-gotten wealth with full "legal" backing, hence the validity of oxford's inclusion of the subjective word "dishonest" to go alongside the plausibly objective term "illegal". Still, both words could be said to be subject to various interpretations.

The word "crime" is defined as "an illegal act or activity that can be punished by law."[2] Additionally, crime could be described as an action or activity considered evil, shameful, or wrong. Generally, this book is a voluminous account of the various crimes committed against the Nigerian state and its people. In particular, this chapter and the next will be specifically dedicated to financial and other related crimes. Therefore, in looking at financial crime, we can define it as "all crimes committed by an individual or a group of individuals that involve taking money or other property that belongs to someone else, to obtain a financial or professional gain."[3] It may involve money laundering, terrorism financing, advance-fee fraud, insider trading, tax evasion, embezzlement, forgery, counterfeiting, bribery and identity theft. To put inelegantly and in the Nigerian context, financial fraud is synonymously defined as "*yahoo yahoo*" aka "419". This book examines other financially related aspects of criminal activities such as racketeering, land grabbing, drug smuggling, illegal arms dealing, and human trafficking According to the Interpol website:

Corruption creates a fertile ground for organised criminal activities, even terrorism, as criminals are aided in their illegal activities by the complicity of corrupt public officials. The effects of corruption are far-reaching: it can undermine political, social and economic stability, and ultimately threaten the safety and security of society as a whole.

In Nigeria, a challenge facing the definitions of corruption and crime is the paradoxical aspect of ideological inconsistency surrounding the nature of both words. What could rightly constitute corruption in saner climes is absurdly adjudged as an element of luck or heavenly grace in Nigeria. Beneficiaries of financial crime tend to misconstrue the proceeds from their activities as a portion of heavenly blessing, especially in Nigerian societies where corruption and illicit acts of wealth acquisitions are flamboyantly celebrated.

Corruption and financial crimes are dangerous global problems that eat deep into every society and aspect of human endeavours. Corruption rears its ugly head in politics, sport, business, finance, healthcare, law enforcement, commerce, trade, public institutions, the judiciary and educational institutions. Corruption and fraud could be found in religious institutions - in God's own house; the scope of corrupt persons and their practices is limitless and without boundary. A World Bank publication agrees:

> Corruption is a major obstacle to economic development. It reduces domestic investment, discourages foreign direct investment, inflates government spending, and shifts government spending away from education, health, and infrastructure maintenance toward less efficient (more manipulable) public projects.[4]

The effect of corruption is that it is the umbrella through which all other forms of crimes and criminal behaviour in society are permitted, aided, and abetted. Limiting the definition of corruption strictly to what is

69

constitutionally illegal would mock the Nigerian reality. For instance, we can defiantly agree that the total money accrued to federal lawmakers and their executive counterparts showcases the grand scale of systematic fraud and corruption despite its legal backing.

Financial crimes and corruption are as old as man and very incremental, especially when the available factors for their growth and spread are not adequately tackled. The then governor of the new entity, Lord Frederick Lugard, recorded one of the first documented cases of financial crime in the newly created Nigeria. Lord Lugard was said to have complained bitterly about the extortive practices of certain fraudsters who roamed villages, communities and hinterlands claiming to levy taxes on behalf of the colonialists or other related authorities. They did not stop there. They continued to perpetuate their activities in various colonial and post-colonial settings, where they carried out their acts with impunity to the detriment of unsuspecting natives.

Shortly after independence, Nigeria became so infested with bribery and corruption cases to such an extent that Stanislav Andreski, the respected Polish-British sociologist, coined a new word, "kleptocracy", a word that now describes social, economic, and political practices in Nigeria.[5] That word also defines the link between political and public offices and illicit moneymaking. We could also say that the British unavoidably left a buoyant economy into the hands of thieves and kleptocrats, hence the commencement of the country's fall from grace. Officials of the regional and federal governments were so riddled with acts of bribery, corruption and other related malpractices that accusations and counter-accusations became hotly debated on the political fronts. Federal officers Inua Wuda and Festus Okotie-Eboh, who were ministers for works and finance, respectively, were both said to be aggressively corrupt. Suppose the reader would permit me to make an opinion from credible sources and gathered pieces of evidence. In that case, I could strongly assert Festus Okotie-Eboh as Nigeria's founder and pioneer of grand political corruption.

As you will read, the effects of bribery and corruption came crushing. Local and foreign businessmen, knowing they could get away with anything and everything lobbied for contracts they did not intend to fulfil. Proposals designed to cheat the public were taken to commissioners, ministers and other public officials for approval. Foreign companies and individuals, counting their luck at the fortune of non-regulation and lack of scrutiny, ran amok and took as many profits as possible. Companies and individuals setting forth to engage in business with government officials reportedly had to factor into their overall budget the amount paid as bribes to such officials. Simply put, government projects that should have cost £1 million were pencilled at £1.1 million, with the extra £100,000 being the cost paid to individuals as bribes. That was then; today, things have gotten even worse.

Financial crimes and corruption grew surreptitiously well after independence into the 1970s, judging at least by today's operational bar. Nonetheless, we could largely agree that grand corruption in Nigeria started in the 1980s for two major reasons. The first was that the Second Republic of Alhaji Shehu Shagari coincided with a period the country experienced an economic downturn, and citizens began to perpetrate whatever action they deemed necessary to make ends meet. Secondly, the military administration of General Ibrahim Babangida differed greatly from the highhandedness and zero-tolerance approach of its predecessor, Major-General Muhammadu Buhari. Babangida's government seemingly gave a wild card to citizens to do as they pleased. The lackadaisical attitude of both the Shagari and Babangida administrations gave sharp rise and embracement to financial crimes and corruption.

Crime and corruption in Nigeria are big, large, and extremely profitable. Organised crime in Nigeria guarantees so much return on investment that its major players sometimes worry less about consequences or punishments. Corrupt and shady dealings can cross multiple sections, making investigations and crime fighting to be time-consuming, complex, rigorous and at times impossible to fight. As documented, corrupt practices are

71

interwoven and intertwined, making it nearly impossible to separate acts of corruption perpetrated in one sector from the other. Analyses of corruption and similar misconduct in various subchapters below branch into one another due to their inseparability, for instance, fraud in the travel sector will spill into the banking sector. Fraud in the banking sector without repercussion often affects other industries due to ongoing dishonesty in the accounting, legal and judicial sectors. Corruption in the oil and gas sector relies heavily on a similar trend in the public sector. They all enjoy some immunity due to a breakdown in prosecutorial diligence, political governance, or corruption in the judiciary.

Nigeria is a country where crime and corruption have become societal cancer. Street smart Nigerians are suspicious of how celebrities wake up to sudden life of unexplainable wealth despite inconsistencies in what they do and what they claim to earn. As part of a team of private investigators for an anti-crime agency, I uncovered that deposits were made into the bank accounts of not less than 20 famous Nigerian celebrities and public figures whose accounts had been used to siphon and launder illicit money. The deposited funds were billions of cash laundered separately from prominent drug barons and money launderers who had consistently used their connections to evade justice. Sadly, the report was never made public, and I am not permitted to comment further on the topic. Separately, a torch investigation into some of the country's celebrities and socialites returned evidential acts of financial crimes, money laundering and other related crimes. Many of the country's famous faces are themselves, money cleaners to corrupt politicians, launderers, fraudsters, traffickers, and sometimes terrorists.

As you will read, the cost of preventing crimes will forever be cheaper than the cost of fighting and punishing its offenders. Reprehensible individuals have little or nothing to lose when they perpetrate their activities, but the damaging impact of their actions will always be colossal. For instance, according to the NBC News Network, the November 2015 Paris attacks cost the attackers less than $10,000. But the impact on the Paris economy was an estimated catastrophic $2.1 billion loss.[6] Similarly, the 9/11 attackers reportedly spent an estimated $500,000 in expenses to carry out the attacks. The attacks resulted in a tremendous loss of $40 billion in insurance losses and two consequential wars with a $6 trillion cost to the United States.[7] Nigeria itself continues to suffer from the effects of corruption and other criminal activities as investors abandon our geographical corner for business-friendly regions.

The title of this chapter is not accidental. Monumental acts of fraud and financial-related crimes that took place in so-called saner climes mysteriously and inexplicably found their way to Nigeria or involved its citizens. For instance, during the infamous Lockheed bribery scandals that rocked the global world of aviation, investigators uncovered that the company paid $3.6 million in bribes to Nigerian officials on a deal worth $45 million.[8] Similarly, the collapse of one of London's most prestigious banks at a time, Johnson Matthey Bankers, was partly traced to the usual Nigerian factor of corruption and fraud. Shady and fraudulent dealings in Nigeria, including granting unsecured loans for politically related activities, led to the bank losing an estimated $170 million.[9] And when the BCCI scandal rocked the global world of banking in 1991, again, Nigeria featured. Time magazine reported that Nigeria received $1 billion in loans from BCCI London following violent anti-government protests in 1989.[10] Other disgraceful international cases such as the Haliburton and the Siemens scandals had the imprints of corrupt Nigerian officials. As regards the cases I cited in this paragraph, foreign authorities pursued the perpetrators aggressively and made them answer for their wrongdoings. In Nigeria, however, none of those involved was ever convicted. Some got elevated up the social, political, and economic ladder.

As you will read, encapsulating real-life historical examples are cited to give the reader a better insight into the level of corruption behind the curtains of our national and societal affairs. Behind the curtains reside state actors and perpetrators who go to every length to ensure that such matters never make it into the public domain. The scandals cited in this book are just a few appalling cases that inevitably made it out to the public domain. If they do make it out to the public domain, a judicial intervention impudently acquitting such ostensibly corrupt or criminal individuals makes it discouraging to cite them in this book for managerial and legal reasons. Aggressively exaggerated headlines by undisciplined and corrupt journalists and media outlets to sell snow as charcoal to the public are some reasons why some high-profile cases will be snubbed so as not to fall victim to the dirty propaganda net of some ill-intent elements. Hence, as a forewarning, some notable cases that should typically be referenced are intentionally omitted. Likewise, the cases cited in this chapter and the next, can be used to understand what has transpired and continue to transpire daily in social, economic and political Nigeria.

Contract and Procurement Frauds

Contract and procurement fraud is one of the first recognised types of financial corruption that started to rear its ugly head in the period leading to independence. These types of fraud were perpetrated by public officials looking to make additional gains for themselves through inflated sums in the amount billed for procurements. They received bribes from contractors who then added up amounts paid through bribery to their overall cost. Private citizens also participated fully in contract fraud by inputting excessive amounts during invoicing, especially in business relationships with less educated or unsuspecting buyers and businessmen who sought their services.

As early as the First Republic, some public officials were nicknamed "ten-percenters" by those knowledgeable for their notorious acts of demanding bribes in the region of 10% of total amounts awarded before such contracts could be approved.[11] This later became a norm and a virus that spread throughout financial dealings in the country. Contract and procurement frauds were perpetrated brazenly during the country's post-independence period when it gained a normative status. For decades, contract frauds went on without respect for accountability or consequences until one of the most disreputable cases in global history occurred in the 1970s, under the administration of General Yakubu Gowon.

Under Gowon, Nigeria experienced its "best years", and things went smoothly, as per the hype and belief from those who inappropriately concluded that Nigeria was tremendously rich. Ironically, the country had just recovered from a bloody civil war and Gowon and the FMG were desperate to put Nigeria right back on track. Therefore, Gowon's FMG thought it necessary to embark on massive infrastructural projects. Events from around the world helped the price of oil to soar to heights never imagined. Military barracks, police stations, bridges, roads, schools, public buildings, and other infrastructures were to be newly built or repaired. In other words, massive public works were set to commence, and resources were needed in huge supplies. The Yakubu Gowon administration estimated 3 to 5 million metric tons of cement would be required for the infrastructural projects and made orders to such effect; except there was a significant and embarrassing problem that came screeching.

Despite the estimated figure being put maximally at 5 million metric tons, it was discovered that an estimated 16 to 20 million tons had been ordered and were on their way to the shores of Nigeria; a devastating problem was looming. By 1975, ships from countries where the cement orders were placed started to dock at the Lagos Port, hoping to disembark. Embarrassingly, a Lagos Port at the time that could only take an estimated delivery of 1 million metric tons within a year had more than 20 million metric tons of ships converging at its seaport concurrently. Soon afterwards, details began to emerge about what had gone wrong. It was discovered that public officials, government agents, and private contractors hoping to profiteer exorbitantly had placed orders in significantly high numbers and at highly overpriced figures. They carried out their activities without cohesion, accountability or due process, obviously in a bid to outdo, outsmart and defraud the country. The resultant effects of their actions were shattering.

If the probably lay reader needs further explanation on actual numbers and figures of losses incurred during the shameful episode, I will gladly elaborate further. A ton is calculated at 40 units of 25kg bag of packed cement product; 20 million tons, therefore, equates to 800 million 25kg bags of cement. Even worse, buyers fixed a fraudulent amount of $115 per ton, which was said to be 2 to 3 times the average cement price in the global market. That meant the Nigerian government owed $2.3 billion ($1.4 Trillion in 2021 exchange value) for the dishonest acts perpetrated by a few. In addition, the figures did not consider the cost of shipping, logistics, or the estimated $4000 per day cost of demurrage for an estimated 500 ships that could not load.[12] It was also discovered that as the country was losing by paying demurrage fees incurred from the actual 20 million tons of cement at the Lagos Port, some ship owners and their cohorts took advantage of the imbroglio by loading cargoes filled with inferior goods to collect unmerited demurrage fees and other applicable fraudulent payments from the government. Credible sources have highlighted this national disgrace as the final blow that nailed the Gowon administration and eventually got him toppled from office in July 1975.

The "Cement Armada" episode is enough illustration of how Nigerians perpetrate contract and procurement fraud and also illustrates the devastating effects that accompany such type of fraud. In many public and private organisations, contract and procurement fraud have become a disease that the infected persons are not in a hurry to do away with, except to infect anyone that can collude with them. MDAs sabotage societal and national growth by awarding contracts to unqualified, inexperienced, incompetent, or blatantly unscrupulous contractors to embark on social and infrastructural projects.

Every time we lament the country's bad shape and look for whom to blame for our national woes, we must be reminded to look at the man in the mirror. The Dasukigate scandal and other military cases cited in this book's prequel illustrate the country's colossal loss to procurement and budgeting fraud. In August 2018, the MD of the Transmission Company of Nigeria (TCN), Usman Mohammed, announced that the organisation had finally recovered 693 containers of power equipment abandoned at different ports in the country. He shocked reporters when he alleged that some had been at the port for more than 15 years.[13] In a country in dire need of emergency solutions to its energy issues, how it was possible for such items to be purchased and left to rot at the port will forever be a mystery, or perhaps not. The lack of accountability in Nigeria has created a fertile ground for theft, fraud and sabotage of all kinds.

Another aspect of contract and procurement fraud is the intentional purchase of substandard products. Public officials acting in connivance with private contractors often purchase substandard products after circumventing established rules and procedures for procurements, hence short-changing the government. To avoid ethical scrutiny and procedures in the bidding processes, private contractors would submit extremely low figures to secure a bidding advantage and eventual approval over other competitors. Afterwards, they purchase low-quality materials that wear off rapidly without facing the consequences of their actions.

Private investigation in Nigeria is very challenging. The skilled investigator must harden his emotions and prepare his mental wellness for the inundated cases of shock and gory he is sure to encounter. Most private investigators would confirm that virtually all the cases contracted to them are at the farthermost side of vice lines where man's cruelty to man is exhibited. On one similar occasion concerning contract fraud I investigated, a government agency once awarded a contract valued at N17 billion to a contractor to construct a major road. Although the N17 billion was approved, the contractor only got N10 billion apportioned to him, while the rest of the N7 billion went their separate ways to respective "heads" of the awarding agency. Of the remaining N10 billion, N3.5 billion went into the coffers of intermediaries, oversight, regulatory and potential "whistleblowing" bodies. The contractor was left with N6.5 billion naira to do the N17 billion job. I assume the reader of this book to be a regular user of Nigerian roads and need no reminder on what the outcome of such unholy arrangements mostly leads to.

Nigerians are unfamiliar with noticeable infrastructural developments in their communities and regions. Schools, roads, markets, public buildings and structures awarded for construction or repairs quickly become an eyesore as contractors crudely embark on using substandard products or lack the necessary experience to engage in such activities in the first place. Nevertheless, billions of naira are said to be earmarked annually for government projects that citizens do not see or feel the impacts.

Contract and procurement fraud affect us collectively. Our hospitals are left without the necessary medical equipment and facilities. Schools are left with shortages of books, laboratory items and research materials because some people think their interests should come first before the education of innocent children. As seen in the Dasukigate scandal and other previously cited cases, security weapons and gadgets for our law enforcement and security personnel are substandard, inefficient, or insufficient because some believe that personal financial security is more important than state security. Building contractors and developers intentionally use inferior materials to construct homes that eventually collapse because what matters to them are rental fees and not the safety of their tenants. Procurement officers knowingly purchase defective mechanical equipment without considering the haphazard consequences of their action on field workers who could get maimed or even killed while using the faulty equipment.

In Nigeria, many officials are "permitted" by law to carry out contract and procurement thefts due to the absence of proper laws, rules, guidelines and mechanisms that should have guarded against potential theft and fraud.

While on a private investigator assignment for a particular organisation, I discovered that a principal officer was engaged in a significant level of contract fraud with the support of archaic contract guidelines and regulations. On knowing that any contract that is to be awarded and valued below N50 million can be approved at his sole discretion without being subject to approval by the organisation's board, the official systematically dodged the stipulated system in place. Of the 102 contracts awarded during his four-year term at the helm of affairs, only 17 were above the N50 million threshold. However, the individual values of most contracts he awarded were far more than the N50 million threshold. What he did was simple. He split mega contracts that would have fallen above the N50 million threshold into separate units. That enabled him to approve contracts to whomever he pleased without board approval. Perhaps, his activities could have been ignored if corruption and theft were not allowed to become the causal factor of monumental fraud and loss for the organisation. I discovered he was taking 20% kickbacks of the total cost of awarded contracts from the contractors he gave out jobs to. The effect meant that of the 102 contracts scrutinised for performance test, an unacceptable number of just 21 passed the appropriate validity test. Others failed deplorably, all thanks to the corrupt activity of the man at the helm of contract approval.

To understand how devastatingly corrupt we have become, it is relevant to know that procurement fraud is cultured as normative and standard behaviour in societal Nigeria. Through acts of negligence, illiteracy, ignorance, client retention tactics or one with intent to defraud, sellers would often ask buyers the specific amount they wish to put on the receipt of a purchased item. This is due to an unspoken but psycho-contractual engagement between sellers and buyers on a general perception that the latter is out to short-change the actual procurer of the purchased items. Such is the general perception that gives social acceptance to financial frauds in our clime. Whichever way we look at the issues raised in this subchapter, they affect us significantly and are responsible for the messy situation the country finds itself.

Payroll and Pensions Frauds

Nigeria is one of the countries with the highest rate of unemployment in the world. With an unemployment rate of around 30% as of 2020, it would take only a satanic individual to deny people access to direct forms of employment intentionally. Modern-day financial technology instruments being put in place by the authorities are beginning to uncover monumental fraud in payroll, labour and pension schemes throughout the country.

Modern fraud detection and verification platforms such as the BVN, TSA, GIFMIS, IPPIS and other biometric mechanisms have led to the discovery of fraud and high-level irregularities in payments relating to salaries and pensions. As these mechanisms are new and relatively dispersed across the country to curtail the presence of payroll and pension frauds, it became clear that some criminals have participated in this aspect of fraud for decades. While Nigerians have been lamenting high unemployment rates for decades, some people were simultaneously drawing salaries on inexistent personnel (popularly called "ghost" workers) at various government tiers.

According to the former finance minister, Dr Ngozi Okonjo-Iweala, the introduction of the GIFMIS and IPPIS led to the elimination of 65,000 ghost workers from the system by 2015.[14] In February 2016, the finance ministry says it detected 23,846 ghost workers and effectively removed them from its payroll system.[15] Additionally, the Federal Government announced a further removal of 50,000 ghost workers from its payroll system, saving the country an estimated N200 billion annually. Ghost worker fraud is not a menace solely associated with the federal government. It is rampant across the two lower tiers of government and in the workforce of private companies.

The Borno state government claimed in 2016 that it had detected more than 10,000 ghost workers in its civil service, which is almost half of its entire 25,000 workforce. It did not stop there. Later, in early 2021, Borno authorities claimed they detected more than 22,500 ghost workers, which included massive discoveries in the local government workforce. The Borno government said the fraud cost the state a monumental figure of over N420 million monthly.[16] Similarly, it was reported that between September 2013 and May 2015, over 110,000 ghost workers were paid a staggering N220 billion from the federal government alone, while ten state governments lost N318 billion to this evil and shameful menace.[17]

At local government levels, ghost workers or inflation of the labour force is used regularly by top officials as high as local government chairmen and administrators who rely heavily on the state tier of government for funding. Across the three tiers of government, labour and pension frauds are mostly undetected for many reasons. This is mostly due to the absence of a well-organised system for verifying the reported labour force figures in respective MDAs. Dr Ngozi Okonjo-Iweala lamented that after she was appointed finance minister in 2003, she discovered that no one knew the actual figures of the total workforce in the federal civil service.[18] If that were to be believed, then it must be understood that Nigeria has operated a civil service system that was carelessly or intentionally designed to be wholly fraudulent.

The private sector is not immune to this ugly practice. The practice, however, is a bit impossible to accomplish since most private entrepreneurs have first-hand knowledge and direct information on the number of personnel who work for them. One way to perpetrate payroll fraud in private establishments is through hiring. As a condition for hiring, recruitment managers or other top executives hint applicants about the compulsive removal of certain deductions from their salaries after eventual selection.

Payroll fraud is also carried out due to the lackadaisical attitude of an entrepreneur or the company's managers. A foreign-based individual once hired me to investigate certain practices engaged by the manager of his manufacturing firm back home in Nigeria. I discovered how his company manager was drawing payments for inexistent personnel. I discovered that the personnel working at the manufacturing firm did not match the numbers of reported staff he claimed to have hired. The manager cheated his employer of an estimated sum of N3.2 million monthly, despite the company making an average profit of N400,000. Payroll fraud denies unemployed people from getting job opportunities and runs businesses to the ground, creating further problems in the employment sector.

In May 2021, the BBC aired a documentary exposing Nigeria's pension fraud. The investigation uncovered civil servants' dirty and greedy nature in bribe-for-payment pension schemes.[19] They demand bribes from pensioners after systematically denying them their pension entitlements. Pensioners unable to keep up with the physically and mentally demanding bottlenecks involved in collecting their pension payments are left with no choice but to cough out money they do not have to facilitate the clearance and eventual settlement of their pensions. Others are not so lucky. They die penniless without ever receiving their pensions, despite contributing enormous savings into the pension savings systems during their time as public servants. As uncovered by the BBC, the fraudulent acts have gone on for decades and have become accepted as a sad norm for the country's pensioners. Pension fraud in Nigeria is perpetrated from the very top to the lowest person in the organisational structure.

My first encounter with the pensions bottleneck in the country was in the 2000s during periodical visits with my grandmother to various government-designated locations to facilitate her pension payments. There, as a young teenager, I noticed that after my grandmother and other pensioners had received their pensions (usually at the City Hall in Lagos Island), they proceeded to a certain office to pay a certain amount, which I believe was in the region of 5%-10% of their pension payments. I misunderstood the money the pensioners removed from their pensions as a standard practice. Now, as an adult, I have deduced what went wrong and perhaps is still in practice. Pensioners who passed the standard clearance process and are qualified to receive benefits are compelled to "drop something". Failure to do that would have their subsequent pensions delayed or denied. Physically challenged pensioners unable to meet stipulated conditions for clearance, such as physical appearances at the screening centres, are forced to pay kickbacks to officials before rendering them the necessary assistance they deserve.

Payroll and pension frauds are among many other ways that top political and public officers make monumental wealth at the expense of people's sorrow and anguish. Transparency groups have alleged how fake identities are created and used to draw the benefits of living pensioners. The genuine beneficiaries hit a block when they eventually set to collect their rightful pension because someone else with access to their information had drawn their payments. When a pensioner dies, civil servants in the know orchestrate means to continue drawing their pension for as long as possible. Pensioners across the country continue to decry various forms of injustice inflicted on them by relevant agencies charged with disbursing their payments. They decry being owed for months or even years. There are encapsulating examples that should point to the direction of where the funds are being held.

The case of John Yakubu Yusuf, a former Assistant Director of the Police Pension Department who pleaded guilty to a N32.8 billion pension fraud scheme, is a relevant example of how people's sweat, blood, tears and cries are drawn to satisfy the needs of fraudsters. The EFCC charged Yakubu Yusuf alongside the department's former director, Atiku Abubakar Kigo and others in the fraud scheme. Fraudulent schemes such as that of Kigo and others meant that homes and families must be wrecked, people impoverished and left unfed due to the greed and satanic thirst of a few corrupt monsters.

Similarly, in November 2021, an Abuja Federal High Court sentenced Abdulrasheed Abdullahi Maina to eight years in prison for diverting over N2billion pension funds for personal use. Maina's role and activity were all the more shocking, considering his position as head of the Pension Reform Task Team (PRTT), a reform team set up by the federal government to look into leakages in the pension system. It would seem that there is a supernatural force behind the fraudulent character of citizens when a man like Maina, who was tasked with stopping leakages, became the eventual facilitator of the leakage.

Settlement Frauds: Judgement, Hidden and Compensatory Damages

A judgement debt is when a defendant has been judged to owe a debt by a court of law. Judgement debts arise when a government ministry, department or agency defaults on a contract, especially in its payment, and is sued by a contractor or service provider, otherwise known as the judgement creditor. Disagreements between government MDAs and contractors are not new, and such disputes occur in different circumstances. However, when such disputes are not properly handled, they find their way into the court of law for proper administration. The natural disagreements between individuals or groups and respective government MDAs are not the subject of discourse but that of negligence, greed, fraud and unholy alliance among parties whose mission is to steal from the public purse.

The disproportionate numbers of court cases against MDAs are particularly suspicious due to a fraudulent pattern that shows an unholy alliance involving public officials and private persons with the sole aim of cheating the government and the people. It has been discovered that public officials enter into backdoor agreements with certain contractors and service providers for rightful payments to the latter to be delayed or for certain aspects of the contracts to be dishonoured. Such agreements are reached so that when contractors and servicers approach the court of law, they not only seek for the actual debt to be paid but also for financial damages to be awarded in their favour. Another unholy alliance involves lawyers appointed by the MDAs who intentionally ensure that the lawsuits against the MDA favour the litigant. The participants involved in the type of fraud, having duped the government, then share the proceeds from the awarded judgement debt and compensation.

Although some of the cases I scrutinised had fraud and corruption written all over, others were out of negligence, incompetence or abuse of office. Whichever way, they bleed our economic purse devastatingly, unknown to many, in the quietest ways of national catastrophe and loss. For instance, in March 2014, the Federal High Court in Abuja presided over by Justice Adamu Abdu-Kafarati, gave a **$15 billion judgment** in favour of Petro Union and its directors in a suit against the Federal Government of Nigeria, the CBN and Union Bank PLC. Subsequently, an appeal filed by Union Bank PLC failed when in June 2018, the Court of Appeal sitting in Abuja upheld the lower court's judgement and dismissed Union Bank's appeal. The matter is currently before the Apex Court at the time of publishing this book.

Notwithstanding, it is important to find out why and how such an astronomical figure, half the size of the country's 2021 total budget expenditure, got awarded against the country by two courts of competent jurisdiction. It is also appropriate to find out why the legal might of the CBN and the Federal Government was not active in such a case of national importance to the extent that Union Bank PLC was left to shoulder much of the legal responsibility and challenges of the civil case. While I am not permitted by law to comment further on this issue for obvious legal reasons, I am forced to ask the type of country we live in where a 15% interest per annum could be allowed to be incurred on a "debt" for 26 years. The judgement makes the sum of interest paid four times higher than the said debt. A potential loss of such magnitude makes it the single most catastrophic financial loss documented in this book and worthy of rigorous scrutiny.

Sadly, scrutiny is an absent word in the lexicon of Nigerian policymakers, and that has become a loophole for aggravated fraud and sabotage against the Nigerian state and its people.

On January 31, 2017, a tribunal sitting in London made a final award of $6.6 billion together with pre-and post-judgment interest of 7% against the FGN over a botched 20-year Gas and Supply Processing Agreement (GSPA) with British firm, P&ID.[20] At the period of finalising this book, **our country seems to be heading for a colossal loss in the essence of $12billion.** If this does not alarm the reader at this point, I do not know what else would. The reader must be wondering what went wrong and how the country found itself in such a situation of colossal loss. Well, it happened, and it is safe to assume that a few citizens, along with their foreign collaborators, made it so through negligence, greed, fraud, sabotage, or even treason. Those are people's fathers, and those are people's mothers. Unashamedly, they have also been decorated with elegant traditional titles and are applauded as they take seats at public functions.

Similarly, following the aftermath of the disgraceful "Cement Armada" episode, then Head of State General Olusegun Obasanjo berated the activities of those the Federal Military Government assigned to guide the government on judgement debts awarded against the country. After the disgraceful episode, which cost the country billions of dollars in financial losses, judgement creditors impounded some of the country's assets and properties in certain parts of the world. They affected seizures after the FMG denied them payments they deemed were owed to them. Obasanjo bitterly lamented how civil servants, lawyers and officials who advised the government, turned around to act as commission agents for the creditors.[21] Armed with the foreknowledge of government reserve positions on the matters, they sabotaged the efforts of the FMG to have a fair agreement with the creditors or even to pursue legitimate claims against the creditors in court. Hence, Nigeria lost astronomical monies due to the greed of people's fathers, mothers, uncles and aunts. Most who have children today lamenting on the state of the nation that their bloodlines created.

Former finance minister Dr Ngozi Okonjo-Iweala equally complained about judgement debt scams. She gave credence to my earlier assertion, saying:

> But there were plenty of stories involving dozens of people. Some had to do with connivance between contractors, ministry officials, and the courts in an unholy alliance, where amounts owed by the government, interest, and penalties were inflated and all parties shared in the proceeds after payments. Others had to do with genuine court proceedings that were defended less than vigorously by government lawyers, thereby leading to loss of the case, heavy fines, and again the sharing of the proceeds among the involved parties. Another set of stories had to do with arbitration and out-of-court settlements that were unfavourable for the government.[22]

Dr Okonjo-Iweala further claimed that between 2012 and 2014, judgement debts amounting to N11.6 billion were verified, certified and paid out to appropriate creditors, while a balance of N68.4 billion was saved by her ministry in funds that should have gone out to unscrupulous elements.[23] In a twist of event, the incumbent Attorney General of the Federation, Abubakar Malami, admitted, "there exists over N150 billion judgment debt against the interest of the federal government, as at 2015 when this government came into being".[24] Either way, when we consider the lamentations of Okonjo-Iweala and Malami, we can rightly conclude that some fellow citizens have made it their mission to turn sufficient gasoline on the Nigerian economy and to light it on fire.

Some of us have never held political or public offices at any point in time and might be unaware of the key challenges facing well-meaning public office holders. Suppose the stories told by credible past and present public/political officers were to be believed. In that case, some frauds deliberately sabotage the country's economy at the merit of a few evil individuals. In fact, outside of the typical rumours that emanate from the aggressive, biased and ever-hyperbolic media news headlines, it is often instructive to listen to first-hand accounts from inside players. Therefore, I must take out this subchapter to show Nigerians what their citizens do in collaboration with foreigners to sabotage and destroy the nation's economy. Dr Ngozi Okonjo-Iweala, in her book *"Fighting Corruption is Dangerous"*, told two believable stories that should corroborate my assertions.

In her first story, she recollected how she was called to the office of the then president, Goodluck Jonathan, sometime in July 2014. The latter had called her to join him in an urgent meeting that involved the country's Chief of Naval Staff (CNS), a senior presidential aide and two representatives from a Middle East shipbuilding company, Privinvest.[25] The CNS informed the minister of the need to finalise a deal with the foreign merchants to help the Navy carry out its objectives as that military branch faced several inadequacies and challenges. The Privinvest representatives claimed that they were ready to invest $2 billion to help the Nigerian Navy achieve its purpose of refitting and modernising some of its key assets, among other things. Puzzled, when the finance minister asked what the catch was that would require a private company - that was not a charity organisation - to invest $2 billion in the country's military expenditures, she realised a suspicious agenda. Privinvest would seek out a loan in their name to invest on the condition that the Nigerian government would guarantee it. Privinvest's mission was to profiteer ludicrous amounts of money from Nigeria through the streams of revenues sufficient to repay the said loan and a margin left over for the investors. In addition, Privinvest was not going to be responsible for any risk of default; that would have to be carried solely by the Nigerian government.

Luckily, the finance minister turned down such a shambolic agreement that could have seen the country lost not only $2 billion in an opaque investment deal but also the consequences of such an agreement. Coincidentally, Privinvest did not approach Nigeria alone for such an opaque deal. They also approached the southeast African country of Mozambique for a similar deal during the same period they approached Nigeria, claiming they could help the country's fishing and maritime industry. Unfortunately, as the case was, Mozambique agreed. Through then president Armando Guebuza, the Mozambican government approved three loans totalling $2 billion to finance the construction of the shipyards, the creation of a fishing fleet, and the deployment of coastguards to curb piracy and illegal fishing.[26] These deals immediately became subjects of controversy in Mozambique and the global financial market.

If the dramatic turn of events in Mozambique were true as it seems, perhaps Nigerians owe deep gratitude to its former finance minister, Dr Ngozi Okonjo-Iweala. This I conclude, despite many public condemnations against her on several other matters, for at least not following in the footstep of her Mozambican counterpart, who was said to have received $5 million in bribes to sabotage the Mozambican economy.[27] It was reported that a total of $136 million were paid in bribes during the Mozambican affair. Indeed, any deal involving the payment of $7 million or $136 million in bribes is bound to be catastrophic. Moreover, the word catastrophic became the result of the Mozambican affair, as the IMF punished the country when it withdrew funding, thereby causing a collapse of the country's currency collapse.

What manner of people destroys their own country for money that they and their generations may never be able to spend comfortably due to the often-catastrophic consequences of their action? The answer is evil-minded people who have found their

way into every corner of our political and public offices. They are ably supported by citizens who welcome them glamorously through sycophancy and prevalent impunity culture.

In another story told by the honourable finance minister, a consortium of Nigerian and foreign project sponsors had sought the permission of the federal government to fund projects to the tune of $2 billion to $3 billion, provided certain conditions were met. [28] According to her, the deal presented to the federal government was "too good to be true", and no one would give out billions of dollars in grants in the manner the consortium had proposed. It eventually turned out that she was right.

People besiege federal, states and local governments in the country with various ideas that is purportedly rich on paper but destructive in practicality. It becomes even worse and detrimental to the public purse if the perpetrators have inside functionaries working with them to help destroy their own country. As we realise, some of these inside functionaries are lawyers, representatives, public officials, political appointees, local government chairpersons, governors, lawmakers, commissioners, ministers, and so on. They sign opaque and extraordinarily fraudulent deals that only serve their selfish interest and those of their allied saboteurs. Nigerians continue to witness the alarming rate at which the country's national debt piles up yet have no idea where the borrowed money ended up. Some of the problems analysed earlier on, hopefully, answer their curiosity. Several debt lawsuits are being filed in separate local, federal and international courts against various tiers of governments and their respective MDAs. These cases seriously jeopardise our economic purse and threaten our national economy, yet they are unacceptably underreported.

One other type of fraud that I detected as a private investigator in Nigeria is compensatory fraud. That arises from an unholy union involving treacherous citizens, law enforcement officers, legal practitioners and their cronies in the judicial arm of government. Law enforcement officers, mostly involving police officers, would inflict fabricated physical harm on a suspect, who then heads to court to plead his case over a perceived breach of his fundamental rights. The plaintiff would demand that compensatory/punitive damages be paid to him for injuries he incurred due to the purported actions of the law enforcement officers. Sometimes, such plans are well orchestrated to prove to the court that, in truth, the plaintiff had lost a significant amount of financial loss due to the events that transpired. Although there are credible events tendered in court to prove the same, they are false and fictitiously arranged to help the "aggrieved plaintiff" to secure a judgement. A backdoor agreement between parties involved would therefore see ludicrous amounts awarded to the plaintiff; a sum that would then be shared by the parties involved. By my estimate, billions of naira are lost to this particular type of fraud nationwide every year. These are true-life stories of how Nigerians dupe Nigerians. However, it is just one out of many scenarios that this subchapter is unable to cover at its extensive length.

Nigeria's Bank Frauds

The banking industry is a natural pillar of economic growth and progress of any society. It has played an effective role since the Banking Ordinance became effective in 1952. Despite relative success, the banking sector continues to experience its share of the Nigerian problem of chaos and setbacks. Setback and distress in the banking sector often have devastating effects on the economy as a whole, as both are inseparable aspects of each other in our modern world. Investors, depositors and the general public started to lose money as indiscipline, unethical practices, maladministration, corruption, and other accompanying features of fraud and criminality began to find their way into the banking industry.

In the private and commercial scheme of things, the banking industry is the chief enabler of all forms of corruption, theft, fraud and other financial crimes against the citizens.

According to the Nigeria Deposit Insurance Corporation (NDIC), a total of 45 failed banks were closed and had their licences revoked by the CBN between 1994 and 2006.[29] The NDIC also disclosed that it had carried out liquidation activities on 425 financial institutions since its incorporation in 1988. While it is only right to acknowledge that certain macro issues are responsible for bank failures, it is equally sad that we have to deal with intentional human culpabilities.

Banking crises are universal, as banks are susceptible to various risks such as credit, liquidity, interest rate, and other environmental factors. Systemic banking crises can damage affected economies into deep recessions and sharp current account reversals. According to the World Bank, some causes of banking crises are unsustainable macroeconomic policies, excessive credit booms, large capital inflows, and balance sheet fragilities, combined with policy paralysis due to various political and economic constraints.[30] Financial chaos and cataclysmic consequences are very certain to trail a nation's economy when factors such as corruption, fraud, manipulation, forged trading, money laundering, sham loans, investment fraud and other unethical practices are eventually added to the list.

Today, it has become obvious that Nigerian banks are not just a haven for fraud and criminality but also an instrument of legality through which state resources are plundered. They have become the legal backbone of theft and financial crimes of all kinds are perpetrated against the state, societies, groups, businesses and individuals. The various type of fraud and related activities executed in the banking industry includes internet fraud, ATM/card-related fraud, letter of credit fraud, account opening fraud, suppression of customer deposits, general cheque fraud, cheque kiting, unauthorised credits, currencies manipulation and theft, diversion of bank charges, loan and credit fraud, wire transfer fraud, and other unethical managerial and banking practices. There seems to be a direct connection between the banking industry and kleptocracy. Babatunde Ogala (SAN), a former member of the Lagos State House of Assembly concurred with this notion and had this to say about sharp practices in the banking sector:

> ...Institution in Nigeria today that in my opinion that supports corruption are the banks. I was a member of the (Lagos State) House of Assembly. On the day after my election, before inauguration, four banks offered me loans, 100m naira each. I looked at my salary, my salary as a member of the house came to about 700 and something (sic). How was I going to pay that over four years? One of the banks had given me a credit card with a credit line of $20, 000; (I had) no account with them. One of the banks had printed check books for me; yes, just like that. so easily, for a four-year tenure of N8.4 million a year, times four, is about N32million, I already had a credit facility of N400million to access. How was I expected to pay back? The banks are only telling me, take this money, find a way to steal it, and pay. So, the banks in my opinion, is the biggest industry corruption in this country.

To expect some Nigerian banks, especially commercial ones, to be ethical and law-abiding is like expecting a wolf to become a sheep overnight. Some banks were created solely to mastermind fraud and criminal behaviours that pertain to money and financial transactions. In the words of an informant:

> No one gets near the middle-level position of the banking industry in Nigeria with the behaviour of a saint. It would help if you were street-smart and carry criminal-like behaviours. Getting to the banking league's top hierarchy means you must be a top criminal.

As you will read, his submissions to me were not far from the truth. Furthermore, if the reader needs any vital example of how true this could have been, or perhaps continue to be, the emergence and the failure of the BCCI is a crucial example. When global investigators determined to discover the reasons behind the collapse of the BCCI, they uncovered fraud of astronomical proportions relating to its activities in Nigeria. To put things the way they were, BCCI was nothing other than a bank created to launder drug money, keep stolen funds, engage in the destruction of the naira and help sabotage the economy. Throughout its existence in Nigeria, the bank fraudulently worked with state authorities to give the naira a pretentious feeling that it was equal to the dollar and that they were here to help the Nigerian economy.

In 2017, I stumbled upon a confidential but very credible report that some bankers were hiring commercial sex workers under the guise of financial marketing to meet set goals and objectives that their banks had put forward. It was an under-table agreement where the recruited "bankers" sought after people of means, befriended them and got them to bring their money and financial assets into the bank's portfolios. That explains why other naive but diligent bank personnel work tirelessly but effortlessly to meet the targets of their "colleagues" in the marketing departments of the banking industry.

Most commercial bankers seem to act under prevalent corrupt and fraudulent practices rather than the typical day-to-day operations for which bankers are universally known. With the connivance of top public officials, bank officials would open new bank accounts for MDAs on certain terms, usually to acquire higher interest rates. The benefits of the newly opened accounts, such as the accumulated interest rates, are then shared among the bank and public officials. This ravenous act of corruption became a norm to allow public servants' and pensioners' salaries and pension payments to be delayed enabling the participants to gather profits from the interests on deposits.

Nigerian banks have become so targeted that government officials and policymakers who introduced overhauling policies in the banking sector have had such policies antagonised by immoral and criminal minds. In that regard, when Nigerians talk so ill about their leaders, they fail to address their own involvements and collusions. The sad case of the People's Bank of Nigeria (The Bank of the Poor), which was created under the General Ibrahim Babangida regime, is a stark reminder of our complicity in tearing down our country through dishonest and fraudulent acts.

The People's Bank was created on October 1, 1989. It was charged with extending credits to lower- and middle-class Nigerians who could not ordinarily access such loans from other orthodox banks. It was reported that Nigerians rallied to receive such loans from designated service points without genuine repayment plans. Insider practices by fraudulent bank officials and representatives who gave out loans to "ghost" persons would eventually crumble the bank a few years after its creation. Field officers assigned by the bank to monitor the utilisation of the loan and possible repayments were given kickbacks by potential defaulters. Corrupt citizens also used fictitious documents to apply for funding and explored the use of other mechanisms, such as "ghost" borrowers, to enable them to garner larger funds. These, of course, they successfully did in connivance with top management officials and personnel of the People's Bank. The bank's chairman, the respectable educationist and activist Tai Solarin, shocked by the alarming rate of financial corruption and fraud by senior bank officials, resigned in protest in 1992. A committee chaired by Alhaji Ahmed Joda in 1999 to look into the bank's failure discovered that an astonishing 80% of the loans taken from the bank were never repaid. The People's Bank scenario is a microcosm of citizens' readiness to "eat and destroy till there is no more". However, the People's Bank situation is just one out of many. The activities that ran the People's Bank to the ground are also perpetuated in every other similar financial program that should typically help citizens in their business and commercial affairs.

Commercial banks are the most notorious sector in the banking industry. After the appointment of Sanusi Lamido Sanusi as the new Governor of the Central Bank in June 2009, he discovered and made it known to the public that prominent heads of the country's commercial banks had systematically diverted billions of depositor's funds through one mechanism or the other. Shocking details emerged about how some of the country's most respected commercial bankers took advantage of various loopholes and backdoors to drag the country into near economic collapse, if not a perpetual one. Those accused were Cecelia Ibru of Oceanic Bank, Erastus Akingbola of Intercontinental Bank, Sebastian Adigwe of Afribank, Barth Ebong of Union Bank PLC, Okey Nwosu of FinBank, and Francis Atuchie of Bank PHB. They were not alone. Authorities discovered that bank directors, managers, executives and private citizens had amassed bad loans estimated at N1.1 trillion, almost three times the 2009 budgetary proposal of Lagos.[31] Billionaires, multi-millionaires, political leaders, churches and corporations were also alleged to be part of those that had taken advantage of the "bad loans" loopholes. It later occurred to Nigerians that depositors' funds had been badly managed and disproportionately disbursed to people with ulterior motives.

Several other financial institutions such as Micro-finance Banks (MFBs), Development Finance Institutions (DFI's), Bureaux-de-Change (BDCs), Discount Houses and Primary Mortgage Banks (PMBs) are also partakers in the grand scheme of financial fraud. I am going to pass on the Central Bank. That is because the CBN's inability to perform its supervisory role is automatically an indictment of its credibility and general establishment, not to mention the cases of abuse that its management and staff have reportedly perpetrated. Simply put, every wrong noted in this subchapter automatically indicts the apex bank.

As time evolves and banks continue to render digitalised products and services, our banking industry has failed to equally put in instruments to checkmate fraud and forgeries, thereby exposing their customers to all forms of theft. The inability of some banks to secure and update themselves with modern-day fraud prevention mechanisms facilitated a sharp rise in the reported cases of fraud and forgeries. A 2021 report by the NDIC shows that 1,199 cases of fraud and forgeries were reported in 2006. That figure grew to 3,786 in 2010, 12,279 in 2015, 37,817 in 2018 and an unbelievably astronomical figure of 146,183 by 2020.[32] The increase in the value of frauds and forgeries is just as shocking and monumental as the reported cases. The figures released by the NDIC show that the total amount of funds lost to fraud and forgeries in 2006 were N4.83 billion. That figure grew to N21.29 billion in 2010, recorded N18.02 billion in 2015, saw a rise to N38.93 billion in 2013 and a skyrocketed figure to N120.79 billion in 2020.[33] I must add that 2019 recorded the highest figure with a massive N204.65 billion lost to frauds and forgeries.

Bank officials and personnel collude with fraudsters to defraud unsuspecting victims. According to the NDIC, 474 bank staff were involved in fraud and forgery cases in 2020, a reduction compared to the 899 and 835 in 2018 and 2019, respectively. While the reported cases and figures are bizarre, it is even worrisome that they only reflect the number of reported cases and not the actual statistics of incidents considering a society like ours, where citizens lack enough convictions to report criminal cases. The categories of those who perpetrate such fraud include supervisors and managers, executive assistants, cashiers and clerks, messengers, cleaners, security guards and some temporary workers.

It has been widely alleged that bank personnel often issue credentials and confidential information such as signatures to third-party check forgers to enable them to steal depositors' funds. Anti-fraud mechanisms set up by banks and authoritative bodies are manipulated and sometimes deactivated in the best way possible to afflict financial grief on bank customers and investors. Bank staff would sell their customers' telephone numbers and emails to fraudsters who use robotic tools to lure victims into providing their sensitive details.

A client once told me how his bank statements were sold on the black market. Unknown to him, crooked travel visa agents had submitted his bank statements to a foreign embassy as proof of sponsorship for intending travellers. Other victims had it worse. People's bank statements were used alongside other fictitious documents to borrow loans and other credit facilities, rendering the account owners in debt. Other victims are forced to prove their innocence to appropriate authorities after fraudsters use their identities to commit grievous criminal acts. Bank personnel connive with fraudsters to steal funds of vulnerable, incapacitated, uneducated, unsuspecting, physically challenged or even dead depositors. In 2016, I investigated and uncovered a fraud scheme where a bank officer systematically diverted over N80 million from a late client for personal use. Undetected by the bank and unknown to the victim's family, the official used fictitious documents of representation to divert the victim's deposits.

Commercial banks looked the other way in the heydays of internet fraud as fraudsters used their monetary services to perpetrate fraud and money laundering schemes of all kinds. Fraudsters used banking services offered through third-party providers such as Western Union and MoneyGram to steal monies from mostly foreign victims using fictitious identities and aliases. Perhaps, internet fraud aka *yahoo yahoo* would not have gained a fertile ground in Nigeria without the recklessness of banks and their financial partners. The failure of Western Union and MoneyGram to crack down on fraudulent financial transactions mostly related to 419 scams drew the attention of US federal regulators and the US Justice Department. In 2017, Western Union admitted to anti-money laundering and consumer fraud violations and forfeited $586 million in settlement with US authorities.[34] Similarly, in 2018, MoneyGram agreed to pay $125 million for failing to crack down on fraudulent money transfers.[35] The mark of Nigerian fraudsters was written all over both cases against Western Union and MoneyGram. Obviously, they had contributed to the emergence of *yahoo yahoo* in Nigeria.

When Nigerians gather to talk about the factors that led to the country's woes, specifically concerning the issues of unemployment and lack of foreign investments, they do so with disrespect for pragmatism. I am curious to know what sort of foreign investor would put his hard-earned investment in a country with bad banking practices or where the banking institution is as volatile as the country itself. I wonder what investors, who are brilliant in thoughts and careful in deeds, would want to put their money in a country where those charged with safeguarding funds are crooked and untrustworthy. I must say that even after the death of former dictator Sani Abacha, the actions of his bankers and others who helped him launder Nigerian's common wealth to banks abroad must not go unpunished. Ultimately, Nigerians are people who continue to fetch water into a broken bucket yet expect it to hold water. We have allowed our parents, families, neighbours, friends, associates, kinsmen, mentors and mentees to get away with grievous acts. With such acts, trust in our economic systems and nation as a whole is eroded. Sadly, the consequences of such activities are economically devastating.

Oil and Gas: Its Politics and Fraud

The oil and gas industry accounts for a significant chunk of the country's source of revenue and foreign earnings. However, it has become the beehive of corruption, fraud, theft, crime and violence; a paradoxical assurance of setback for a country that relies heavily on the same sector. Since the discovery of oil in Oloibiri in the Niger Delta region, it has become more of a curse than a blessing for our country. Nigeria moved from a land once prophesied to become one of the world's major economies through agriculture and other natural resources to one that suddenly developed into a state of economic collapse and socio-political chaos.

Since the 1970s, we have shifted from an agriculture-based economy to one heavily reliant on oil. That has also caused the abandonment of other sectors that would have been vital to the nation's economy and citizens. It later became evident that there was a catch to it. Something sinister was going on that made several political leaders, business people and a few crooked citizens see the oil and gas industry as a haven for massive financial gains, to the detriment of the entire citizenry.

One arduous part of discussing the oil and gas industry in Nigeria at its extensive length is the compulsory involvement of politics. In the Nigerian terrain, oil and politics are inseparable aspects of each other. It would also be impossible to discuss Nigeria's oil and gas industry regarding corruption and fraud without analysing the dirty politics surrounding it.

Immediately after the discovery of oil in the southern region, foreign oil firms started to pay homage to the country's new leaders. Mobil, Tenneco, Gulf Oil, Chevron, Agip and Elf all trooped in as hungry ants that had just come across a heap of sugar mixed with honey. They made the Tafawa Balewa government understand why they had come and their missions. They informed the Balewa administration that a tremendous source of economic revenue had been detected in the country's southern region. If Balewa and the northern oligarch were in doubt or needed better information, the oil firms readily provided sufficient details. They humorously told them that the newly discovered oil was nothing like the palm oil that Balewa and others knew or were used to. They informed them that the much-known palm oil only serves to feed a family for a short period, but the oil that was discovered helps to provide not just the family but also an entire region for generations to come.

Genuine to their words and to back up their prophetic depictions of profitable future, foreign oil magnates, barons and businesspeople started to roll out money for investment purposes. Monies were paid into open government accounts, and of course, bribery and kickbacks equally followed. From there, the problems began aggressively. As the foreign companies and individuals trooped in, requests for licenses were made, solicitation and blessings of social and political leaders also followed. Similarly, the need for alliances and partnerships with indigenous participants became habitual.

Nigeria had a list of pioneering problems even before the discovery of oil. However, the discovery of oil was what catalysed monumental fraud, corruption, marginalisation, disunity and enmity. For instance, when the July 1966 mutineers, consisting of mostly northern soldiers, attempted to secede from the country, they were quickly reminded that the North was a barren land compared to an ongoing economic boom in the southern region. The northern soldiers immediately held back. Rather they took charge of the country's affairs, just as their civilian counterparts had done a decade earlier. A year later, when Colonel Dim Odumegwu Ojukwu decided to pull the Eastern region away with some parts of the newly discovered oil territories, the same northern military soldiers who had threatened secession waged a three-year war to keep the country together.

Politics and economy in a heavily divided country like ours, especially one that reached its bitterest heights in the 1960s, only benefitted a few aristocrats. When the foreign companies started forging the needed alliances needed for the extractions, production and sales of oil and petroleum products, they did so without much approval from the indigenes of the Niger Delta. People of mostly northern extraction who were in power for most of the 1960s and 1970s started to put themselves in prime positions to benefit from the gains and profits of a now impoverished region. However, it would be disingenuous not to mention that, intermittently, indigenes of the Niger Delta and other people of southern extraction equally took full advantage of the corruption melee without bothering to care for the needs of their masses.

The subsequent years after the civil war period were not any better politically, socially or economically for the Nigerian people. While the country's leaders were caught in a hostile and bloody political engagement with each other, the oil companies and their Nigerian partners went to work. The oil companies went about committing all sorts of environmental degradation. They perpetrated more woes on the inhabitants of oil-discovered areas, who were already aggrieved at being left out of the accompanying benefits. The Niger Delta region, which was once incredibly endowed with natural resources, including palm oil, a wide variety of crops and products, economic trees and fish farming, suddenly became devastated and poisoned as a result of activities from oil exploration.

The Niger Delta people were so impoverished and cut off from the country's newfound source of wealth to the extent that necessities such as food and drinking water became impacted. The health implications have been very grievous as inhabitants continue to witness sharp rises in malaria, tuberculosis, cholera, typhoid, dysentery and other diseases. The oil companies and ground personnel went about their explorations with a "we have paid your leaders, leave us alone" approach. Curiously, it is instructive to ask which leaders the companies paid money to and where the money went to. Indeed, the oil companies made payments to people they thought were the representatives of the Niger Delta region but, indeed, were only on the lookout for their personal interests. Monies were paid to traditional chiefs, indigenous intermediaries, local tribe members, military administrators, local council presiding officers and everyone who held political, social and economic positions.

Lobbying became a prominent feature of the oil and gas industry. The concomitant features of corruption and fraud intensified in full force after General Yakubu Gowon nationalised the oil industry by creating the Nigerian National Oil Corporation (NNOC) in 1971. Lobby groups and individuals saw the newly formed corporation as a means to create personal wealth, perhaps rightly so, if only their intentions were merely capitalistic and genuine. The lobbyists used machinations to short-change the corporation, the government and the entire country in connivance with public officials. People charged with ensuring sanity in the newly created corporation that should typically serve as the nation's money house were unconcerned with the fraud and patronage system, which later became a catalyst for hostility.

That was unsurprising. After all, the perpetrators of fraud and corruption in the oil industry were (and still are) the cohorts of political leaders who were being rewarded for their political services to the powers that be.

In 1977, the Nigerian National Petroleum Company (NNPC) was founded to regulate and participate in the country's oil sector. Unfortunately, any economic policy that puts corrupt officials in charge of affairs has the proverbial carriage of hiring thieves as security watchdogs of a house they had long targeted. Under Shehu Shagari's Second Republic, an estimated $16 billion was stolen by oil fraudsters and corrupt persons, according to reports. The money stolen constituted 20% of the oil revenue within that period, a massive figure in a country facing financial hardship and a consequent recession.

Theft and corruption varied and were perpetrated with impunity, ranging from oil theft to awarding of illegal licenses, fraudulent contract approvals, extortions of private individuals and companies, oil subsidies fraud, and connivance and conspiracy to theft and sabotage.

Subsequent military administrators who claimed to have brought correction and sanity to the country and the oil sector only proved even worse. In 1994, a report issued by the Panel on the Reorganisation and Reform of Central Bank of Nigeria, which Dr Pius Okigbo chaired, discovered that $12.4 billion had mysteriously disappeared from the county's treasury accounts. The missing monies were additional proceeds paid into separately opened accounts to receive a windfall of oil proceeds emanating from the Gulf War. Nigeria has lost an estimated $400 billion of oil revenue to theft, corruption or misappropriation since the country's independence.[36] In a country that bleeds of lack of social amenities and other basic needs, such stolen funds would have greatly impacted the economic and social lives of citizens. Today, corruption and fraud in the oil industry are so vast that it requires an entire book of analysis to capture.

Oil theft became the oil industry's most notorious aspect of criminal activity. Oil theft is perpetrated in many ways and carried out through different means, mainly hijacking oil cargoes by militants/pirates, illegal diversion, and bunkering. *Bunkering* is a term used to describe transporting fuel or oil from one boat to another. It involves the illicit transfer and smuggling of petroleum products into ships and vessels for illegal exports, refining and eventual sales to places other than the legally channelled destinations. Through oil theft, a few amounts of powerful people and their foot personnel make money off smuggled items and are not inclined to give up this act of theft, waste and sabotage. Analysts have claimed that between 10% and 25% of the country's daily oil productions are smuggled by oil thieves, thereby creating Pandora's box of problems, especially financial and environmental problems.

Nigerians have always wondered why the fuel scarcity issue has become a regular occurrence in the country. Nevertheless, something more sinister lies behind their curiosity and suspicions. One of the greatest ironies of our socio-economic existence is that despite our country's abundance of oil reserves, we remain one of the world's highest importers of petroleum products. Since the 1970s, Nigerian oil products have been smuggled out of the country and found their way to countries where higher amounts are paid. Nigerian oil has been smuggled to neighbouring African countries, Europe, Asia, the Americas and others. Oil marketers, oil tankers and fuel station owners divert government-subsidised petroleum products for sale to neighbouring West African countries to benefit from huge profit returns, thereby short-changing the government and the citizens.

As far back as the 1970s, the Nigerian government had surreptitiously introduced fuel subsidies to cushion the adverse effects of the period's national and global economic meltdowns. Subsidy programs which had been regarded as one of the common masses' saving graces, soon became another among a list of blessing-turned-curse programs introduced to our national life. Systematic diversions of funds or subsided products benefit a rich circle of people with privilege and connections to people within the corridors of power. That tiny circle includes politicians, godfathers, political office holders, public officials, elite private citizens, foreign collaborators, and every other person in such a corruption circle. Nigerian citizens continue to be hoodwinked by the dirty propaganda messages of those who believe in the continuity of the fuel subsidy program. On subsidies fraud, the former minister of finance, Dr Ngozi Okonjo-Iweala, had this to say:

> These fraudulent dealings went beyond the smuggling of oil shipments over the border into neighbouring countries such as Benin and Niger, where prices were much higher. Allegations were rife that companies were claiming subsidies for shipment of oil never delivered. For shipments of kerosene, allegations swirled that corrupt payments were being made to assign the rights to import cargos of subsided kerosene to certain companies, which then sold the kerosene to consumers at nonsubsidised prices.[37]

Subsidy programs will continue to be eclipsed by the selfish desires of fraudsters in our country, where exploitations of all innocuous mechanisms have become a biological curse for many. Military personnel and security forces primarily stationed to watch and curtail the activities of militants and oil thieves have inversely become the service dogs of those same people. They abandoned their patriotic assignments and acted as armed escorts for stolen petroleum products and to gather intelligence that helped oil saboteurs avoid the authorities' radar. Militants and criminal gangs continue to enjoy substantial backing from political and military personalities in the country. Hence, they never lack financial, logistics or any other material support. Undercover reporters and security agents have exposed unscrupulous military personnel and other state actors who provide security to buildings and vicinities where stolen oil products are kept.

Oil exploration and production licenses in the country are awarded to people with ulterior motives or those who are profit-driven and unconcerned with other external factors. Licenses are granted to people with no knowledge or experience in the oil and gas industry but are given as a reward for patronage and returns for political favours. The habit of awarding contracts on a nepotistic basis gives people a lack of moral responsibility or any duty of care to respond to issues other than that which have to do with sales and profits. For all they care, the region, societies and the entire country can burn to the ground as long as money is made and profits are accrued to them personally.

Contracts in the oil and gas industry to address specific areas that need quick government intervention are improperly carried out, mismanaged, maladministered or never carried out. Armed with a criminal-minded opinion that the petroleum ministry has unlimited budgets at its disposal, contractors unjustly abandon full implementations of works awarded to them, thereby leading to neglect and further deterioration of intended areas where interventions are needed. Officials and inspectors from the Department of Petroleum Resources (DPR) and other relevant agencies responsible for monitoring pollution and other environmental degradation have become the actual pollutants through acts of gross negligence, corruption and abuse of office. They are known to go after compliant companies and threaten them with hefty fines to extort them. At the same time, those who engage in pollution, environmental degradation and other anti-societal behaviours pay bribes to escape fines and prosecutions.

It is unclear who controls the oil and gas sector in Nigeria between the government or some powerful few cronies. It has been proven that politicians, lawmakers, past and present political office holders, powerful warlords, communal chiefs, traditional rulers, military personnel, and militants have been identified as owners of illegal refineries in the country. The NNPC is arguably the most corrupt institution in the country's history as it is home to some of the most opaque and unaccountable practices Shambolic practices and maladministration in the NNPC are responsible for the country's loss of billions of dollars since its establishment.

Maladministration, lack of transparency and improper oversight of NNPC's functions have given birth to accusations and counteraccusations of missing funds that often end without anyone being held accountable for reported fraud and crime. As far back as 1978, a year after the NNPC was founded, an allegation surfaced that monies in the region between $2 billion and $3.5 billion were missing and not remitted to the nation's treasury by the NNPC. Such reports were not properly investigated and fizzled into thin air. In 2011, the audit firm KPMG found that N28.5 billion was illegally deducted for subsidies between 2007 and 2009. In December 2013, Central Bank Governor Sanusi Lamido Sanusi claimed that an estimated $50 billion of proceeds from oil sales was not remitted to the federations account; although a reconciliatory committee later revealed the figures to be around $12 billion. Sanusi shocked the nation again when he suggested that the unremitted figures were $20 billion. Whichever it was, $50 billion, $12 billion or $20 billion, it has become as white as snow to Nigerians that a few satanic individuals have decided to hold the entire country hostage.

Also, in March 2016, the Auditor-General of the Federation made another shocking revelation when he announced that the NNPC could not account for the $16 billion the NNPC was meant to pay into the federation's account. The NNPC countered that the federal government owed its corporation $6.8 billion. In the same month, the Revenue Mobilisation and Fiscal Affairs Commission (RMAFC) claimed that the NNPC was yet to account for N4.9 trillion of monies it failed to remit, further affirming the Auditor General's reports that something sinister had gone wrong with funds that were meant to go into the nation's purse.[38]

As I have stated repeatedly, the list of those who set out to steal from Nigeria and its citizens is endless. In March 2017, The Senate shockingly revealed that it had uncovered an alleged fraud of N10 trillion that NNPC officials carried out in connivance with other public and private officials between 2006 and 2016. Those accused of probable theft and complicity were officials of the CBN, FIRS, Nigerian Customs, Nigerian Ports

Authority, NIMASA, independent marketers, oil and gas companies and other agencies.[39]

Trust in our agents of socialisation and those of our social, economic and political systems are eroded. That is because figures are sometimes brandished to instigate the public against certain individuals, thereby killing the shock value aspect that should naturally accompany such breaking news stories. Transparent systems can help citizens hold public and private officials accountable and not rely solely on accusations and counteraccusations that often emanate from politicised and biased media outlets. An April 2015 independent forensic report by the audit firm PWC to look into the alleged missing $20 billion that shook national headlines suggests that the model through which the NNPC operates was faulty and almost non-functional.[40] The report also indicated that activities of the NNPC lacked transparency and sustainability.

Lack of transparency and accountability in our economic systems has allowed kleptocrats like a certain former minister of Petroleum Resources, Diezani Allison-Madueke, to steal billions of dollars traced to several local and international bank accounts. Properties and items worth billions have also been forfeited through court orders, as the former minister had no problems abandoning them for a life in exile. She is just one out of several others who have decided that the blood of innocent Nigerians is a joy for them and their generations to feast upon.

It is factually correct to reprimand people from other regions other than the Niger Delta for being the major perpetrators of the dirty politics of the oil business in the region. Nonetheless, we cannot excuse the greedy, dirty and self-sabotaging acts of Niger Delta indigenes. Those who claim to be fighters and activists from oil regions are no better than those they criticise. They perpetrate significant anti-people acts when given a chance to make corrections, policies or actions capable of bringing positive changes to their communities. For instance, to bring social developments to the Niger Delta people, the Umaru Musa Yar'Adua-led administration created the Ministry of

Niger Delta Affairs in 2008 to oversee crucial agencies such as the NDDC, which the Obasanjo administration had set up in 2000. Indigenous leaders who were charged with helping their Niger Delta communities also got infected by the typical Nigerian disease and took turns betraying their people. One of such infamous discoveries was acted dramatically in an Oscar-like performance during a live hearing organised by the House of Representatives Committee on the Niger Delta. The lawmakers were looking into allegations of N1.5billion financial misappropriation when the Acting Managing Director NDDC, Daniel Kemebradikumo Pondei, collapsed when faced with daunting questions he could not answer. This development came shortly after the former MD of the same NDDC, Joy Nunieh had accused the Minister of Niger Delta Affairs, Godswill Akpabio, of fraud and corruption. It became clear to the people of the Niger Delta that their sons and daughters had allegedly misappropriated N40 billion that was earmarked for the development of their communities.[41] What also became clear to them, if it ever did, was that contrary to the propaganda that was spread out, their sons and daughters were not as innocent from acts of theft and crime against their region as they had thought.

Furthermore, Nigerians have been fraudulently swindled by organisations that often sell pretentious ideas as activists and crusaders of their rights. Associations like the Petroleum and Natural Gas Senior Staff Association of Nigeria, Nigeria Union of Petroleum and Natural Gas Workers, the Depot and Petroleum Products Marketers Association, Independent Petroleum Marketers' Association of Nigeria, and Major Marketers' Association of Nigeria have all become the antithesis of everything they claimed they were established for. These bodies are everything wrong with citizens and their inability to purchase and consume petroleum products affordably and contentedly. Most of the activities relating to corruption, fraud, racketeering, oil theft and diversion, manipulation and propaganda that have been relayed in this subchapter are also orchestrated by these organisations and their members, who act under the devious umbrella of unionism and activism.

This chapter cannot do enough justice to the fraud and corruption in Nigeria's oil and gas industry. The incidences are limitless, the suspects' names are humongous, and their activities seem endless. Still, the culprits are relentless and in no hurry to give up their disgraceful criminal behaviours. Sadly, and as usual, the Nigerian citizens remain the colossal losers.

Law, Accounting, Auditing and Insurance Frauds

In December 2008, American authorities effectuated the arrest of American billionaire and former NASDAQ chairman Bernard L. Madoff. He was subsequently charged with securities fraud, investment advisor trust fraud, mail fraud, wire fraud, and money laundering.[42] Before Madoff's downfall, he was acknowledged as one of the most important names in US financial markets and had successfully pioneered one of the largest companies in the world. Simultaneously, he was defrauding thousands of victims through phoney investment schemes. The list included celebrities, businessmen, banks, charity organisations, socialites, prominent hedge fund managers and everyone else to the tune of "at least $50 billion." [43]

After pleading guilty to the charges filed against him in March 2009, Bernard L. Madoff was sentenced to 150 years in federal prison and was ordered to pay $170 billion in restitution. Having been defeated by the tactical manoeuvrings of such a significant fraud, US authorities left no stone unturned and went after everyone they identified as accomplices. Authorities were able to secure criminal convictions against key co-conspirators while others were issued hefty fines, made to forfeit their assets or engage in civil settlements with victims.

Nigeria, as a state and a geographical entity, continues to be a fertile ground for criminal activities of all kinds due to the presence of an impunity culture that allows all sorts of criminals to escape punishment. Combinations

110

of crooked lawyers, accountants, and auditors who have become caught up in the country's "get rich quick" syndrome facilitate such impunity culture. They do not only look the other way when acts of financial and economic crimes are carried out; they actively participate in it and engineer the escape of perpetrators from punishment. Many Nigerians have seen people like Madoff and his conspirators, who committed devastating atrocities, escape punishment. While many do not understand the reasons behind masterminds of criminal activities escaping punishment, they do quite well understand that corrupt lawyers and their cronies within the judiciary are primarily responsible.

Crooked lawyers are a major impediment to our social and criminal justice systems. It primarily amounts to a bias of some sort to write about the judiciary in hugely unfavourable terms, as I did in the prequel to this book, without highlighting the upsetting roles played by the country's lawyers. Regardless, we must draw the line between what may be considered legal or lawful vis-à-vis what is morally reprehensible.

Many of the criticisms I levelled against judicial officers have the handwriting of some notorious lawyers. For instance, I mentioned how lawyers would often pay court clerks to ensure that their court dates are manipulated, either much nearer or to a much further date. While it is true that court clerks and other judicial staff are notoriously corrupt, their corruption did not start overnight. A lawyer who, for certain reasons, wants his case to be heard promptly would offer mouth-watering bribes to court officials to ensure that such occurs. Also, a lawyer who wants his appearance date extended further for dishonest reasons would easily bribe his way through. The various methods used by lawyers to help circumvent the rules and ethics of the legal profession are abundant, and they use every mechanism at their disposal to achieve their goals.

Corrupt individuals who work as prosecutors or counsels in the office of the Directorate of Public Prosecutions or other law enforcement agencies have seen their position as means of extortion and enrichment. That is due to their power to determine who gains freedom from possible prosecution or otherwise. Right there, the market of freedom from prosecution is often negotiated. That is why some scandalous allegations that rocked the nation and were once on the front pages of every media outlet suddenly fizzle out into the dust. A legal practitioner and High Court Judge in Enugu, Comfort Chinyere Ani (PhD), put it succinctly:

> The officers in the Office of the DPP, upon perusal of the case file, render necessary advice on the appropriate line of action, as to whether to prosecute the accused person, if so, what charges to prefer against him. In his exercise of discretion to prosecute, a law officer may exercise the discretion negatively or positively, depending on the party whose bidding he wants to do, where he has received or been promised a reward. In the same manner, he might decide to oppose or not oppose a motion for bail, depending on the party he received gratification from. Such an officer could intentionally fail to direct the police to carry out further and better investigations where he observes that there are some arrears in the evidence that needs to be clarified by further investigations. He could also frustrate a case by employing delay tactics, either in writing the legal opinion, or during the prosecution, by absenting himself in court, etc., all in a bid to cause a deadlock of the case.[44]

As evident in several high-profile cases in Nigeria, several lawyers have abandoned the acts of counselling and advocacy for money-sharing law enforcement and judicial officers. These unscrupulous lawyers set out to make money by all means and abandon the principles and ethics of their renowned profession. Being privy to the financial buoyance of their clients, they would constantly extort their clients by telling them of payments that are needed to pave the way for certain judicial processes or to bribe officials even when it is untrue.

112

Nigerian lawyers derive joy in stalling trials longer than necessary by employing frivolous applications, motions, and filings, all in a bid to achieve extended delays and adjournments. Frivolous applications to frustrate criminal proceedings have seen many cases stalled or even neglected due to the implausibility and unfeasibility of prosecutors using state resources to pursue such cases. The late Emeritus Professor Adedokun Adeyemi aptly surmised thus:

> What do we see today in the Legal Profession? We see legal practitioners misleading the courts, being discourteous and, sometimes disrespectful to judicial officers and vice-versa, embezzling their clients' monies, converting their clients' properties, being dishonest and dishonourable to their fellow legal practitioners. In fact, some legal practitioners have become agents for the corruption of administration of justice, by colluding with clients, the courts, police personnel and fellow legal practitioners to engage in the use of gratification in the administration of justice. The situation is so bad today in some places that the gratification has become an accepted part of legal practice by many young and some old practitioners and their clients.[45]

A list of high-profile cases that have stalled for several years, some for as long as 10 to 15 years, have been documented by various transparency groups.[46]

Nigeria needs enabling mechanisms and systems to flush corruption and financial crimes. However, the bodies and institutions meant to achieve that have been greatly compromised. Nigeria's accounting and audit firms are silent collaborators of everything wrong with our socio-economic and political systems. The various MDAs, banks, corporations, private companies and every establishment that stole public funds were all examined and audited by accounting and audit experts. Curiously, one is forced to ask the actual significance of Nigeria's audit and accounting sector when frauds of open and astronomical proportions are carried out daily on our national soil. From time to time, elated shareholders of publicly listed companies would wake up to discover that they had purchased shares on false assumptions or based on cooked audited financial statements.

Acts of accounting and auditing negligence and corruption are a global syndrome. For instance, American energy giant Enron was caught up in an accounting fraud where it was discovered that its leadership had fooled regulators with fake holdings, income inflations, and off-the-books accounting practices.[47] As a result of this shady practice, among other things, Enron's shares went from $90.75 at their peak to $0.26 at bankruptcy. At the height of its manipulations, the company had fooled the world of business, finance and economics to the extent that it was named "America's Most Innovative Company" for six consecutive years.[48] The collapse of Enron affected thousands of its employees and shook Wall Street, with investors losing $74billion to a much-undetected aspect of corporate fraud.[49]

Back to Nigeria, the word "endemic" best illustrates the situation of things in our country regarding almost every activity of insanity that fellow citizens mete out on one another. If Enron could commit such an act on US soil despite the effective watchdog system authorities there have in place, one wonders what must have been happening in Nigeria where audits and accounts are whatever we are told. Jointly, financial institutions and regulatory organisations in Nigeria are hell-bent on ruining the country and leaving it to waste as long as they benefit. Although many of these cases escape regulators and stakeholders' radar, there are few instances where, by chance, Nigerians got wind that they have been duped. As I have said repeatedly, Nigeria has the media underreporting numerous failed systems and many happenings in the country. As Nigerians, we wait for a catastrophe of irreparable proportion to occur before we set out our gears of activism, but more than often, the damage has been done.

On April 11, 2008, shareholders of the leading African maker of confectionery, Cadbury Nigeria PLC, woke up only to discover that they had been duped. Cadbury was said to have "overstated its accounts by a whopping N13.25 billion through stock buyback, cost deferrals, trade loading and false stock certificates of suppliers to manipulate its reports that were filed with SEC and the Nigerian Exchange (now NGX) and issued to the public."[50] Investors who had been joyous when Cadbury's share price surged to an all-time high of N65.52 were left to count their losses as the share price dropped below N9.00 by 2009.

The banking fraud scandal that rocked the nation in 2009 was carried out with the connivance of some auditors and accountants. Auditors had given a clean bill of health to the banks in question before the CBN exposed their unholy alliance and certified them as distressed entities. Many thefts and embezzlements at various civil service levels have the support of auditors and accountants, some acting as key participants. In what would look like a contradiction and absurdity of institutionalised fraud, many state and federal attorney-generals, auditor-generals and accountant-generals have been charged with economic and financial frauds, some amounting to several billion. Nigeria has become that country where the gatekeepers have not only become inefficient on the job but have become the actual thieves.

The insurance industry in Nigeria is very redundant and seems to defy either reactive or proactive measures necessary to cater to the insurance needs of Nigerians. For most Nigerians, insurance is an afterthought after the eventuality of a sad occurrence. The average Nigerian does not see the need to assure his life or property against future doom. Some major insurance problems in Nigeria are due to the convoluted aspect of verifying claims made by the insured party and the complicatedness of making payouts by insurers.

Insurance frauds are perpetrated by elements who pose as the insured parties, insurance brokers or officials of insurance companies. With collaborators in insurance companies, political and public office holders draw insurance payments on government properties that are not in use. Abandoned public buildings, electric generators, elevators, vehicles and other items are inappropriately insured, with the monies being shared by the collaborators. I was reliably informed that a public building in Ikoyi allegedly belonging to the Ministry of Defence and abandoned for several years was still being insured inappropriately. Funds (estimated to be billions) under the purported guise of being insured were budgeted and disbursed for its elevators, electric generators and other equipment that had not been used for over a decade.

Insurance fraud is perpetrated to inflict fraudulent costs on insurance companies. Some notoriously perpetrated frauds are autos fraud, life and disability fraud, worker's compensation fraud, intentional damage to insured properties, excessive damage, and staged accidents. It has been proved that some Nigerians buy cars at undervalued prices and insure them at extremely overvalued figures. After that, they stage auto accidents with the insured vehicles to defraud insurance companies. I have reliably gathered that such a trend has been ongoing for some time and applies to other properties such as houses, businesses and cargoes. Shamefully, some of these acts would have been impossible without the connivance of collaborators in the insurance sector. Inside collaborations by industry players and actors are a major reason foreign investors would rather not choose our country as an investment destination. Hence, a national loss becomes the resultant effect of the activities of a few shady and crooked citizens.

Professional bodies like the NBA, ANAN, NAA, ICAN, and IIA must also hold their members and others within their jurisdiction to account for acts of misconduct. It must be noted that those same institutions are quick to rally in support of members charged by relevant authorities and are quickest to call legitimate prosecutions witch-hunts. Trust is greatly eroded in our systems; ironically, watchdog agencies have become the chief collaborators of everything they should stamp out of our social and economic systems.

Charity and Donation Frauds

During the last quarter of 2020, people, mostly youths, angered by incessant police harassment, torture and extra-judicial killings, took to the street to offer their civil discontent against police authorities and the government. Unexpected events led protesters to discover acts that had long been perpetrated behind closed doors and were undetected for decades. They found out that relief items meant to serve as "palliatives" for citizens facing setbacks and hardships due to the COVID-19 pandemic had been diverted and housed in various warehouses across the country.

As if they had struck gold, starving residents sprung into multiple warehouses across the nation and looted the palliative materials for consumptions or sales. Although authorities denied that the items were improperly diverted, several factors and evidence indicated otherwise. Widespread disbelief and condemnation followed the discoveries of the hidden relief materials. Nonetheless, it became evident that Nigerians did not understand the various degrees of theft that had gone on for decades by their fellow citizens. Of course, they are aware of pervasive corruption; they do not know how such corrupt acts are carried out.

The illegal diversion of aid and relief materials is not a strange occurrence. Public officials in Nigeria usually divert earmarked funds for social intervention or poverty alleviation programmes. Since most of these activities are cash-based (to cater to less privileged people in rural areas), officials conspire with other actors to create a fictitious and inexistent list of charitable programs and people for purposes of funds diversion at the expense of poor and vulnerable people. Cash-based projects were heavily subject to fraud, diversion and abuse before the introduction of anti-fraud mechanisms. Still, a backdoor mechanism was created by the notoriously corrupt set of officials. They go into rural areas to gather impoverished and vulnerable persons who welcome whatever stipends come their way. The officials then effectuate negotiation for a certain percentage of whatever the government grants to them before proceeding to include them as beneficiaries of government welfare programmes.

Charity fraud in Nigeria continues to be a prime illustration that "politicians and leaders" are not the only problems we have to contend with. As I have opined repeatedly, unethical, crooked and dishonest citizens in every corner of geographical Nigeria continue to make it difficult to measure the success or failure of leadership in Nigeria adequately. The moral compass that ought to highlight the success or otherwise of certain leaders has been broken and shattered by the greed, fraud and dishonesty of a large chunk of citizens themselves. It is mystifying how unprincipled citizens thought it prudent to steal relief materials and charitable items meant for the poor.

My investigation into charity frauds discovered widespread malpractices unknown to many Nigerians. For instance, on some occasions, I found widespread discrepancies between allocated items meant for distribution and the eventually distributed materials. I also found out that items projected for distribution but not yet distributed did not tally with the list of items that private donors had signed off from their point of departure. Where did the items go, how did such occur, and what took place? Were these accidental or intentional acts to defraud and cheat donors and victims of relief supplies? Systems lacking transparency and accountability will continue to open doors for fraud, theft and corruption. Thefts are likely to occur from the point of departure, especially when such items emanate directly from the government, where corrupt public officials ensure their own "cuts" before the final dispatch of items. The cuts eventually make their way to awaiting electorates who erroneously see them as gift items from their political messiahs. Ministry officials, charity workers, camp managers, supervisors, care workers, and security agencies are active partakers in this show of shame.

Relief materials given to charity organisations, aid groups and IDP camps are repackaged for sale on the black markets. IDP camps have become an eyesore and are places where man's inhumanity to man is presented to attentive first-time visitors. They are also places that show the real nature of greedy people whose conscience is inflexible to take advantage of bleeding and dying persons under their care. There have been credible reports that babies and children of displaced persons ended up in the hands of human traffickers. A credible source told me that IDP camps are a cheaper and safer place for "baby-making factories", a practice that cheats legitimate people with legitimate problems, the governments, donors and the larger society. Innocent children are also used in extensive alms begging schemes. Babies, as young as a few weeks old, are used to solicit for alms under unfavourable weather conditions. Unsuspecting people who give monies to these innocent children are, by extension, encouraging all the ills accompanying child abuse. The more disgraceful actors make profits, the more innocent babies and children are procured to engage in the alms begging fraud.

It must also be noted that some charity organisations and so-called private foundations in the country are founded for money laundering, trafficking of persons and other illicit acts. They are used to "wash" proceeds from illegally gotten funds and to escape the radar of relevant authorities, among other things. Our country is home to various NGOs (registered and unregistered) masquerading under the guise of empowerment programs, poverty alleviation organisations, welfare homes, and children and orphanage care centres, among others. With conspirators or even sponsors in top public and private organisations, they fraudulently divert funds into fictitious organisations. The conspirators then share the proceeds at the expense of genuine charity/welfare organisations and others in need.

Charity fraud is extensive and carried out through various means by individual fraudsters, in units or as a group. A private client contacted me a few years back to help investigate a matter of urgent concern. Some individuals had access to pictures of his ailing wife that he had innocently posted on his social media pages to celebrate her birthday. Armed with pictures of his bedridden wife, they launched a fundraising campaign through GoFundMe (a crowdfunding platform) to help secure treatments for "their ailing and dying mother". By the time their plan was thwarted, they had secured donations of up to $62,500 on the GoFundMe platform.

Some others have devised a fraudulent practice where they directly engage unsuspecting sickly patients in a bid to help them solicit funds for treatments. The unsuspecting patients, naturally glad and expectant of such generous gestures, prepare themselves to work with the fraudsters by agreeing to have themselves recorded and having their graphic details displayed to members of the public. The fraudsters then distribute the patients' graphical images and recorded videos for fundraising and other support. Once a relatively large amount of funds has been secured, they count their gains, never to be seen again, leaving the patients and the donors as victims of an unholy fraud.

Charity fraud kills the trust system and messes up the good natural psyche of well-meaning people to render help and offer support to those who are genuinely in need. Many donor organisations and countries worldwide have consistently lamented that their donations do not often get to the right sources. Genuine charity organisations are bleeding support and hardly ever get the patronage support they need unless they agree to dance to the tune of some immoral patrons and shadowy donors. For most of them, getting help from societal elites comes with the ability to pay back in kind, such as agreeing to whatever promotional and publicity stunts such persons have arranged, mostly for politically affiliated or even sinister reasons. Again, in all of these, genuine Nigerians with genuine needs tend to be the ultimate casualty.

Inelegant Conclusion

During one of the country's recession periods of the 1980s, a global leader curiously asked why the country was so poor and in so much debt despite having numerous rich individuals capable of singlehandedly paying off our national debts. The country is home to multi-millionaires and billionaires who offer almost no economic or financial value to the nation. That is why solving the country's high unemployment rate has been difficult. Shamefully, most of the country's stupendously wealthy individuals with no legitimate business traced to their name do not like being questioned. A former Senator who fit into such a profile, Dino Melaye, once approved the notion by saying that his source of wealth should not be a worry for anyone, and neither should anyone bother to investigate it.

Nigeria is a land of people with so many excuses. So sophisticated are these excuses that they have become the basis for which financial frauds and crimes have been allowed to become a norm. For instance, it is a well-known fact and a global norm for criminal suspects to have their day in court. In Nigeria, however, offenders do not need to have their days in court; they have lawyers who know what to do to ensure such people escape punishment. When you ask them, they will tell you they are doing their "job," and that is something no one can dispute. I must also do my job as an investigator and a writer who knows them too well.

A handful of lawyers in the Nigerian criminal justice system are no different from insurgents and terrorists. The latter resides in forests and wields guns and ammunition to wreak havoc on citizens, while the former hide behind their fanciful wigs and gowns to perpetrate criminal acts of all kinds. It is equally important to note that lawyers have Latin maxims to orchestrate their activities while the terrorists and bandits have weapons and ammunition. Either way, both are a curse to society, and neither should have their actions justified. Nigerian lawyers and judicial officers continue to use various means to free ruthless criminals from punishment. They should not be surprised when the same criminals use similar or other avenues to inflict harm upon them or those close to them.

Top public officers in areas that demand near piety are by themselves the country's most notorious and crooked individuals. Attorney-generals, accountant-generals, solicitor-generals, chief prosecutors, electoral chairpersons, chief justices, lead counsels and their synonymic titled associates in public and private offices all have damning levels of accusations that had the marks of guilt written all over. Recently, some of the country's top guardsmen and watchdogs of our national treasury have been accused of grand thefts to the tune of billions of naira. What a hopeless situation we have on our hands when people who occupy such offices have become the antithesis of their establishments. We cannot continue like this. Many of such people have exquisitely looking children all over social media displaying their parent's pictures elegantly as the "best" fathers and mothers in the world. Even annoying is that, due to their elegant lifestyles and portrayals, gullible and money-worshipping youths follow them in droves, and in a way that bares the mark of sycophancy. And we claim to want a better Nigeria? We are joking!

Nigerians must be made aware that no one has a monopoly on crime, no matter the stylishness used to define such criminal behaviour. Oil and gas fraudsters, real estate criminals, payroll and pension scammers, crooked bank officials and other white-collar criminals must be reminded that they are in the same league as kidnappers, bandits, terrorists and insurgents. Elegant use of English, corporate attires, fanciful looks, self-embellishments, and air-conditioned rooms and offices do not exempt or exclude their behaviours from the umbrella of criminal misconduct.

The mammoth level of financial crimes in the private sector has proven that the country's citizens need rigorous sanctification before they can morally hold their political leaders accountable or demand dividends of good governance. Sadly, it would appear that the fight against financial crimes and political corruption will continue to hit a stumbling block so long as citizens participate in such acts gleefully. I have to admit an inelegant truth: I have always believed that Nigerian citizens who lament corruption and financial crimes are merely jealous of their political leaders and other perpetrators. That belief is concluded upon the fact that they do not frown on the illicit acts perpetrated by their political and socio-economic leaders because they find such acts inappropriate and detrimental to societal building; they frown on them because they are not personal beneficiaries of such acts. With a large segment of a grossly corrupt and fraudulent citizenry, political and large-scale corruption is certainly a long way from becoming a thing of the past.

3: FINANCIAL CRIMES AND CORRUPTION II

Although Nigeria today has become a sanctuary for all sorts of financial crimes and atrocities, Nigerians did not invent some of such acts. The anarchy and impunity culture that was allowed to become part of our sociopolitical culture was what permitted such acts to become widespread and innate characteristics of today's unacceptable proportion of citizens.

Pre-colonial non-indigenes perpetrated the first documented cases of financial-related crimes. Called "obtaining by trick," foreign merchants disguised as legitimate traders swindled inhabitants into parting away with their commodities for inferior goods. They earned so much from cheating inhabitants that the thought of leaving the country became unfathomable. Rather, they chose to stay in the region for over 100 years, in which the theft of resources and the repatriation of wealth back to their nations became commonplace and legitimised: the construction of what has been elegantly termed colonialism. Regardless, their acts will not be documented further as this book does not aim to focus on non-indigenous actors and players.

Financial-related crimes have become so interconnected that it has become tasking to differentiate them from one another. They all carry one single motive: the conning of victims of their financial earnings or properties. Financial frauds, interchangeably called "419", preceded the country's independence. As far back as 1922, the then British Secretary of State for the Colonies, Winston Churchill, had received a letter from the headmaster of the Hope Waddell Institute, the Rev. J.K. Macgregor. Macgregor bitterly lamented that foreigners were taking advantage of the postal system to dupe

Nigerian pupils.[1] Macgregor complained that hundreds of mass-mail advertorials of "mystic charm" and homoeopathic medicine were being sent to his pupils from India, Britain, and the United States to con unsuspecting students who believed in the magical and superstitious wonders of such items.[2] The charms and medicines were nothing other than a valueless piece of materials to ensure pupils part away with more money should they need more powerful charms than the ones sent to them.

The late British historian and Africanist Stephen Ellis had even suggested that as early as 1921, a certain "Professor" Crentsil was already engaging in the practice of "419". "Professor" Crentsil also took the infamy of being the first person to be charged with the offence after writing mass mails offering magical powers for use to victims. Ironically, again, according to Stephen Ellis, the "Professor" was not a Nigerian citizen but a Ghanaian (from the former Gold Coast).[3]

Another wing of financial crime that has been documented is trafficking. In general, trafficking is not new to the region of Nigeria. Human trafficking has been around for centuries, dating back to the periods of human enslavement and the slave trade. Other aspects of trafficking, such as currency and drug trafficking, have inflicted us with series of economic and social injuries. As you will read, these acts of financial crimes and others perpetrated by Nigerians only serve the actors but impede general economic growth and development. In addition, a dangerous culture of impunity and tolerance for crime created a fertile ground for financial criminals in the country and one that today has become nearly impossible to curtail.

Haven for Smuggling and Trafficking

Prior to the financial recessions of the 70s and the 80s, peoples and societies of the Nigerian region were overwhelmingly conservative. Generally, they

124

were hostile to liberalised habits such as smoking, alcoholism, abortion, prostitution and other acts that they deemed immoral or even taboo. It is not to say that such acts were strange or were not perpetrated in the early stage of the country's development. Still, they were acts associated with only a very few deviants. Incidentally and unknown to the general populace, a more dangerous trend had commenced but had gone unnoticed; the scourge of drug and human trafficking.

Smuggling itself is as old as the country. The colonialists in Lagos Colony had put checks in place to curtail the menace of smuggling as far back as the late 19th century.[4] Subsequent colonial reports (as early as 1900) show that colonial authorities were lamenting the smuggling of items such as cowries, spirits, tobacco, adulterated palm oil and even humans into various regions and areas of their respective jurisdiction. Nobody could tell when drug trafficking kicked off in our geographical terrain. Although there are reports that drug smuggling had gone on as early as the 1950s, there is little evidence to accept that to be factually correct. Regardless, the earliest period it got the attention of the authorities was in the 1970s.

Smuggling of all kinds started to take shape in the 1960s and well into the 1970s. Smugglers took advantage of the three-year Nigerian civil war to start a business that had been in practice for so long and also made it a national worry thereafter. Unsure of whose side to take between Nigeria's Federal Military Government (FMG) and the Biafra government, foreign and local business people started smuggling currency notes and material goods, evading sanctions and border control agents. Others continued the smuggling business that preceded the civil war and that had just become lucrative. Exports and imports of smuggled goods benefited the smugglers and negatively impacted the country's overall economy. Subsidised goods relating to farm produce, petroleum products and currency notes were illegally exported outside the country to neighbouring countries to make substantial profit returns and short-change the public purse.

Heavily taxed foreign manufactured cars were smuggled into the country through Benin and other neighbouring countries, while stolen cars were inversely smuggled out for sale into the same countries. Smugglers were not done. Currency smuggling, which was done to help Biafrans to circumvent financial sanctions by the FMG, continued well after the war ended. In fact, after the war ended, currency smuggling became a major revenue source for smugglers. At the same time, it was reported that the number of smuggled currencies was more than that of legitimate transactions that had taken place in the currency exchange market. I also gathered from credible underground sources that the profits from smuggling were so lucrative that legitimate business people started to abandon their initial businesses for full-time engagement in the smuggling and trafficking of legal and illegal items.

Smuggling and trafficking were activities that would have been impossible without the involvement of state actors. The two political administrations that allowed crime and corruption to be pioneered under their watch were the Shehu Shagari civilian administration and General Ibrahim Babangida's FMG. Under both leaders, crime and corruption thrived freely. Therefore, it was not a coincidence that the period from 1980 to 1990 recorded newly introduced forms of criminal behaviours alien to or imperceptible in Nigeria. Drug trafficking in Nigeria did not develop on its own. Arguably, it can be said to be attributed to incidents that occurred elsewhere around the globe but eventually made foot movements right here to our national soil. Those movements became criminal practices were permitted and eventually allowed to grow, develop and succeed.

By 1971, the United States government under President Richard Nixon had declared drug abuse as "public enemy number one" and one that must be fought aggressively. In 1973, the United States Drug Enforcement Administration (DEA) was formed to tackle the menace of drug smuggling and distribution within its jurisdictions. During that period, powerful drug cartels emerged from Mexico, Colombia and other regions of the Americas. As the US government stepped up its efforts to fight drug abuse and

126

trafficking, homegrown and neighbouring cartels also increased their activities to a growing number of consumers in the US and global market. These events meant that rerouting locations were needed to get drugs into the United States and Europe at all costs. That was where Nigeria and the then-new generation of ever-ready criminal minds stepped in.

Nigerians were not immune to the global financial crises of the 1970s and 1980s. With corrupt and incompetent leaders at the helm of affairs, itinerant unemployed youths who had returned to the country brought dangerous cultures of crime and indiscipline. The returning citizens could not believe their luck, as they met unsecured national borders (air, land and sea), corrupt officials and archaic immigration and customs control system in the country; all the needed resources to engage in the free activation of their new-found inglorious trade. Global demand for psychoactive drugs and a badly unmonitored aviation system catalysed Nigeria into one of the world's most infamous routes for drug trafficking. America, of course, was not the only destination they had in mind. They targeted neighbouring African countries, Europe, Asia and the rest of the world. Ironically, as Nigerians got alerted to the activities of drug traffickers, a strange set of events showed great conspiracies and complicities by powerful men and women in the same corridors of power.

It was not an erroneous act to omit General Muhammadu Buhari from the political leaders that permitted crime and corruption under their watch during the 1980s. Events vindicated him as a no-nonsense leader, perhaps an incorrigibly incorruptible one at that. When Buhari took office on the morning of January 1, 1984, Nigeria seemed to have found a man who would return the country to its "glory days". The era of indiscipline, corruption and criminality seemed to have found a vibrant terminator. His introduction of the War Against Indiscipline as a vehicle to rid the nation of its ills was widely applauded. Ready to live up to his promise, Buhari enacted Decree 20, a law that prescribed the death penalty for persons convicted of drug trafficking and illegal bunkering. Shortly after, convictions were carried out, and executions followed. At the time, those unaware of the devastating effect of drugs harshly criticised the death penalty that General Buhari promulgated. Today, governments worldwide have imposed similar penalties against drug trafficking, and the US government has launched deadly strikes on drug cartels and their foot soldiers, especially in Latin America. Sadly, as Buhari and his deputy Major-General Tunde Idiagbon went to work, other members of the military government were not in agreement.

As you must have read in this book, the propensity of Nigerians to commit crimes despite the grave repercussions that follow is not new. As far back as April 22, 1985 - a few days after the executions of three convicted drug dealers - officials at the Aminu Kano International Airport arrested a woman named Gloria Okon. She was arrested on suspicion of possessing several kilogrammes of banned substances en route to Europe. Strangely, Gloria Okon was not able to face trial as she was found and pronounced dead some few days after her arrest in very mysterious and suspicious circumstances. General Buhari immediately ordered an investigation into the cause of Gloria Okon's death. A judicial panel of inquiry was commissioned to submit a report on its findings. Incidentally, Buhari had one thing going bad for him. He was ignorant of the personality of the men who surrounded him or was just too helpless to act. A few months after the Gloria Okon saga, Major-General Ibrahim Babangida deposed General Buhari, and the commission's report never saw the light of day. But that was not the end of the story.

A year after the Gloria Okon incident, a journalist Dele Giwa was said to have discovered a link between Gloria Okon and members of Buhari's inner caucus. Independent investigators alleged that Gloria Okon, who herself was a wife of a top military officer, was also an associate of Maryam Babangida. At the time of Gloria Okon's arrest, Maryam Babangida was the wife of the country's Chief of Army Staff, General Ibrahim Babangida. Babangida had become the country's head of state when Dele Giwa uncovered the connection. Dele Giwa was reportedly working on a connection linking drug

128

trafficking to the corridors of power. His investigation followed a tip-off over strong allegations that Gloria Okon was not dead but had been smuggled to London to escape punishment. On the heels of his investigations about to be published, Dele Giwa was assassinated through a parcelled bomb on October 19, 1986. Giwa's death had all the marks of the government's connivance or those within the corridors of power. Obviously, there is no smoke without fire. The incidents, all within a year, were too related to be just matters of coincidence. The death of Gloria Okon in custody (true or otherwise), Buhari's removal from office despite the heavy penalty of death that comes with a coup failure, the suppression of the commission's report, the death of Dele Giwa by state actors, and the failure to successfully investigate the circumstances of Giwa's death all stink of a significant hidden plot.

The Gloria Okon and Dele Giwa stories were not the only incidents that showed excessive collusions involving government officials and traffickers. The 1980-decade was filled with drama and highlights of public officials' penchant to do as they pleased, without much care for how the public viewed them. The government's inability to furnish its citizens with complete information on perceived negligence of conduct by top officials was enough to enrich the conspiracy theory and rumour industries. For instance, in 1984, the Buhari administration put strict measures at the country's airports to control the menace of currency trafficking after changing the country's currency notes impromptu. Buhari also ordered that suitcases and travelling luggage of all passengers must be checked irrespective of class or status of the traveller. However, a story regarding "53 suitcases" (as it was later dubbed) that had passed through Customs without proper clearance made national headlines, rocked the polity and tainted the anti-corruption crusade of Buhari's military government. It was alleged that the suitcases belonged to the Emir of Gwandu and his entourage. It was also alleged that the Emir's son, Major Mustapha Jokolo, the Aide-de-camp to the Head of State General Buhari, unduly facilitated the clearance of the suitcases. A journalist,

Onukaba Adinoyi-Ojo, hurriedly ran the publication without accurate information and with a sensational motive. Regardless, something else indicted the Buhari administration but was unknown to the public at the time.

Coincidentally, the flight that had the Emir of Gwandu also had Ambassador Dahiru Waziri, the country's Ambassador to Saudi Arabia. Ambassador Waziri had just been posted to serve as the Chief of Protocol at the State House. He was relocating back to the country with suitcases totalling 20 and had an entourage of family close to a double dozen. Through overzealous behaviour or intent to bypass Customs for ulterior motives, officers attached to the newly appointed State House's Chief of Protocol transported the luggage from the aircraft straight to his house without going through customs. The Area Administrator of Customs at the Murtala Muhammed International Airport at the time was Alhaji Atiku Abubakar, who later became the country's Vice-President. General Muhammadu Buhari and Major Mustapha Jokolo, who later succeeded his father to become the Emir of Gwandu, later confirmed the collusion of certain officers attached to Ambassador Dahiru Waziri in the disgraceful saga.[5] The illustration of the "53 suitcases" incident is to paint a clearer picture of what transpires behind closed doors of political power and authority in Nigeria and why many crimes continue to be perpetrated with unfathomable impunity. Although the contents of the Emir's suitcases had been clarified as household and personal items (its trueness is another topic), to date, no one has been able to confirm the actual contents of Ambassador Dahiru Waziri's suitcases or why it was not screened contrary to Buhari's direct order. Even if parties involved in the saga had no ulterior motive, the story's relevance is to create a pictorial view of how smuggling and trafficking were easy to perpetrate by people in positions of power.

Several other episodes illustrated to Nigerians how men of the underworld enjoyed the support of those in power to carry out their activities. In regard to drug trafficking, one similar episode was the inglorious exit of the first chairman of the newly created NDLEA, Fidelis Oyakhilome. Perhaps, to rid the country of illicit drugs, the Babangida administration created the NDLEA by promulgating Decree No. 48 in December 1989. A decorated police officer, Fidelis Oyakhilome, was made chairman of the organisation, but his tenure was short-lived. He was dismissed for allegedly having an amorous relationship with a businesswoman and socialite, Jennifer Madike, who had been arrested and later indicted for drug-related offences. Jennifer Madike was also said to have collected $80,000 from arrested drug suspects to facilitate their release through her connection with Fidelis Oyakhilome. The story made Nigerians to understand further, the nexus between crime and political power.

The drug business is a very daring business to engage in. It requires guts and connections with those in the corridors of power. In the prequel to this book, the roles played by unscrupulous agents of the NDLEA and other agencies in smoothing the operations of traffickers were documented. By 1990, traffickers had recruited the services of travel officials such as pilots, stewards, hostesses, airport officials and luggage handlers to participate in drug movements aboard aircraft. Public officials, celebrities, diplomats, military men, socialites, and security officials who were deemed not liable to rigorous checks became recruited as movers of drugs, narcotics, and counterfeit currency notes.

Nigeria is a country with an ever-present aggressive battle between suspicions and rumours versus facts and accuracy of events. The rumour mill industry of Nigeria is assuredly rich with accusations that some of the country's political elites, socialites, entertainers, celebrities and public figures are engaged in the scourge of drug trafficking. In matters of honesty, there are strong anecdotal connections to arrive at such conclusions. However, as a competent court has never indicted the suspected individuals, it becomes a matter of mere gossip even when trueness exists. Such suspicions cannot be featured in this book despite many temptations to do so. Two similar cases of relevance were the arrests of two popular Nollywood actors.

In September 2006, popular Nollywood actress, Taiwo "Wunmi" Akinwande, was arrested on suspicion of trafficking in cocaine at the Murtala Muhammed International Airport. The NDLEA made her to excrete sizeable wraps of cocaine that she had ingested. She was charged to court and was given a three-year jail term with an option of N1million fine by a Federal High Court in Lagos. Similarly, popular Nollywood actor and comedian Babatunde "Baba Suwe" Omidina was arrested in October 2011 by the NDLEA on accusations of drug possession. However, after more than three weeks in a detention facility and 25 bowel movements, he was released and freed on bail.[6] Baba Suwe pressed charges against the NDLEA, and he was awarded the sum of N25 million in compensation for breach of his fundamental human rights. People in the know claim there was more to the incident and that Baba Suwe was not as innocent as claimed. Drug smuggling was a common "side hustle" among those in the entertainment circle.

Nigeria conveniently became one of the control centres of the trafficking business because of the ease of operations and the inefficiency of law enforcement operatives in tackling the menace. Today, several Nigerians languish in jails worldwide for their roles in drug trafficking. Some have been executed in countries with the death penalty in place for convicted offenders. Not all Nigerian travellers arrested or eventually convicted by foreign authorities for drug-related offences were guilty. Some became victims of circumstances or ignorance. Getting wound of information that a particular individual is about to travel abroad, drug dealers, mostly acting as middlemen, would lure an intending traveller into a well-orchestrated scheme to use them as conduits in drug movement operations. The most common method is to present the intending traveller with a package for transportation abroad under the guise of delivering it to a third party in the destination country. Packages of such nature have carefully concealed drugs that eventually get detected by Nigerian or foreign authorities, thereby igniting a long legal battle for proof of innocence by the unsuspecting traveller. Proving innocence is an implausible task for many, who end up serving lengthy jail terms or even getting executed for a crime they know nothing about. There is a true-life story I feel inclined to bring to the reader's attention which will further underpin my belief that so many of the country's citizens who carry innocent faces and could be seen in some of the most pious social settings are the actual devil on earth.

Some years ago, I was contacted by the family of a local Imam in a community in Ogun, South West Nigeria, to intervene in a case that had their patriarch languishing in a foreign prison. The Imam, from a noble and humble background, had been approached by a respected Muslim community member in the area he presided, on the premise that he would be sponsored to Saudi Arabia for Lesser Hajj. The Imam joyously accepted the offer as a one-time opportunity and one he deemed a heavenly blessing. He was elated and thanked his sponsor. He also summoned members of the Islamic community, which he presided over, to help appreciate the sponsor and to make special prayers of thanks her way. On his way to the Lesser Hajj, he was given a briefcase and was told to pass it on to a third party in Mecca. That was not a problem for the intending traveller since he had not much luggage as it never dawned on him that he would ever travel out of the country's shores, much more for Hajj, a dream for Muslim faithful. However, his travail started when Saudi authorities accosted him at the King Abdulaziz International Airport in Jeddah, Saudi Arabia. They told him that items in one of his luggage (the particular luggage handed to him by the travel sponsor to give to a third party) had carefully wrapped blocks of heroin weighing 15 kilograms. That was the beginning of his long ordeal and a three-year journey before successfully proving his innocence to Saudi authorities. Many have not been that lucky, and they languish in jails all over the world, thanks to people who sleep well at night spending money from drug trafficking no matter the accompanying cost.

Nigeria is home to a host of superstitious beliefs, where some assume the "blood money" phenomenon is not just real but works and can make them stupendously rich. From my understanding and interpretation, illicit wealth that involves the destruction or taking away of human lives is narrow enough to enter the wide definition of what constitutes blood money. As regularly dramatized in Nollywood and the country's pop culture, Nigeria itself carries the paradoxical illustration of sadness and hilarity combined. Many citizens are unaware or naïve of how evil and despicable their parents are. The beautiful girls on social media whose parents thrive in wealth and financial glory from selling fake and expired drugs that destroy innocent lives could also be found among a crowd of civil protesters, perhaps demanding good governance. The son of a drug trafficker whose happy destiny was arrived at through the destruction of innocent lives is on social media, celebrating his drug-trafficking father as the "best father in the world" or other fanciful pictorial portrayals. Many Nigerians of today who live in abundance do so from the tears and destruction of innocent lives.

Drug trafficking is very profitable to its players and actors, except for members of the larger society. Customs officers and other authoritative bodies are inundated with abandoned drug-laden luggage and cargo at various entry points or exits. Despite continuous seizures of drug items, sometimes worth as much as billions of naira, more drugs continue to flow in and out of Nigeria, a sharp reminder that it is indeed a lucrative business. So lucrative is drug trafficking that despite the death penalty in most Asian countries, recalcitrant youths continue to engage in such an unholy business in those same regions. Ill-gotten wealth in Nigeria concerning trafficking is not solely attributed to drug trafficking. Satanic individuals carry out other similar demonic activities on our national soil.

Nigeria continues to suffer from the scourge of human trafficking that has become a cancer in various societies. The United Nations defines human trafficking as:

> The recruitment, transportation, transfer, harbouring or receipt of people through force, fraud or deception, with the aim of exploiting them for profit...Men, women and children of all ages and from all

backgrounds can become victims of this crime, which occurs in every region of the world. The traffickers often use violence or fraudulent employment agencies and fake promises of education and job opportunities to trick and coerce their victims.[7]

As I noted earlier, human trafficking in this corner of the earth precedes the country's formal existence. Every tribe, group, and almost every wealthy individual of pre-independent Nigeria took part in this sad inhumane behaviour. Human enslavements for the financial prosperity of individuals and societies were an unspoken rule that developed as a regional norm.

The buying and selling of children was a distastefully practised behaviour among some members of the Igbo community to such an extent that colonial authorities launched massive raids against traders and practitioners well into the 1940s. The Afikpo, Owerri, and Cross River regions were infamous for their roles in the slave market ordeal as recent as the 1930s, a hundred years after the colonialists abolished slave trade. Trafficking and kidnapping gangs were not the only parties involved in the inhumane practice. Across the region of Nigeria, women, men, landlords, debt collectors, and husbands had innocent victims (wives, children, servants, pawned individuals) to sell to ready buyers. The practice was hard to detect by colonial authorities due to the systematic and well-orchestrated manner involved in the trades.[8] A British colonial report said:

It would seem there is evidence to support the fact that children of both sexes are being illegally procured and sold, but the matter is complicated by the fact that it is difficult to establish proof of parentage when children alleged to have been stolen were too young to remember their parents, while in other cases the so-called " slaves " do not desire to leave the custody of the persons with whom they are found and therefore render very little help to the investigating officer.[9]

135

That was the colonial report back in 1934, a hundred years after the abolition of slavery by the British. Sadly, things do not seem to have changed up to this day. Understanding the menace of human trafficking in Nigeria is very dicey. That is because, in many cases, people who ought to be categorised under the definition of "victim" never see themselves as such until the wheels come off, in very ruinous circumstances. Traffickers take advantage of vulnerable citizens desperate to leave the country's shores for a better life abroad and recruit them into a well-organised plan of fictitious promises. Young girls and women from underprivileged backgrounds in villages and rural townships are mostly targeted for eventual recruitment into a world of sex trafficking, prostitution or slavery abroad. After being told of "too good to be true" jobs and promised better life abroad, girls and younger women are recruited willingly or coerced by parents/guardians to be repatriated abroad.

Abroad, they discover things are not the way they have been told. Their passports are seized, and they are forced to undergo the worst form of physical and psychological rituals to prevent them from absconding. They are forced to succumb to a new world of forced labour and sexual enslavement; this they do till they can pay up the monies they allegedly owe to their traffickers. With this practice, many young girls, hungry and desperate for patrons, are seen roaming the streets of foreign countries, a disgraceful stain on our national pride and collective existence. From Italy, Holland, Turkey, Cyprus, Ukraine, UAE, Saudi Arabia, Kenya, South Africa, Egypt, Qatar, Oman, Jordan, and Brazil, to name a few, young Nigerian girls are engaged in the world of voluntary and involuntary prostitution. Surprisingly, you could also find them in some of the world's harshest regions, such as Libya, Sudan, Iraq, or Somalia, mostly as domestic servants or what locals refer to as *shagala*. They did not get there of their own pure volition; rather, some fellow citizens thought it wise to enslave other people's children to improve their own children's lives.

The word "lucky" might be deemed insensitive to describe victims of human trafficking who find themselves in the dungeon of forced labour or sex trafficking exploitations. But such victims may have to count their luck when they hear gory details of other victims. Illegal immigrants looking to use pathways of countries such as Morocco and Libya to gain access to Europe are hardly ever lucky. Trapped in a foreign region (sometimes stateless regions), they fall prey to the hands of human scavengers, who capture them and prepare them for eventual enslavement or sale in underground slave markets. After being sold, they are made to work in slave camps, with only food and water as compensation, in a well-calculated manner to ensure their survival as enslaved people who are seen as mere commodities by their captors. Some victims who are caught by kidnapping syndicates are tortured or even maimed in a bid to extort ransom payments from their already impoverished families back home. Others are sold to cruel agents who butcher them and harvest their body organs for sale in covert black markets.

Human trafficking has become predominant in all regions of Nigeria, and activities regarding it differ by region. For instance, in the North, children are trafficked to solicit alms and into forceful early marriages, while some find themselves in the hands of insurgent groups and terrorists. In the Southeast, young boys are lured to smuggle drugs abroad. In the South-South, girls are mostly trafficked for prostitution and sex slavery. Young girls and women are trafficked to mostly Arab countries as domestic servants and into forced labour in the southwestern parts of the country. The scourge of human trafficking has brought disrepute, shame, and disgrace to Nigeria. Quite a handful of Nigerians who live abroad have at least a memory of discrimination and racial profiling based on their nationality. What they do not know are the factors responsible for such disgusting treatments by foreign natives.

No one could tell for sure or with accuracy how Nigerians historically became a people disreputably afflicted with the scourge of prostitution and sex trafficking around the world. As it has been said, prostitution (or commercial sex as elegantly called) is one of the oldest forms of labour on earth. It is a global curse and one that exists in every society in the world. Typically, prostitution is insignificant to gain a mention in this book. The problem is that it has become disreputably attached to the Nigerian people.

From my personal examination, I traced the source of global sex trafficking that involved Nigerians in its notorious form to the usual Nigerian factor. Some early set of Nigerian immigrants in most European and Asian cities found out that they could make money quicker and faster from commercial sex activities than from their day-to-day job and wasted no time making a switch. They did not stop there. They sent messages to friends and colleagues back home about the lucratively new "job" they had encountered. As time went by, two things happened synchronously. Firstly, the first sets of prostitutes grew older and were naturally not sought after by sex seekers and clients. They knew they had to quit the job that had become mouth-watering and they had depended on their entire life. Not to be left behind, they sought younger girls from cities, suburban areas and villages back home in Nigeria. Secondly, those were coincidentally the period the country degenerated into chaos, and the younger generations were jumping at any available offer from abroad. Young itinerant Nigerian females who once gained access to several regions of the world unhindered soon found themselves restricted by foreign embassies as the country and its citizens suddenly became red-flagged. The restrictions meant hopeful immigrants had to go through trafficking agents who lured them through fanciful talks of a better life abroad. Societies and regions whose women - later known and referred to as *madams* - first came in contact with prostitution syndicates got affected the most. The *madams* became the ringleaders in the Nigerian axis. Areas such as Benin, Warri, Sapele and some neighbouring parts of the South became the hub of prostitution and sex trafficking up to the present day.

Nigerians are aggressively stubborn and are sharply intransigent to warnings of chaos and disasters, so long as the opportunity of hope presents itself. One must agree that some Nigerians were lured, tricked, or forced into trafficking. Also, it is misleading to pretend that others did not willingly ask for it. In a bid to escape the country's shores at all costs, some people quickly jumped into whatever offer they encountered despite being aware of the paradoxical bifurcation of their action, which presents mild success or disturbing cruelty. To be straightforward, the advent of social media and news-sharing platforms has made even the least educated person in heavily targeted areas aware of the dangers of sex and human trafficking. Nevertheless, people stubbornly agree to embark on such journeys of unlikely return. News updates constantly warn itinerant hopefuls to desist from making attempts into Europe through areas of the Mediterranean Sea due to the accompanying risks. It would seem as if some had made up their minds to enter a pot of doom as cooked meals by ever-ready scavengers who await them en route to Europe. As we know, "it never rains, but it pours."

Untruthful and dishonest itinerants returning to their respective hometowns became the chief enablers of human trafficking, albeit unintentionally. Returning to their various localities from foreign countries and in a bid for self-aggrandisement, they misled families, societies and communities about their experiences abroad. They hid true accounts of life realities that are sometimes related to pains and agonies. Some intentionally sold distorted information, lies, deceits and misleading notions to every individual they came across, that travelling abroad is the only way out of impoverishment. The returning itinerants did not paint the true picture that life abroad is unkind to unskilled, uneducated and illegal migrants. That singular thread of behaviours created a false sense of belief among hopeful travellers and became the major catalyst for people's obduracy to relocate abroad by all means necessary.

The excuse factory of the average Nigerian is rich and abundant enough to last a lifetime. There is an excuse for every of our criminal and immoral engagements. We have become a people that sleep comfortably, with our children tucked safely under our roofs, feeding fat off the blood of innocent children elsewhere. We sleep well knowing that horrific acts condemned and outlawed some 200 years ago have been picked up and used to enrich our pockets and used as a source of comfort for our children. Our brothers and sisters are sold off in underground markets to face a daily life of excruciating pain, agony and torture. Individuals and families are left in tears because of the thirst and greed of their fellow citizens. Likewise, societies and communities continue to welcome despicable traffickers into their midst, where they are met with respect and reverence from immoral money worshippers and praise hunters. Cultural and religious institutions are not any better as front-row seats are given to people whose sources of wealth stink in blood, tears and anguish.

I opined earlier that sometimes discussing the menace of trafficking could be a dicey one as regards people who should typically fall under the "victim" definition do not see themselves as such. I could also contend further that some "victims" could count their "luck" when they compare their predicaments with those of other victims who fall into the widely thrown-out net of the victim definition. For instance, child slavery is a very condemnable act and one that should be frowned upon and never excused. Legality and humanity are on one side of the coin, and pragmatism is on the other. Thousands of children today work as domestic servants to mostly middle-class and upper-class families. They have been denied their basic right to education and made to live an adult life while being compulsorily denied their childhood. If I were to write as an egregious hypocrite, I would blame those harbouring them and label them ignominiously. However, the reality says otherwise. Many child-servants are people who were originally failed by their own parents and the general society. People failed to ensure that children brought into this world must be catered for compulsorily and without any iota of excuse for such.

In most cases, children who work as manual labourers are not orphans. They are given out by parents who could hardly tell if a child is missing due to the odd numbers of such children within their fold. Defying logic and law,

140

and although condemnable, child-servants live and enjoy a better standard/quality of life than what could have been made available to them under the roof of their negligent parents or out there in a cold world where nobody cares. That is the sad dilemma facing enslaved children in the homes of comfortable families all over the country today.

Nigeria is a country with many challenges, and the challenges continue to cloud over any little progress or achievement the country ever tries to make for itself. While drug and human trafficking are well-known types of trafficking, the prevalence of arms trafficking continues to destroy the fabric of societies that tolerates them. Illegal arms trafficking prevents peace and stability and is responsible for many nations' economic and sociopolitical regress.

As a reminder, societies where traffickers and smugglers are allowed to gain a stronghold will continue to see insurgencies and other forms of violence on the rise. People with devastatingly ulterior motives easily procure guns, ammunition, drugs and children in Nigeria. Societies that spend more on arms than socio-economic development always pay for their foolhardy stance. Also, any society where arms are traded freely and illegally, especially by non-state actors, has ensured a parting from peace and stability. Sadly, Nigeria is an example, and we are paying a high price for such an anomaly.

Land Grabbing and Scams

The "This House is not for sale" inscription that has become a permanent feature on houses, buildings and land fences in Nigeria is not a fabrication of people's figment of imagination, but an indication of possible danger. It is actually out of valid fear and suspicion that originated from horrible incidents involving victims of land fraud and theft. Some scams are deeply rooted and intertwined with historical, social and structural factors. One such example can be found in the *omo-onile*/ajagungbale syndrome, which is predominant in the country's southern areas. I had earlier written about the rise of land grabbers in various societies of Nigeria, especially in societies and communities that carried the historical "king owns everything" connotation and phenomenon.[10] Through such a belief system, principal architects and beneficiaries of land ownership were not subjected to questioning. Kings, chiefs, war generals, aristocrats, and oligarchs could arrogate lands to/for themselves, paying no attention to the probability of ownership by common people.

The parlances *"omo onile"* and *"ajagungbale"* are used interchangeably and have easily relatable translations and etymologies. *Omo-onile* means the land's owners (first settlers), while *ajagungbale* means the one who fights to collect lands. They take lands with impunity and determine with so much audacity who owns the land, what can be done and when projects can commence, most times in a bid to extort land buyers. Nonetheless, these groups of people who have become a menace actually have fair historical precedence on how they became so relevant and perhaps powerful in their own right.

A significant rise of the *omo onile* in southwestern areas of the country dates back to the periods of the Yoruba Civil wars of the 19th century (at least by recent historical analysis). However, before that period, generalissimos of Yoruba states did not live inside city areas with the paramount ruler. Rather, they are designated to outskirts and surrounding areas to live. From there, they could detect incoming raids and neutralise enemy forces before the invasion of their states. That was the case in Oyo, Lagos and their fragmented states. The areas and lands that were commanded by the generalissimos, their warriors and their offspring, gave birth to both the *omo onile* and *ajagungbale* phenomenon.

The traditional rulers of pre-colonial states later became renowned for giving lands and settlement areas to indigenous war generals and mercenary fighters. Rewards were mostly for their loyalty, fearlessness, and bravery in fending foreign attacks. The heroics of these warriors were so notable that rulers gave them permanence of ownership for particular lands and areas to establish full autonomy and control for the setup of military command posts to monitor the activities of hostile forces.

Some overzealous warriors later began to use their infantrymen to encroach into other lands under the guise of monitoring the activities of those within their boundary and jurisdiction. Armed with enough warriors and resources, they began to take advantage of the system of unwritten agreements relating to land ownership to decide who owns what and who gets what. They passed on their notoriety and entire practice from generation to generation. Each generation saw themselves as the rightful owners of lands given to them "legitimately", including lands their previous generations had acquired inappropriately and forcefully. This book is not historical, and there are discussions about the history of land scams and violence that this book cannot cover. However, I can conclude factually that most people today who arrogate the "right" and "legitimacy" to award lands up to this day are generations of blood-thirsty, fraudulent and monstrous land thieves and usurpers.

Land grabbers are not just some regular members of society; they are well connected due to their affiliations with traditional and political leaders, making it a safe assumption to refer to them as political stalwarts. They have numerous "boys" behind them who are readily available to cause mayhem and chaos on those who challenge their right to ownership of lands they set out to acquire. The large numbers of boys at their disposal make them prime assets for those who need their services; a client list that includes politicians, socialites, warmongers and social disruptors, to name a few. Communal members also use them to dislodge one another in civil conflicts arising from land disputes, debt resolutions, financial disagreements, family feuds, and intra-tribal clashes. In fact, it could be credibly concluded that land grabbers played a pivotal role in establishing several violent cult groups in the country. The deadly *badoo* cult group that once terrorised the residents of Ikorodu and its axis were attributed to notorious land grabbers in the same area. As

Nigerians, we tend to give rise and encouragement to activities that ought not to have been condoned or allowed to gain momentum in the first place.

Like every other scam, they are characterised by deceit, concealment, or betrayal of the trust system. They focus heavily on using fake documents and fictitious "signals" to lure unsuspecting victims into believing all is well. From using a forged Certificate of Occupancy (C of O) to selling lands to multiple individuals, fictitious documents, hidden buyers fees, land tax debt, history of incomplete transactions with third parties, and sale of lands with possible litigations, to name a few. Some of these acts are carried out on a one-off basis by individuals who are in a desperate bid to cut losses incurred from a previous ploy they themselves were a victim of. For some others, it is a career assignment and an everyday job.

Relatives and associates of land scammers are not immune either. Wayward children are known to sell land properties that do not have the express permission of the rightful owners. Similarly, it has been reported that married spouses dispose of properties belonging to their partners without due consent. Individual cases such as these should typically not be enough to gain a notable mention in this book, except that they are widespread behaviours that create a trust deficit in our societies.

Land conflicts due to the activities of grabbers and scammers in villages, rural and suburban parts of Nigeria have led to the destruction of lives and property and the displacements of people. In some rural communities, the activities of *ajagungbale* gangs have terrorised people and forcefully dispossessed them of their ancestral lands, instigating tribal and ethnic tensions between/among warring parties. Land disputes affect the societal and national economy because manipulative practices from grabbers and scammers dissuade potential investors from bringing potential economic activities to areas where fraud and manipulations are prevalent.

Visa and Travel Scams

Trafficked victims, especially those desperate to leave the country's shores, were not the only victims of crooked activities. Victims of travel and visa frauds were also given a compulsive bitter pill to consume.

As early as the 1980s, visa and travel fraudsters began hunting citizens desperate to leave the country's shores for greener pastures. The resultant effect of their activities was that foreign authorities got alarmed about the need to view Nigerian travellers with deep suspicions. The various types of visa and travel frauds perpetrated by Nigerians need no introduction or further analysis. They have become well understood by both Nigerians and foreign authorities. Activities regarding visa and travel fraud are perpetrated in the open and without a burden of care to consequences. A foreign ambassador once said at a forum organised in Lagos that his home country stopped asking Nigerians to provide specific documents for scrutiny because they found out travel fraudsters easily procure any document required of them. Such is the culture of impunity in Nigeria, where travel agencies impudently run advertorials on helping itinerant hopefuls secure travel visas using fake documents.

Economic crises hit Nigerians so bad that many became desperate to leave the country's shores. Rightly or wrongly, they viewed the country with so much disdain and hopelessness. Desperate to leave, yet unqualified to be granted travel visas, at least by the standards established by foreign countries, they began to arm themselves with other alternatives. The "*yoju*" syndrome came to the rescue of such people and was their immediate recourse. *Yoju* was a carefully orchestrated type of travel fraud where stolen international passports of victims found their way into the hands of fraudsters, who then sold them to aspiring travellers by removing the picture of the original owner. The stolen passports were either foreign-issued or Nigerian passports that carried valid visas that the conniving traveller could not meet up to the condition of its issuance. The desperate use of fraudulent travel documents in a bid to travel, perhaps never to come back to the country, eventually gave birth to the '*japa*' phenomenon.

It has become our innate character to blame our leaders for all that is wrong while intentionally giving fellow citizens a free pass. As regards travel and visa fraud, many have been sent into a state of perpetual poverty, while some have committed suicide because of the atrocities of travel fraudsters. A true-life story illustrates the sad occurrences of travel fraud in Nigeria.

In 1995, Samuel Adelaja (not actual name) won a scholarship granted to him by an NGO to study medicine at the University of Leeds in the UK. Samuel was a 20-year-old child from a family of four and had just completed his secondary school education in his hometown of Atiba in Oyo. Samuel joyously informed his aged father, a retired pensioner, of the good fortune which had just smiled upon him. The NGO informed him that his school tuition fees for 5 years would be paid for and that a travel visa would be secured for him. Conditionally, he would have to facilitate his flight ticket and must cater for his accommodation and daily expenses while studying; these, the NGO set aside to ensure that students contribute their minimal quota to study. The conditions were fair enough for Samuel, who could never have imagined his family having to train him through a Nigerian university to study medicine, much more in a foreign land. He was happy and received the offer. He put in his documents and was approved for a student visa.

Knowing he was bound to travel, Samuel beckoned on his pensioner father to seek help to procure a travel ticket. Knowing well that a travel ticket was not the only thing needed per the condition for the scholarship, his father even went further to solicit additional funds to help his son have enough funds for his accommodation and daily expenses. Pa Adelaja sold his farmland, which he usually leased out to make ends meet, and borrowed funds from a local loan shark, using his only house as collateral. Phew! The prices parents pay to ensure their children's happiness is guaranteed! Pa

Adelaja gave Samuel the proceeds from the land sale and the loan funds to enable him to commence his travel plans.

Samuel, having been told that flight tickets are sold only in Lagos, embarked on a journey to Lagos to purchase a flight ticket. He had been told where to go and what to do, and he did as he was told. He purchased a flight ticket to London and returned home to Oyo to prepare for the final journey. His father was delighted, his family celebrated, and even the village head chief gave him his blessing. Their son would become a foreign-trained medical doctor in a few years. Things were going well for Samuel, but then Nigerians happened to Samuel. I said Nigerians, not Nigeria; that was not a grammatical error. You read that right.

In August 1985, Samuel got set to depart for London for a life abroad. His flight ticket was tendered for check-in procedure at the Murtala Muhammed International Airport to the appropriate officials, and that was where his troubles began. Samuel was told that what he thought was a flight ticket was a counterfeit piece of valueless documents. Almost arrested, Samuel was relieved to have been released after narrating his ordeal, one that airport authorities were already familiar with. Samuel was cautioned and told by authorities to only purchase tickets from official sources in designated offices.

Samuel missed his scheduled flight and started to seek immediate recourse. He was desperate not to let down his father, his family or the entire people of Atiba. Unprepared but undeterred, Samuel sought assistance. He thought he had met his helper; a middle-aged man dressed in an official airline uniform who noticed Samuel's "JJC" demeanours and approached to help him. The helper informed him that even if he had been allowed to board the flight, he would have been turned back on getting to the UK because his currency notes were in naira and not British pounds. Samuel's helper offered to help and asked for his passport to enable him to procure a valid flight ticket and to change the notes from naira to pounds sterling. To Samuel, his helper would soon arrive with the flight ticket and exchange currency notes. He was later to find out that he had been conned. His passport containing his 5-year student visa and his money had all been taken away from him.

A 20-year-old inexperienced boy from a village in Oyo, how could he have known that anyone would want to dupe him, especially in an environment like that of an airport? How was Samuel to know that the "helper" was just one of the hundreds of fraudsters who roamed airports seeking victims? Airport authorities found Samuel dead in one of the public bathrooms that night. He had committed suicide because of the possible shame that would likely follow his failure to proceed with his education abroad.

Sad stories like that of Samuel are numerous, more often happening than being told. Bogus passports, false visas, forged flight tickets, counterfeit travel documents, and fake currency notes have been reasons Nigerian citizens had their dreams squashed right before their eyes. The story of Samuel is indeed a sadder affair. Unlike some who intentionally used fraudulent documents, he had everything legally going well. Some citizens never know that they have been duped until they have disembarked from their foreign-bound flights, only to be turned away by foreign immigration officials.

Using globally standardised biometric international passports prevented fraudulent acts like that of *yoju*, but it did not deter travel fraudsters. Rather, they began to use fictitious documents like false bank statements, affidavits and forged certificates to help secure travel visas for intending travellers. Such illegal activities were a win for them, but a collective loss for us as foreign embassies kept scoring the country low on trust, morality and legality. According to a 2006 report, The Home Office (UK) fingered Nigerians as the nationality most frequently detected at UK ports of entry with fraudulent travel documents.[11]

Embassies became more restrictive and imposed stringent conditions for intending visa applicants. In fact, embassies and consulates began to take more cautious, rigorous, and even extensive time checking travel documents that applicants submitted for potential frauds and malpractices. At that point, it was obvious that Nigeria was in trouble, desperately bleeding moral consciousness, but nobody cared. Nigerian travellers with tons of fraudulent documents that are mostly hard to detect besiege foreign embassies, offices and airports. According to the UK Visa office, between September 2005 and January 2006 (a 4-month period), 500 false passports were among tens of thousands submitted for visa applications.[12] Even children's passports were not left out of the scheme. Stolen children's passports were altered and used to help facilitate the travel of children of cronies who then accompany adults overseas.

It has become common for foreign authorities, especially the US and UK, to issue moratoriums, at will, on prospective Nigerian travellers. Contrary to a popular perception that foreign embassies were cheating Nigerian applicants by charging exorbitant amounts of non-refundable money, it is Nigerians who should be held responsible for aggravating scenarios that should never have been problematic in the first place. Recalcitrant fraudsters continue to impede whatever strategy foreign embassy officials put in place. Recently, British and US officials asked people to book their visa appointment/interview dates through telephones, couriers, websites and other means. As usual, the "ever resourceful Nigerian fraudsters hijacked the phone lines and charged applicants huge sums of money to arrange visa interviews."[13]

Today, seeking to outdo one another and outsmart fellow citizens, visa facilitators, travel agents, ticketing officers, immigration officials, bankers, public officials and every other individual have joined hands to soil the country's reputation in the chaotic water of infamy and ridiculousness. They have shattered the dreams of innocent Nigerians hoping to travel abroad for various legitimate reasons. Conversely, fake visa agents and their collaborators have been responsible for why some of the most morally bankrupt persons in the country have found their way abroad, thereby presenting moral discolouration on our nation's reputation. Fraudsters, cultists, violent gang members and sex traffickers have found their way abroad and are erroneously perceived as a representation of the Nigerian people. In all of these, we continue to wonder why our country has become a symbol of regress and failure; the same regress and failure that we have sworn to ensure must come to pass.

The Open World of 419 and its Many Siblings

I must again emphasise that, although the various types of financial crimes documented in this book have gained a foothold in geographical Nigeria, they are not unique to us as a country or as a people. While it may be true that Nigerians reshaped the practice and architecture of financial frauds, the most common financial crimes did not originate from the country or its citizens, as history recalls. Even the frauds that have become commonly associated with the Nigerian people today (especially advance-fee frauds) were not invented by Nigerians but only commandeered and orchestrated by us more widely than the actual inventors did.

Some forms of financial-related crime (a term that I use synonymously and interchangeably as financial crime, fraud, scam, and financial fraud) have been part of societal Nigeria, even before independence. In Nigeria, educated citizens who travelled out of the country's shores were the first to perpetrate some financial crimes. Available documents show that prior to independence, foreign authorities were already looking into strange activities by some Nigerians who hid under various pseudo-titles such as King, Prince, Chief, Heir, or Reverend Father to defraud unsuspecting foreigners through unsolicited bulk postal mails or spam advertorials. For instance, between 1940 and 1960, foreign newspapers innocently received ads and publications from several Nigerian "princes" who were portraying themselves as the rightful heir to the Nigerian throne or any other territory they alleged to be rightly theirs. One of such persons convicted for fraud was Dr Nwafor Orizu, who went on to become the country's first senate president after his seven-year sentence for his engagement in scholarship fraud.

Similarly, Nigerian newspapers were filled with advertorials of different natures that went unchallenged for decades. Fraudulent educational scholarships, money doubling, black money scams, magical item sales, employment opportunities, grants and loans, marriage enticements and other fascinating offers filtered newspaper advertorial pages, most of which had the intent to con victims.

Other Nigerian fraudsters took a clue from global swindlers by offering inexistent fashionable and luxurious items (ivories, diamonds, oil supplies, artefacts, gold, and antiques) for sale to unsuspecting buyers. Charity fraudsters also took the stage by sending postal mails to unsuspecting people abroad who innocently, and out of the abundance of their charitable minds, were obliged to send funds for help. As a clear reminder, these activities preceded the country's independence.

Modern-day frauds have become sophisticated that it has become impossible to capture them all under a single list. Nonetheless, it is possible to focus on some aspects of financial crimes based on their prevalence or impact on victims. Major fraudulent activities and financial crimes such as Obtaining by Trick (OBT), racketeering, identity theft, advance-fee scam, Ponzi scheme, pyramid scheme, currency fraud and manipulation, counterfeiting, internet fraud, and money laundering continue to metamorphose over time. The list of financial-related crimes is long, and their mode of practice differs based on varying circumstances and factors. Acts of fraud have become so scattered, unpredictable, and different from other aspects of criminalities. Analysing fraudulent activities tends to be tedious considering the mysterious way the activities are carried out.

One common form of financial crime is the "black money" scam. The scam involved the swindling of carefully targeted people who are often shown a box purported to contain large sums of money (usually foreign currencies) that need cleaning. So audacious and systematic was this kind of crime that carefully selected notes were picked and handed out to the potential victim for use. In this case, the victim is told that all that is left for the millions in the box to be cleaned is the purchase of certain chemicals. This particular pattern, perhaps with slight amendments, is done to victims abroad. Brazenly, some fraudsters walk into banks, lodge in five-star hotels, dine in top-class restaurants, and roam freely around airports and other commercial areas looking for potential victims. The number of those who fell for their sham is unbelievably staggering.

Most recently, the most common aspect of financial crime is perpetrated using the internet, commonly known in local parlance as *"yahoo yahoo"*. The etymology of the *yahoo yahoo* parlance could be traced to the late veteran Nollywood comedian, Babatunde "Baba Suwe" Omidina.[14] His popularisation of the term came about due to the prevalence of internet crimes that were facilitated through the most commonly used email domain (Yahoo) back then. Other local parlances such as *client, update, maga, mayee, cash out* and *bomb* have become popular within the circles of Nigerian fraud syndicates. Financial crimes are perpetrated with so much impunity that they carry a street slogan that tells them "it is legal to be illegal in an illegal society".

Nigeria itself is home to various violent and deadly criminal activities. Hence, internet fraud has come to be regarded as understandably permissible and erroneously seen as a victimless crime. Indeed, the Nigerian populace has come to acknowledge financial crime as a necessary evil that should be tolerated in a nation with a disturbingly high unemployment rate. Today's internet fraudsters mostly come from poor but educated backgrounds. And with access to the internet and a social structure that acts as a fertile ground for free participation, it is no wonder that a many young individuals are involved in such aspects of fraud.

Indeed, financial crime in Nigeria has a long and illustrious history. Internet crime is a successor to prior forms of fraudulent activities that disrupted Europe and the rest of the world in the 1980s and the 1990s. Immediately after the Second Republic kicked into life, corruption, fraud and other similar crimes followed the attendant economic problems that tormented the country. In the early 80s, Nigeria descended into socio-economic chaos like never before, and all sorts of criminal acts rapidly became commonplace. The eventual loss of jobs and mass retrenchments of civil servants also had calamitous effects and became the catalysts for the spread of white-collar crimes. The former officials, now unemployed but armed with the practices and loopholes of operational activities in the public and private sectors, took full advantage of the loopholes to perpetrate financial frauds systematically. Activities such as money laundering and fund diversions initially confined to top public officials started to spread throughout societal Nigeria.

Nigerians returning from overseas were disappointed to meet a country worse than they had left. They met a country with a high unemployment rate, indiscipline, corruption and an unfriendly business climate. Like the private citizens who lost their jobs during the various economic recessions, they armed themselves with information on socio-economic and financial practices from the foreign countries they had returned from and started to take advantage of the Nigerian system to carry out significant financial crimes. At first, financial crimes and other related activities surreptitiously gained notoriety among educated unemployed people. Their activities were carried out by taking advantage of a trust system, a hallmark of civilisation. Later, in the 1980s and 1990s, the country descended into moral chaos. Sadly, financial crimes were allowed to flourish by respective political administrations, perhaps to cushion the effects of the economic crises on the citizens or to save face from the public shame that stemmed from their political inefficiency and maladministration.

The practice of *yoju* took a swerve into banking fraud where people's bank withdrawal booklets, which carried their pictures, were manipulated. After replacing passport photographs of original account owners with theirs and also armed with necessary details, cheque forgers confidently walked into banks to withdraw large sums of the victim's deposits. The digitalisation and enhancement of security features on travel documents and other financial documents did not deter fraudsters. Rather it opened more doors for them. As companies and financial institutions began to upgrade their products and services with enhanced security features, fraudsters proved equal to the task by upgrading the modus operandi of their tricks.

By the mid-1990s, Nigerian citizens' activities had gained notoriety, and they became synonymous with fraudulent activities and financial crimes. Foreign countries suspiciously watched Nigerian travellers, who once had unfettered access to several countries of their choice. Our international passport was green in colour, but in reality, it bled red; a sign of risk and danger. Citizens and businesses began to suffer from the accompanying effects of fraud and criminal behaviours. Yet, the country's military leaders and public officials decided to leave the country on autopilot. That was when the citizens decided to steer the country's flight in the direction of perpetual frauds and criminalities of all kinds with audacious impunity.

By the end of the 1990s, the game of financial fraud had kicked off in full gear, thanks to the introduction of internet cafes in Nigerian towns and cities. Financial crimes such as mail-wire frauds, which started in the '80s through posts and fax machines, were fortified by the introduction of phones and the internet. With the introduction of the internet, financial fraud became more systematic, cost-effective and covert. The introduction of internet cafes saw engagement in internet fraud as a legitimised occupation and one that carried an attached hilarity to it. In some areas of Lagos, especially Surulere, Ikeja, Ilupeju and Lagos Island, fraudsters took up office hours in internet cafes with booked times similar to those of office hours. They dressed in corporate attire and carried demeanours and outlooks of formalities similar to any other white-collar employee. Others booked night browsing spaces in cyber cafes to enable them to meet up with the time disparity with targeted victims around the globe. Public officials were also on the ground to use state resources to help fraud syndicates, to dupe victims to the tune of unbelievable amounts. In some cases, the word "unsuspecting" did not necessarily apply as a prefix to the word "victim". That is because when eventual victims suspected a game was up, near-perfect features were applied to manipulate victims into dismissing any thought of being conned.

Interestingly or not, Nigerians gained a notorious reputation for themselves, not just by news reporting alone but with actual stories containing real-life victims. For instance, a former US ambassador and a former US House of Representatives member, Edward Mezvinsky, was taught by Nigerians the nature and consequential effect of greed and criminality. He was swindled out of massive sums of money and later became a fraudster himself, for which he was convicted.

After the turn of the new millennium, several factors had come in to crown the city of Lagos as the de facto headquarter of financial crimes and fraud-related activities in Africa and, arguably, the entire world. As early as 2003, fraudsters had well-established networks in Oluwole and Isale-Eko, both on Lagos Island. They also operated in converged networks in the Shitta and Ogunlana Drive areas of Surulere, Empire in Yaba, Association Avenue in Ilupeju, Allen in Ikeja, the inner areas of Apapa, Oyingbo, Ijora, Ebute-Metta and Shomolu areas of Lagos. Any document (even one sought with a nearly 100% feature of the original) that could not be found in those areas is a document that does not exist anywhere in the world. To tag Nigeria of the early 2000s as the most fraudulent country in the world is not one touching on a lack of patriotism but a factual reality. Although the period after 2005 could be one that witnessed the rise of financial fraud in Nigeria, significant incidents before then had catapulted the country into infamy.

- Regarded in January 2004 as one of the largest "419" busts, Dutch police arrested 52 people, mostly believed to be Nigerians, suspected in connection with various levels of financial fraud. A task force of 80 officers raided 23 apartments, seizing computers, fake passports and 50,000 euros in cash. The arrests came several months after the conviction of some Nigerian citizens on a similar offence. Interestingly, a Swiss academic professor whose estimated loss amounted in the region of $482,000, helped authorities track down the criminals.[15]

- In 2004, a survey of 220 packages sent from Nigeria to the UK unearthed forged cheques totalling £46.1 million in British and foreign currency. Following up on this incident, £20 million in forged cheques and postal orders in courier mail from Lagos was discovered later in 2005. It was estimated that advance-fee fraud was costing the British economy an annual loss of £150 million during this period.[16]

- According to the Guardian UK, 310 people, many reportedly Nigerian nationals, were arrested in connection to fraudulent activities bordering on advance-fee and lotto fraud schemes that were thought to have cost victims in the region of £70 million. The arrests brought to more than 700 the number detained in operations against so-called "Nigerian frauds" in Spain since 2003.[17]

- In September 2005, Nigerian authorities clamped down on the notorious Oluwole area of Lagos, where more than 100 individuals were arrested. Items discovered included foreign cheques, local and foreign passports, foreign visa templates, money orders, certificates of occupancy, and educational certificates. Airlines tickets, copies of insurance papers, bank statements, classified government documents, local and foreign driver's licences, debit/credit cards and other financial instruments were also found. The items were discovered, in their tens of thousands, all forged and entirely fraudulent. Sophisticated printing machines and hardware were also recovered during the raid.

As severally noted, three conjoining factors worked simultaneously to make Nigeria the arguable global headquarter of financial crimes; a population of extremely brilliant minds, the prevalence of anarchy, and persistent socio-economic crises. Nigerian fraudsters who had chosen European cities such as Amsterdam, Madrid, London and Dublin as their favourite operation centres soon found out that their days were numbered as authorities cracked down on their activities across Europe.[18] By 2005, thousands of Nigerians in Europe had been arrested by various authorities. Some were jailed, while others were deported back to the country.[19] The deported Nigerians quickly linked up with their counterparts at home to form a formidable force that involved sharing trendy fraudulent ideas and tools to perpetrate more activities in the most profitable ways. Coincidentally, luck and other events bordering on socio-economic activities in the country made things even easier.

After the country emerged from military dictatorship in 1999, the new administration of Chief Olusegun Obasanjo was determined to rid the country of corrupt and fraudulent practices. After paddling through the muddled waters and dirty politics that often asphyxiate newly constituted republican governments, the former military head of state geared up and began to act true to his words. In 2003, the Economic and Financial Crimes Commission (EFCC) was created to look into the activities of financial crimes and other related activities. Immediately, the EFCC sprang into action and began to effectuate the arrest of citizens and leading personalities of financial crimes in the country. Ordinarily, the activities of the EFCC against fraudsters were meant to deter intending recruits. Well, if only authorities knew how unmanageable and determined Nigerian citizens had become in matters relating to financial crimes.

The creation of the EFCC coincided with the period the Global System for Mobile communications (GSM) was introduced to Nigeria. Telecommunication companies sold products and services to readily available buyers, and cyber cafes spread more into urban and suburban areas. Simultaneously, as the EFCC was rounding up certain individuals for their alleged roles in retroactive and recently committed crimes, Nigerians began to equip themselves with their new-found means of communication. As the EFCC busied itself with the announcements of the arrests of major fraudsters and how they perpetrated their acts, individuals who were initially oblivious to such acts but now armed with such information, along with newly improved and sophisticated tools, went fully into action. Soon, stories and exploits of certain notorious fraudsters became sources of near-folklores and inspiration to an inquisitive and eager generation rather than bases of deterrence as erroneously thought by anti-corruption agencies.

Throughout the first decade of the new millennium, the exploits of fraudsters gained admiration by mentees and public sycophants to such an extent that some notoirous fraudsters enjoyed pop culture reverence. Names such as Dr "Prince" Abyssinia Nwafor Orizu, Ademiluyi Adedeji "Ade Bendel" Alumile, Fred Ajudua, Dele Ilori, Emmanuel "Frank" Nwude, Emmanuel Ofolue, Nzeribe Okoli, A.A. Adele, Maurice Ibekwe, Victor "Ezego" Okafor, Christian Anajemba, Amaka Martina Anajemba, Hilary Okey Amadi, "Prince" Modupe David, "Prince" Peter Eket Inyang Udo and Obum Osakwe became notable examples of those who cemented their place in the hall of infamy of Nigeria's history of financial fraud and other related crimes. Interestingly, the acts perpetrated by some of the names mentioned were retroactive but only gained prominence after arrests were made. Also, from my investigations, many of them became mentors and guide-gurus of subsequent internet fraudsters who later became communal and perhaps national celebrities in their own right, at least by "street" weight of credibility.

Curiously, as reports began to spread, many educated people could not believe the monetary figures earned, nor could they believe the ease of operation in perpetuating the fraudulent acts. For instance, they could not comprehend how anyone could be so gullible as to believe that an individual owned a country's Central Bank and therefore possessed the right to put it up for sale. They wondered what kind of intellect anyone could possess to believe the country's National Stadium or National Arts Theatre could be sold through unorthodox processes like the ones used by internet fraudsters. Why would anyone believe that the late General Sani Abacha's $1 billion is stacked somewhere, with half of the funds to be shared once a particular sum has been paid to facilitate the release of the stacked funds? Again, why would anyone assume a country's head of state or central bank governor would need the help of a stranger through email to access and repatriate millions of dollars for any purpose or under any guise whatsoever? When the hopefuls got answers that people actually believed the stories and that, for decades, such stories and patterns of fraud had made actors stupendously rich, they calmly got to work; hence, the Internet fraud syndrome became fully birthed in widespread proportion.

The rapid movement in technological evolution also boosted the inelegant e-fraud industry. The introduction of upgraded technological tools and devices such as laptops, smartphones, the internet and other devices into the Nigerian market intensified the ease of perpetration and the ability of fraudsters to carry out their activities individually, independently and from the comfort of their various domains. The larger society also began to feel the impact of internet fraud. Students besieged tertiary education campuses and their environs with flashy cars that even their lecturers could only envy. The social life industry encompassing nightclubs, restaurants, bars and lounges flourished and became the "home away from home" for the fraudsters. The entertainment, hotel, real estate and auto industries witnessed a major boom as younger Nigerians rapidly became their chief patrons. People gaped as younger girls scrambled their way into the lives of young men who have now made so much money than their parents ever did throughout their entire time on earth. But as these fraudsters made temporal gains, a set of ruinous consequences began to follow.

Firstly, the reputation of the nouns "Nigeria", "Nigerians", and "Naija" suffered a devastating setback. We found ourselves on the watchlist of foreign individuals, organisations, companies and authorities. Nigerian individuals and businesses became subjected to hostile profiling and were also prevented from accessing numerous websites of important financial and material value. Similarly, the scourge of fraudulent activities discouraged foreign investors and businesses, many of whom looked at the potential of investing in our country, especially after the return to civil rule. A simple search on Google of the name "Nigeria" returned negative results relating to fraud, lawlessness and criminality.

Today, Nigerian fraudsters are notoriously known worldwide. They have created de facto networks and HQs in areas of and within Atlanta, Dubai, Nairobi, Cairo, Cape Town, London, Houston, Chicago, Johannesburg, Dublin, Accra, Istanbul and Amsterdam. Regardless, the reader and I miraculously expect foreign investors to trust their hard-earned money in the financing, investment and employment opportunities in a country with such a low reputation. As a reminder, financial crime does not necessarily have to be done through the internet. However, the internet has become the fastest and most convenient way to perpetrate the former. Other types of fraud are carried out within Nigeria and outside its shores that do not necessarily involve internet use but equally cause havoc on victims. Here are some of the most infamous fraudulent activities carried out by Nigerian crime syndicates:

- Black Money Scam
- Advance-Fee Fraud aka '419'
- Romance and Dating Scam
- Credit Card Fraud
- Sales and Shopping Scam

- Home Rental and Apartments Scam
- Auto Purchase Fraud
- Employment Fraud
- Wire Transfer Fraud
- Money Order and Check Cashing Fraud
- Currency Counterfeiting
- Identity Theft
- Phishing and Business Email Compromise (BEC)
- Lottery Fee Scam
- Crowdfunding and Charity aid Fraud
- Disaster and Accident Claim fraud
- Shipping Hijacking and Courier Fraud
- Tax Refund and Unemployment Benefit Fraud
- Money Transfer Fraud
- Ransomware
- Pyramid and Ponzi scheme
- ATM/Debit Card Fraud

The above list does not encompass the entirety of frauds being perpetrated, while others are popularly known through various parlances or phraseology. The deadly scourge of internet fraud stung even the normally traditional and deeply conservative areas of most southern parts of the country. Parents broke-shame and force their children into joining the scourge. Wives and girlfriends threatened dissociation from their partners if they failed to level up with their fraudulent peers. Young teenagers abandoned their parents' homes and returned with luxurious cars and other extravagant items. Nobody bothered to ask where they got their money. Rather, everyone supported, celebrated and applauded them. The more successful ones followed the footsteps of previous generations of fraudsters by donning chieftaincy titles and gunning for societal awards and honours.

As I opined earlier, Nigeria's reputation as the one of the world's most fraudulent countries is not by accident and not one without evidence either. In the past few years alone, some Nigerians have been involved in high-profile fraud stories that shook the international community and further enabled them to stiffen their already unfavourable relationships with us. Some high-profile cases became even more disgraceful and tasteless because they proved what Nigerians had known all along; the link between state actors and financial fraud of various proportions.

The reader must be reminded that financial crimes and political corruption are conjoined twins. It must also be noted that the theft of national resources and state funds is the most obvious and notorious example of financial crimes perpetrated against Nigerian citizens. Political corruption is closely linked to the ability to steal state resources with impunity and without consequences; hence, many Nigerian politicians who have stolen state resources will not feature in this book for legal reasons. However, one relevant case I feel inclined to mention was the arrest and successful prosecution of former Delta State Governor James Ibori.

In May 2010, the International Police (INTERPOL) arrested the former Delta State governor in Dubai, UAE. He was subsequently deported to the UK to face money laundering charges that were levelled against him. A speedy trial commenced, and James Ibori pleaded guilty to the counts of money laundering and fraud-related charges at a London court. Prosecutors detailed how the former governor of the oil-rich but impoverished Delta State laundered an estimated $77 million of state funds.[20] Authorities in Nigeria put the actual figure at around $250 million.[21] He was subsequently sentenced in April 2012 to serve a 13-year jail term. Ironically, the successful prosecution of James Ibori in the UK was not a necessary victory for the UK as much as for the Nigerian people. Ibori's conviction was a remarkable victory for Nigerians who had been used to seeing people like him escape the long arm of the law despite their open theft of state resources. At the time James Ibori was getting convicted in Britain, many of his colleagues back home in Nigeria were escaping punishments and had given the notion to an awaiting generation of fraudsters that financial crimes have no consequences. Of course, their message was well received.

In August 2019, businessman Obinwanne "Invictus Obi" Okeke was arrested by FBI agents in Washington, US, on conspiracy charges to commit wire fraud while trying to depart the country for Nigeria. As news filtered back home, people familiar with the "hardworking and clever young man" swore that it was a case of mistaken identity and that the FBI got the wrong person. Just a few years before his arrest, Invictus Obi was a person who had been on the front page of Forbes Africa magazine. Invictus had been acknowledged by the BBC for his inspiring role as a young entrepreneur and had also won several other entrepreneurship awards before clocking the age of 30.[22] Regardless, the FBI was not going to have any of that. They put incriminating evidence right to Invictus's face to let him know that his game was up. In less than a year, Invictus Obi pleaded guilty to a computer-based intrusion fraud scheme that cost victims $11 million in losses, according to prosecutors. He was subsequently sentenced to 10 years in prison.[23] With the rapid manner the conviction of Invictus Obi was secured, he learnt quickly that the United States authorities are not as lacklustre as the ones in his home country. Fraudsters like Invictus Obi in Nigeria continue to fool the Nigerian public by using fictitious businesses and organisations that serve no economic purpose to the country. They peg back the country's growth and development by their continued soiling of the country's name in the international arena. Invictus Obi's arrest was not enough to deter his counterparts from the illicit acts of financial fraud. In fact, some thought they had grown enough wings to fly above the radar of authorities and were above the law; but they guessed wrong.

In a digital world where social media easily portrays the activities of persons through their accounts and self-told stories, some internet fraudsters also introduced themselves and their "hard-earned" wealth to the entire world. With social media, people's penchant for flamboyance grew proportionately in the aspect of competition and unbridled rivalry, as if show-off were a sporting event with a price. Nonetheless, flamboyance on social media has its trophy; it is called social currency. In modern day tradition, social currency is the value of an individual's worth by estimating their financial wealth through their activity, followers and overall influence/presence on social media. Subsequently, the champions of such unorthodox sporting competitions began to emerge, thanks to their decision to participate in a competition that displays their daily activities to the applause of an enticed youthful generation of money worshippers. Like those before them, the fraudulent politicians and financial fraudsters of societal Nigeria, the new social media champions equally began to inspire generations in a fashion that borders on the paradox of criminal heroism. The list of such social media champions who fit into this narrative is long, but I will go with the crop of the top as a singular illustration.

On June 25, 2020, I was with a team of private investigators in Kirkuk, Iraq, when a senior colleague drew my attention to a breaking news story aired on an Arabian TV Channel. It was the arrest of a popular Instagram user (or influencer as he chose to be called) Raymond Abbas, aka "Hushpuppi", by the Dubai Police in collaboration with the FBI. I was unsurprised by his arrest. After all, I did not wander the Lagos streets of Ilupeju, Yaba, Ogudu, Surulere, Shomolu, and Ikorodu, all for nothing. If anything, I grew street smart to identify a fraudster when I see one, no matter the mask they wear. Hushpuppi was arrested alongside Olalekan Jacob Ponle, aka "Woodberry", and ten others in a well-organised sting operation. Dubai authorities later detailed how the group had been on the radar of law enforcement for several months before their arrest. At the time of their arrest, Dubai authorities claimed that a purported plan to steal more than $435 million was underway. An estimated $41 million in cash and 1. luxury cars with an estimated value of $7 million were seized from the arrested suspects.[24] Dubai authorities wasted no time proving they were in a hurry to dispense swift justice. On July 2, 2020, a global audience of enthusiastic observers learned that Hushpuppi and his accomplices had been handed over to the FBI and had landed on US soil for prosecution. If Hushpuppi and his fellow collaborators had thought they were in Nigeria, where they could get off the hook due to the attendant problems of prosecuting criminal cases in the country, they guessed wrong. United States authorities proved they meant business, and in less than a year, court documents released by US officials showed that Hushpuppi had pleaded guilty to money laundering charges.[25]

Nigerians' reaction to the Hushpuppi story underscores my earlier assertion that a very unacceptable portion of the population has erroneously welcomed financial fraud. A dangerous attribute closely associated with financial fraudsters is that they are no respecter of persons and will perpetuate their acts on those close to them when the opportunity arises. They are like the proverbial dogs that eat their fellow dogs when they begin to starve. Thus, it began to happen.

The Rise of "Local" and Investment Scams

Financial fraudsters noted the sweeping changes that had swept through the banking and financial sectors. They wasted no time taking advantage of the leakages to defraud fellow citizens. Called *"local"* in street parlance, they target people using new technological tools such as bulk SMS, phishing, and social media applications to lure unsuspecting victims into one fraud or the other. They perpetuate fraudulent acts, especially those relating to pyramid and Ponzi schemes, ATM/debit card fraud, and bank account compromise. Their targets are mostly uneducated, elderly, uninformed, vulnerable and sometimes greedy persons whose bank accounts get wiped out after their encounters with the fraudsters. Most of their activities concerning financial fraud through the banking sector are documented earlier. However, one aspect that must not go without mentioning is the nature of greed that combines with the ridiculous gullibility of victims.

Patriotism aside, Nigerians, by nature, are a very arrogant group of people who mistakenly pride themselves in the excellence of unsubstantiated remarkable stories. They see themselves as who they are not and allude to possessing things based on figments of their imaginations rather than by fact or reality. We tell ourselves how stupendously rich our country is based on the natural resources we have as against what is available to us for use. Nigerians will tell you how their football team is the best in the world and curse their luck or rain curses on match officials at tournaments despite a lack of preparations for the same tournament they so fantasise to win. We incorrectly brag about how we are the smartest group of people in the world and how no one could successfully con us due to our purported level of street smartness. This apocryphal anomaly is worthy of discourse and I feel entirely obliged to address it as a matter of relevance.

I believe that Nigerians have been swindled socially, politically and economically all through their existence. I also believe that we have been victims of various frauds individually. Nigerians who claim to be the smartest group on earth need to ask themselves what smart person would receive N500 during every electoral period only to be denied his entitlement, which in mathematical terms could be valued at millions later on. This chapter is dedicated to financial frauds only. It is not the place or time (and I doubt whether any page on this book could have afforded me that space) to tell Nigerians how they have been victims of fraud since our emergence to self-rule.

Now, back to the relevant topic, facts and figures suggest that Nigerians are one of the world's largest victims of Ponzi and pyramid schemes. The numbers of Ponzi and pyramid schemes in the country are endless, and the casualty figures are staggering.

To be clear, the perpetration of Ponzi and pyramid schemes in Nigeria precedes some other types of financial fraud, especially those perpetrated through the internet. Popularly known as *'sogundogoji'* (money doublers) in Yoruba parlance, fraudsters roamed the streets of communities and neighbourhoods of a group of profiled people and exploited their weaknesses, especially greed. *Sogundogoji* is a system of pawnship and moneylending operations that has existed for more than a century in mostly Yoruba societies. Ruthless and callous moneylenders involved in *sogundogoji* charged huge interest rates on money loaned to people in desperate need. They would loan out £20 to earn a minimum of 100% interest, expecting £40 in return, hence the etymology of the name *sogundogoji*.

Nonetheless, the inverted characteristics of the moneylending practice were what fraudulent characters used to lure victims. It metamorphosed from a moneylending practice to a "bring money to earn double" practice. In that sense, the literal translation of the *sogundogoji* still sufficiently applied.

Victims were meant to believe they could earn multiple returns of whatever money they devote in the care of the fraudsters. Of course, it never ends well for the gullible and greedy victims. Some victims went as far as clearing out their savings. Others took out loans, while others sold off their properties only to discover that they had been duped. The adventures of the notorious fraudsters did not end with the *sogundogoji* practice. They have camouflaged under several nomenclatures, from wonder banks, investment schemes, finance management, power networks and empowerment programs. By estimate, millions of Nigerians have fallen victim to the menace of this avoidable type of fraud over the last decade alone.

The convicted Russian fraudster Sergei Mavrodi's MMM company that crashed sometime between 2016 and 2017, is arguably the most popular Ponzi scheme to be introduced in the country. The MMM saga caused untold havoc to an estimated 3 million victims and a loss in the region of N18 billion, according to the NDIC.[26] The heavy losses incurred by victims of prior investment scams and the spread nature of the news stories were not strong enough to deter Nigerians from falling prey to similar practices.

Various regulatory and authoritative bodies say they are handicapped in their attempts to flush Ponzi scammers out of business due to the mind-blogging ROIs promised to potential investors. This form of financial fraud purportedly disguised under various investment schemes has been endorsed and promoted by some of the country's most famous personalities. The list of endorsers and promoters of Ponzi schemes are showbiz personalities, socialites, clergies, comedians, business analysts, actors, musicians, celebrities and a wide network of social media influencers. Traditional businesses in the areas of real estate, financial banking, agriculture, and autos, among others, have been heavily used to lure victims into the heinous act of fraud. The new-age business models such as cryptocurrency, online betting, digital marketing and e-consultancy have also been targeted and marketed to unsuspecting victims. They advertise in some of the country's major media outlets, from TV to radio, newspapers, and online. As a result, an estimated N300 billion financial losses have been recorded in the last five years alone, with accompanying cases of reported suicides.[27]

In March 2021, a Twitter user Kalu Aja, with the username *FinPlanKaluAja1,* conducted a poll on the social media platform to inquire from fellow users about their experience(s) as regards investment scams in the country. Responses and details from the poll revealed how swindlers had taken advantage of the lax attitude of authorities in conjunction with the "get rich quick" syndrome of the citizens to perpetuate huge financial havoc. To understand the destructive nature of this particular form of fraud, I feel inclined to list a few from possibly a large pool of those that have caused consequential losses to victims. A compilation of some of them is in the table below:

Pyramid/Ponzi Scheme	Estimated Total Loss

	by Victims
MMM	N18 billion
Imagine Global Solution Limited	N22 billion
Yuan Dong Ponzi	N900 million
Galaxy Transport Ponzi	N7 billion
Famzhi Interbiz Limited	N2 billion
Cowlane	N100 million
Dureil	N100 million
Nospetco Oil & Gas Ltd	N22 billion
Benignant Forte Nigeria Limited	N10 billion
Denkol Farms	N900 million
Twinkas	N1 billion
MBA Forex	N213 billion
Brisk Capital Limited	N2 billion
Tonso Elite Enterprise	N10 billion
Megawill Integrated Global Investment Company	N890 million
Swiss Golden	N3 billion
Wales Kingdom Capital	N14 billion
Quintessential Investment Company	N11 billion
Micheno Multipurpose Cooperative Society	N27 billion
Racksterly	N3 billion
Chinmark Group	N22 billion
Eatrich Farms and Food Limited	N20 billion
Bluekey Investment Club	N2 billion
Menorah Farms	N1 billion

A few weeks before the crash of MMM, the country's apex bank, the CBN had put out a notice that reminded Nigerians of the impending dangers of doing business in such doom-to-fail schemes. The ever-recalcitrant citizens on social media responded with vile messages of attacks and abuses on the apex bank and swore that the MMM was legitimate. My innocent attempt to explain that the CBN was indeed right was met with vicious attacks by a large pool of resolute social media audience, who at the time thought nastiness and greed were enjoyable pathways to the citadel of overnight riches.

As a consultant once told me, promoters of fraudulent schemes will continue to defraud them successfully as long as Nigerians continue to be motivated by an inordinate ambition to get rich quickly in a disproportionate fashion. To put the blame squarely on the government is taking responsibilities away from adult citizens who ought to be able to differentiate right from wrong.

Of course, the millions of Nigerians who fell victims, and continue to fall victims, to pyramid and Ponzi schemes portray the cancerous problems that had swallowed any hope of growth and development the country ever had; the problem of combined greed and fraud.

Contrary to popular perception, fighting financial fraud and other forms of criminality in Nigeria is exhausting. As you will read, we are a devastatingly hypocritical people who continue to think we can mollycoddle criminal behaviours and then expect authorities to use limited state resources to fight the same crimes we help to manufacture, nurture, endorse and spread. The entirety of the criminal and immoral behaviours you have read in this book continue to happen in Nigeria, not just because authorities are lacklustre in fighting them (even as that is the true case), but because Nigerians themselves have created a fertile ground and welcoming environment for fraudulent and criminal behaviours of all kinds.

Financial Crimes: Society and Endorsement

In May 2016, President Muhammadu Buhari seemingly agreed with the opinion of then British Prime Minister David Cameron, who labelled Nigeria as a "fantastically corrupt" country.[28] Several Nigerians were infuriated by the response of their president to what they termed a derogatory remark from a foreign leader. It was an opportunity, as usual, for activists and opposition groups to test their popularity by jumping on the grubby bandwagon of an ongoing debacle.

Many opined that the country's president must be the chief image maker of the country and must project the country in good light to sell a positive image to the rest of the world. However, amidst the uproar, Nigerians inadvertently proved the president correct. It was not just because Cameron said so, not because Buhari agreed, but by asking our president to mislead a global population of people through the pretence that all is well back home.

There is a short anecdote about the Cameron-Buhari situation that I would like to note as a matter of relevance. It is the proverbial story of a critically sored man who visited a hospital for diagnosis and possible treatment. After a further inquiry by the doctor to ascertain the nature of his illness to proffer possible solutions, the ailing man responded alarmingly that all was well with him and that he was hale and hearty. A neutral observer could tell that the man is dying and in dire need of help, and the doctor could see that the man needs help. Nonetheless, they do not understand why a sickly man would leave his house for hospital treatment only to tell the doctor and everyone else that his health is fine and that all is well. That illustrates the character of Nigerians in a nutshell. We have failed to realise that today's global population is not as ignorant as we think concerning matters of fraud, corruption and crime in our geographical theatre. They have their facts handy.

Incidentally, David Cameron was British Prime Minister during the sentencing of James Ibori in London. Nigerians proved to be the naïve ones to have expected the British government to hand over billions of stolen funds that had found their way to Britain, back to a country that claims to be free of fraud and corruption.

Our response to issues like President Buhari's "gaffe" has shown that we have allowed an underground culture of mollycoddling fraud and corruption. We expected Cameron and the British people to acknowledge us as corruption-free people. Yet, a few years before Cameron's statement, he had witnessed, as prime minister, a then serving Nigerian governor, Diepreye Alamieyeseigha, jump bail in the UK and absconded to Nigeria in a manner that showcased his talent as an escapologist. Cameron also witnessed how then-president Goodluck Jonathan had little issue granting a state pardon to Diepreye Alamieyeseigha, who, just a few years before the pardon, had $401,931 in traceable assets seized and forfeited by the US Department of Justice.[29] Alamieyeseigha was a man who had embezzled as much as $55 million according to the New York Times and money laundering activities to the tune of $3.2 million according to British authorities.[30]

Jonathan's history as a corruption endorser also saw him give a posthumous award to a former dictator and tyrant, General Sani Abacha, a man whose stolen funds were still being repatriated back to the country. Jonathan's pardoning of Alamieyeseigha was even more expressive of his corruption status, considering Alamieyeseigha's conviction was one of the very few high-profile cases to be successfully prosecuted in the country. Incidentally, no high-profile case was successfully prosecuted during Jonathan's 6-year tenure as president. In an ironical twist, Jonathan decided that the nation's informal top whistleblower, the former governor of the CBN, Sanusi Lamido Sanusi, was the man who should be reprimanded. Jonathan wasted no time and sacked Sanusi from office in 2014, which plunged the country further into economic chaos.

As regards Abacha, corruption and gaffes, one gaffe that indicts Buhari himself, and an almost unforgivable one, was in 2008 when he noted that Abacha never stole from the public purse. However, that is a sharp contradiction and would surely mock his position as today's president, as his government has become the biggest beneficiary of Abacha's repatriated loots.

The idea of selling Nigeria as a corruption-free country is an absurd one. It defies logic, responsibility and reality. We claim not to be a corrupt group of people, yet it is inscrutable to dissect the massive reception and heroic welcome granted to James Ibori on his return to his home state of Delta in February 2017 after his release from a London prison.[31] The unprincipled hiring of rented crowds to celebrate or drum support for politicians facing corruption charges are not new, but the celebration of a returning convict who had stolen billions of naira meant to cater for his people was an entirely low one. It is relevant to ask how we got to the current state where financial crimes and other related fraudulent activities are condoned, overlooked or expressively applauded throughout our societies and communities.

To understand how much of a fertile ground Nigeria has been for fraudsters and corrupt persons, we need to look at the desperate attempts made by people like Invictus, Hushpuppi, Woodberry, Ibori and Alamieyeseigha to fight being tried abroad for criminal allegations levelled against them. They, alongside people like Abba Kyari, Joshua Dariye, and Buruji Kashamu (a former top police officer, a governor, and a senator, respectively), preferred to be tried in Nigeria because of associated prosecutorial failures right here on our soil. Joshua Dariye, a then serving governor of Plateau State, like Alamieyeseigha, absconded from London before the commencement of his trial.[32]

Their sudden apprehension of the criminal justice system of the societies that they so much cherished demonstrates the reality of criminal prosecutions in Nigeria as opposed to saner climes. Their sudden awakening to the reality that such societies do not create avenues for criminals to escape punishment no matter how long it takes is indeed telling. The trials and convictions of Ibori, Hushpuppi and Invictus were concluded within a year, and all took a similar pattern. All three pleaded guilty in the separate trials against them. Also, all three reportedly hired top-notch lawyers who woke them from their slumber to the reality of life in the Western world, which is bound to punish forms of criminality without respect to class or status. In the UK, James Ibori did not have the people of Oghara, Delta, to help him evade arrest and prosecution as they had done in 2010 when Nigerian authorities tried to effect his arrest.

Besides the country's archaic system of leakages that allowed acts of fraud and criminality to have taken place in the first instance, the involvement of the public in ensuring offenders escape prosecution is worrisome. Many citizens have chosen to be divided along the lines of bias, sentiment and prejudice regarding criminal trials. For instance, under President Buhari, it is very common to see southerners refer to corruption and criminal trials as one of ethnic persecution, even when a mammoth level of evidence indicts people of their ethnicity or association. Our failure to allow for successful prosecution is a driving catalyst for the procreation of more criminal activities in the country today. In Nigeria, some elites have become too powerful that they fail to honour police invitations for alleged wrongdoings. Police investigators and DPOs panic knowing they are to summon certain political, social or traditional rulers in the community within their jurisdiction.

A combination of corrupt and fraudulent prosecutors, lawyers, judges, bankers, auditors, accountants, witnesses and a large chunk of the general populace continues to be the inimical forces behind the fight against corruption and criminality in the country. To perfectly understand the dangerous game often played by these sets of Nigerians, permit me to explain a hypothetical situation that would have occurred had Hushpuppi been arrested in Nigeria instead of the UAE.

As regards Hushpuppi's criminal trial, it would have taken a minimum of 10 years to reach its conclusion, with a high possibility of case dismissal or acquittal. Relating his arrest and eventual deportation to Nigeria, his army of lawyers (likely to consist of a host of SANs) would have a field day in various courts to contest the legality of his deportation from the UAE to Nigeria. It will be recalled that Hushpuppi tried this approach after he landed on US soil but failed woefully and was subsequently told to prepare himself for an eventual trial. Various media platforms and news agencies would have entertained some 'eminent' Nigerians the right to offer their displeasure on how Hushpuppi's fundamental rights are being abused or how the government is on a witch-hunt. He would have gotten the support of notable pan-Yoruba cultural groups who would be quick to tell the world that his trial was premeditated and that he was being hounded because of his ethnicity, not because he was a shameless fraudster. Hushpuppi would have had his lawyers filing various frivolous injunctions and applications at numerous courts across the country. They often do that to frustrate a trial process and asphyxiate the prosecution team's limited resources and the country's justice department. Shadowy human rights groups would have demanded his immediate release. They would have cited constitutional sections of the law and let us know how his rights were violated. Ironically, Hushpuppi was remanded in a US Federal prison for several months, even before the commencement of his trial. He was denied bail for two years before his sentencing, even in a country regarded as the bastion of democracy and citadel of human rights. Lastly, Hushpuppi would have had, as it eventually happened, a bandwagon of support from his mercenaries of social defenders whose mission would be to sell all sorts of deceptive narratives about why his prosecution must not be allowed to stand. Sadly, all these will forever be subjected to conjectures and hypotheses; as Hushpuppi has realised, life in civilised societies does not permit the nonsensical shambles used in the just concluded hypothetical illustration.

Succinctly, the aforementioned hypothetical anecdote illustrates why a large pool of Nigerian criminals continues to escape judicial punishments despite the mammoth level of evidence against them.

175

At the time of publishing this book, a natural observer's look at the Instagram accounts of Hushpuppi and Woodberry shows that the poisonous substance of crime endorsement exists in our society. A week after the arrest of Hushpuppi, I studied the perception of the social media community - the modern-day representation of a group of people – to understand public opinion regarding the Hushpuppi saga. The return was shocking. I discovered on a popular media blog, Instablog, that a shocking 65% of the respondents, majorly youths, condemned his arrest and fanatically demanded his release. On his Instagram page, 73% of those who commented on his most recently uploaded post praised him and prayed for his release. Yet, we say we are not fraudulent and criminally minded people.

Shockingly, the support given to the duo has made it unmistakeably clear that a deadly virus has been allowed to spread like a pandemic throughout our societies. Nevertheless, at what point did Nigerians become obsessed with making excuses for crime and corruption? And at what point could we say that the Nigerian public began to embrace acts of crime and corruption as a societally acceptable menace? Truthfully, we are a people who, for several decades, have lived in denial concerning issues that paints us in a negative light when we should have flushed out national cancers like indiscipline, crime and corruption. To support this claim, let me bring you a popular true-life story that has become a common proverbial expression in Yorubaland.

In 1971, a cab driver named Ayodele Muibi Sonubi was stopped by a group of passengers who sought his service. The passengers asked that they be taken to several locations in the Ibadan axis, including an extended ride to areas of the old Western state of the country. On the completion of the trip, the cab driver took his car for an overall wash in a bid to close the day. Later, he was approached by one of the car wash attendants, who informed him of a bag they found in the backseat of his cab. On confirmation, Muibi Sonubi discovered a substantial amount of money in a bag belonging to the passengers who had earlier patronised his service. As the good citizen and morally principled person that Muibi was, he took off to the nearest police station to report the incident and to give an account of the story that transpired. The news media took note of the incident, and it was not long before the news spread throughout the Western state and the country in general. Unknown to him, his act of kindness, good gesture and moral uprightness would backfire. The populace, who should naturally applaud him for his moral gesture, turned against him. They could not believe that someone could be so "stupid" to return wands of cash they had found. Muibi and his wife faced ridicule and mockeries of all sorts from everyone around them to the extent that he was forced to abandon his job as a taxi driver and abandon life in the city of Ibadan for a quieter life back in his village. People taunted him and gave him the nickname *"Muibi ari owo magbe, osi ni o ma ba ku"* (Muibi who saw money but failed to keep it will die in poverty)". That nickname would later transform into a common proverbial way of taunting people with similar acts of moral uprightness in Yoruba societies.[33]

The story of Muibi Sonubi points to the fact that as early as 1971, there had been widespread reception of moral decadence, indiscipline, fraud and corruption among the Nigerian people. What began to occur from that period into the 1980s, and later into this day, is that citizens' complicity in immoral and illegal acts has grown disproportionately higher. Newer generations sought to outdo and outmatch previous activities rather than discard immoral behaviours from previous generations.

The act of worshipping and rendering praises to criminals and morally bankrupt persons had long been part of our national culture, sometimes unknowingly, until it became something done without an iota of shame or remorse. For instance, as early as the 1970s, notable Nigerian musicians were known to render entire full music discography to praise elite members of the society based on the wealth and financial status attributed to the latter. Praises and accolades were rendered that it became a bragging right for shady citizens to get such mentions no matter the cost. One underground source told me the importance of namedropping in the 1980s and how it was seen as an obsessive bragging right, especially within the circle of drug dealers, for elevation and acceptance purposes. Sometimes, abjectly corrupt political and public office holders had their names namedropped by all and sundry. It would take years and sometimes decades for praise-singing musicians to discover the true source of wealth of people that they had rendered an entire music album to their name. Meanwhile, if the early musicians of the pre-2000s praised fraudsters, criminals and morally bankrupt persons without true knowledge of their backgrounds, the musicians of the 2000s did theirs openly and extensively. Today, acts of fraud, crime and corruption are openly celebrated and praised through pop culture and screenplays.

From the early period of the new millennium, when internet fraud gained momentum, musicians took to the studios to render songs that give hospitable habitat to financial criminals. The veteran Nollywood actor Nkem Owoh released a song that celebrated the prevalence of advance-fee fraud rather than its condemnation; Singer "Kelly Hansom" released a song, *'Maga don pay'*; Singer "Olu Maintain" released a song titled *'Yahoozee'*. All songs were hit songs and were just a few notable examples out of several others released during the same period.

After 2010, the country's music industry upped the ante. The music and entertainment industry became money laundering avenue and an escape route for individuals to divert and wash the proceeds of their dishonest means. To understand the nexus between the entertainment industry and fraud (including its acceptance) in Nigeria, two social media uproars sometime in June 2017 and May 2018, respectively, are worthy of recollection and relevance. In June 2017, Nigerian rapper Folarin "Falz" Falana criticised his fellow music artistes, warning them to desist from singing songs that seem to give credence to fraud or praise fraudsters. His innocuous comment sent social media into a frenzy that underpins the notion that Nigerian youths have become unashamedly fraudulent and corrupt in acts and mentality. An unacceptable portion of social media users descended on him and sent threats of all kinds. Behaviours such as those by fraudulent-minded citizens continue to deter others from attempting to criticise society's ills, thereby paving the way for some to erroneously see acts of financial fraud, particularly *yahoo yahoo*, as a welcome development.

Similarly, after the reported arrests of some suspected fraudsters at a nightclub in the Ikoyi area of Lagos, businessman, blogger and showbiz personality Noble Igwe took to his Twitter handle to voice his opinion on the prevalence of fraudsters masquerading themselves as entertainment personalities, among others. Here are some of what he had to say:

> People steal and then turn around to blame the government for making them criminals. Anyone that defends a criminal is a criminal and while we have a list for people advocating rape culture, we should also have one for such people... An armed robber is an armed robber. You are a thief armed with a computer...[34]

His comments sparked off an uproar across the Nigerian social media space, with people giving their share of diverse opinions on the said issue. The sizeable number of citizens, including notable personalities who antagonised Noble Igwe's tweet, showed that Nigerians have come to accept financial crimes and other aspects of criminality as a culture. Noble Igwe and Folarin "Falz" Falana were not the only ones who had been mobbed by an electronically assembled group of demented fraudsters and their sympathisers online. It has become a shameful culture of Nigerians on social media gathering to harass, bully and shout down people who speak against financial crimes. Additionally, the massive support given to suspected criminals and convicted offenders is evident that the country's future is bleak regarding crime-fighting.

As you will read further and should probably have known, it is foolhardy to expect our country to progress as long as we ridicule people like Muibi Sonubi only to celebrate people like James Ibori, Invictus Obi and Hushpuppi.

I must also note that some persons on social media with the highest engagements, followers and patronage are those whose sources of wealth are known to be fraudulent, morally reprehensible or abjectly criminal. They enjoy a massive following from people who readily applaud and salute their everyday activities only to hypocritically turn around to wonder why the country is in such a shambolic state. As regards Nigeria and the culture of impunity and its consequences, I intend to dedicate an entire subchapter to it in subsequent pages.

Inelegant Conclusion

There is an absurd twist to the reality and nature of what has been described in the previous chapter and this particular one. The acceptance of financial crimes in Nigeria is an open secret. Perhaps, it is time for a national consensus among Nigerians to determine if the wide acceptance of financial crimes is something that could benefit us in the long run. Perhaps, it is high time that we did away with the hypocrisy that we frown at financial crimes when we embrace them as part of our national culture. We live in a country where workers are not paid enough to sustain their livelihood, yet employers of labour do not bother to find out how they sustain themselves daily. We know that many employees in the country have ulterior plans to gather illicit and backdoor incomes to add to the meagre salaries they often receive.

Nigeria is where, with impunity, cyber centres were opened in towns to teach teenagers and young adults how to engage in "yahoo," and such are advertised in the open. Recently, there have been open social media advertisements (especially sponsored ads) intended to teach people the basics of financial fraud. On Facebook, Twitter, WhatsApp, and Instagram, fraudsters openly make "*yahoo*" transactional pleas for engagement with others on those platforms. Knowing fully well, at least by now, that Ponzi schemes are fraudulent, people still lure others in schools, workplaces, churches and other gatherings to put their money into such doom-to-fail investments. Various social media accounts teach hopeful itinerants how to cheat visa application systems. Up to this year, some even offered to help itinerants supply "proof of funds" using obviously fraudulent means to bypass checks and systems. Pastors and clergies are invited to the house-warming ceremonies of ostensibly fraudulent and criminal individuals. The list goes on.

Admittedly, Nigeria is arguably the country with the highest number of criminally minded persons as regards financial and economic fraud. It is furthest from my intention to be morally or legally clumsy. However, there are pieces of historical evidence from the global world of financial and economic crimes to attest to such a fact. Unlike some nations that have benefitted from tasteless and negative attributes, could the same be said of Nigeria and its citizens?

Powerful nations of the world today have escaped with the development of their nations through nefarious activities that they carried out, mostly to the detriment of lesser nations and societies. The European countries of today know that the industrial revolution would have been utterly impossible without the criminal and murderous engagement of the slave trade and the effectual colonisation of other nations and societies. They engaged in it viciously and benefited immensely; the rest is history.

The United States engaged in all forms of despicable activities bordering on the imperialism of countries that leaned towards communism during the Cold War era. It asphyxiated uncooperative nations to help gain numerous economic and sociopolitical advantages, gains and successes that were finally achieved to the detriment of the nations it viciously attacked.

Despite the "protective big brother" personae that they sell to developing nations, foreign powers are profiteers of doom in the same nations they claim they are out to help. Western countries, for decades, have become safe havens for storing stolen state funds from Africa, some of which have been repatriated back successfully; others, we might never find out. Regardless, the stolen funds have contributed significantly to the growth of Western nations. Similarly, China is aware of the implausibility of creating jobs for its overpopulated citizenry and has intentionally looked the other way as its citizens profiteer from producing substandard foreign products for cheap exports to mostly underdeveloped and developing nations.

These activities illustrate the underground positive influence of immoral and criminal activities globally. In Nigeria, however, it is impossible to attribute any positive outcome to activities that border on financial crimes.

Financial crimes and corruption should be frowned upon, no matter its little carriage or existence. Nevertheless, would our country have been in this present state of moribund if those who stole our country's resources had taken nationalistic steps despite their corrupt behaviours? I doubt so. Political and public office holders have shown to us that they are the devil's key representatives on earth and that Nigeria is where they have chosen as their command headquarters. Millions and billions of the country's stolen funds could have helped the economy if the looters had sprinkled the funds into various segments of the economy. If that had been the case, multiple sectors of the economy would have been functional, unemployment much lower, the naira stronger, exports higher, and, of course, our overall economy relatively far better than what we currently have. Sadly, this has been far from the case.

Political and public office holders who looted state funds quickly repatriate the money into offshore accounts, inflicting more damage to the country's economy. It has been uncovered that some of the country's stolen funds stored in fictitiously registered accounts using fraudulent identities are being held up in foreign banks after seizures. Stolen amounts of money from government coffers, sometimes converted into foreign currencies, have been discovered in septic tanks, farmhouses, abandoned buildings, bushes, and burial grounds. For several decades, the country's economy suffered the effect of stagnation due to these acts of greed, wickedness and sabotage by the same citizens who lament the state of economic regress.

The masses are not any better. Financial fraudsters spend their proceeds on purchasing exotic foreign cars, pieces of jewellery, imported alcohol products and other assets that are, in a natural sense, almost non-contributory to the nation's overall economy. The reader should permit me to quickly bring into discourse an anecdotal demonstration of events unknown to many between 2020 and 2021. It was the period when an unprecedentedly large number of Nigerian internet fraudsters made enormous proceeds due to unprotected backdoors that were left open to them. These occurred during the benefit funds disbursements in the United States meant to cater for unemployed victims of COVID-19. Nigerian fraudsters joined their colleagues across the globe to besiege US states and federal government application websites. They filed multiple applications and received shared proceeds that amounted to tens of billions of dollars. Yes, you read that right! I can confirm that many Nigerian youths became millionaires overnight during that period. And if you have not read it anywhere else, I will tell you here. The astronomical figures earned by the fraudsters encouraged SARS Police operatives to go rogue in pursuit of every youngster that fit into their profiling and in demand for their "percentage". The rogue operations of the SARS officers and their desperate extortions were what alarmed the public to provoke a massive protest in late 2020. Many protested, and rightly so. Yet, many did not know of an existing unwritten and underlying agreement between the fraudsters and the SARS operatives. The SARS officers were hounding profiled internet fraudsters with a clear message: "We know you made so much money; where is our cut."

As I explained earlier, the resultant effect of the financial feats of those fraudsters should have reflected positively on the Nigerian economy and created job opportunities in the country. However, such expectations would be blatantly foolhardy for anyone who does not understand the mentality of our average gawky youth. As funds from the proceeds of their illicit gains (especially that of the COVID-19 benefit frauds) made their way into the country, they inversely headed back immediately. Luxury car lots were cleared out, with auto dealers counting their unprecedented luck. Rolex and Gucci ownership became the new trend among the fraudulent youths, and Apple products were purchased in huge numbers. Illicit drugs filtered the streets as the purchasing power of the young fraudsters became immediately reflective. Hotels and nightlife industry witnessed a sharp rise in patronage, and other informal sectors of the economy benefited largely. In all of these, most youths who benefited from the COVID-19 benefit fraud failed to invest in the nation's economy by creating businesses or investing one way or the other in the employment sector.

Also, the naira suffered a devastating blow because of the underground trade of the naira in the black-market currency exchange and crypto markets. As these went on for an estimated 18 months, even the bests of the country's so-called educated elites were unaware that something catastrophic was happening under their nose. Such is our sorry state, as it has always been, that some people who profess to know it all do not even have a clue about activities in the country. All they know is that the country is bad and the government is to blame, but the activities of their fellow citizens regarding our collective destruction are something they inadvertently overlooked or mollycoddled each time they open their mouths on national television.

I must reiterate that no influential nation of today has got to be where they are with a clean bill of health. The Scandinavians are regarded as the most peace-loving people in the world today. That is a sharp irony and contradiction to the bloodthirsty ravaging monsters that they were some centuries (or even millenniums) ago. Nevertheless, they have profiteered from their activities and built their nations to become the shape they are today. In fact, today, many successful countries rely on the chaos and crises of countries like ours to remain afloat.

I must say that if, as a people, we have decided to accept financial crimes as a national culture, then we must have a national consensus and stop the pretence that we are a pious nation; not like anyone is fooled by the irrational numbers of churches and mosques at every corner on our national soil. We are a bloodily corrupt people, and it might be high time that we started looking at how financial crimes could benefit us, as it has benefitted other nations, rather than us selling a pretence; a false commodity that foreigners are not buying.

4: SCHADENFREUDE AND DESTRUCTIVE ACTIVISM

When the coup plotters who truncated the country's First Republic decided to reach out to Nigerians, a voice purportedly belonging to the alleged mastermind of the plot, Major Chukwuma Kaduna Nzeogwu, broadcasted saying: "you will no longer need to be ashamed to be Nigerians".[1] Such is the audacious arrogance of people whose actions are fashioned by sentiments and sometimes murderous lunacy that they never consider the consequences of their actions but only the unrealistic wishes that reside in their fantasy world.

Today, contrary to what Nzeogwu had thought, it is an unarguable fact that Nigerians are more ashamed of their nationality than they were fifty-six years ago when the coup took place. In fact, Nigeria never recovered from the disastrous actions of the coup plotters who hid under the deceptive umbrella of revolutionary ideals and freedom fighting.

Nigeria has become a home to many so-called freedom fighters like Nzeogwu and the rest of the January 1966 coup plotters whose idea of revolution and freedom fighting is to burn the country to the ground through fanatical ideas and dangerous rhetoric. Misleading and erroneous mythical and fanciful beliefs have overridden logical thought processes in almost all sociopolitical discourses. So many are such beliefs that they seem contradictory to an impatient listener and observer.

To start with, most Nigerians believe that the country is abundantly rich in resources, which might be quite true, but what is not true is their assertion that the country is so rich that every of its citizen should thrive in abundant

186

splendour. On the negative side, most citizens have terrible things to say about the country, such as nothing good could ever come out of Nigeria. While some of the assertions may be correct, some are aggressively exaggerated. For instance, while it may be true that Nigeria is a poor country, it is misleading for anyone to assume that Nigeria is the poorest country in the world, as often put out for malicious reasons. It is also not true that Nigeria is the most dangerous country in the world or the one with the worst sets of citizens. Sadly, some of these things have been erroneously yet doggedly put out to be correct by alarmist groups and political demagogues who think they do the country a huge favour by asserting such inglorious ascriptions to the country.

Again, an impatient observer could sense some paradoxes when analysing the Nigerian situation; one moment, the country is said to be rich, and the next, it is agreeably said to be poor. That is because questions and answers relating to the complexity of the Nigerian situation and theories strongly depend on whom you ask and the authentic purpose behind their response.

Many Nigerians know that their country is corrupt, but they fail to acknowledge that their information bank is equally corrupt. Part of such occurrence is due to a corrupt media that, as we know, has fed citizens manipulative lies, distorted information and disingenuously fabricated stories. Conversations with a vast majority of Nigerians would lead an unbiased individual to acknowledge that many have come to see misinformation and fake news as real historical and factual accounts of events. One thing is unmistakably clear; the information bank of Nigerians is abjectly faulty.

Manipulative media, fraudulent journalists, biased writers, prejudiced historians, unscrupulous social media warriors, ethnic jingoists, phoney rights activists and the propaganda machinery of political demagogues are responsible for this

unholy social feature of our national life, where facts have become fiction and vice-versa.

Bad News is big business; it thrives and spreads fast. Depending on their objective, they derive joy or indifference to chaos, ruin, decadence and collapse. Contrary to the appearance of concern or sympathy they sell, they are joyous to hear news of evil, chaos, calamity or tragedy. Nonetheless, bad news did not become a booming industry overnight as certain circumstances and factors facilitated its growth on our national soil. Unknown to many members of the public, to their detriment, there are social, political, financial, and economic benefits from the spread and success of bad news, especially for the anchors.

Bad news anchors often use their machinery to spread fictitious and damaging news to elicit discontent and stir anger towards a particular group of people. The biblical question "Can any good thing come out of Nazareth?" also apply to the Nigerian situation. That is because sharp divisions along ethnic and religious lines are enough reason for the personality and credibility of individuals to be questioned especially during electioneering. Depending on who steers the wheel of the country's vehicle, hostilities and resentments often accompany such an individual from his first day in office. This ugly pattern had traceable roots to electoral periods when electorates voted based on ethnic and religious sentiments rather than qualification and competence as necessary criteria. The agents of darkness who occupy positions in the corridors of power know well-intentioned individuals who just gained access to political offices. These agents gather all available tactics to destroy such individuals from their first day in office because they are perceived as obstacles to their corrupt practices.

Former finance minister, Dr Ngozi Okonjo-Iweala, once narrated a story about how she got a visit from Dr Donald Duke (former governor of Cross Rivers state) after President Goodluck Jonathan offered her a ministerial role. Dr Duke had come to inform her that some people who wanted the

Jonathan administration to fail did not want her to participate in the administration. They did that in a bid not to "give Jonathan and his administration credibility."[2] Obviously, such agents of darkness were confident of the qualification and capability of the erudite financial expert that they would rather not have her in a position to drive the country's economy forward. That typifies our sorry state of today. People habitually lurk behind the shadows to work towards the failure of an incumbent administration to their merit. They justify their predictions of doom and effect activities for their gains and selfish purposes.

Divisions in the country continue to be the basis for hostilities and resentments against people of different extraction. The venoms of such divisions continue to spill into the already embittered game of politics. Therefore, seeing people of a particular extraction view others in political leadership with suspicions is not strange. Inversely, it has become a trend for certain political leaders to view people of certain extraction or region with an equal sense of suspicion. Such suspicions have become the basis for umbrella activism that, in the real sense, is prejudice in disguise.

Before President Muhammadu Buhari's 2015 electoral victory, the rumour mill and conspiracy theory industry were rich with disseminated information. Some believed he was the chief sponsor of the Boko Haram group, and others believed he had plans to Islamize the country. Others swore that Boko Haram was his manufactured idea to subvert the polity in a bid to damage the reputation of the Goodluck Jonathan administration. They hinted he would pocket his "boys" once sworn into office. Sadly, as history has it, they were following the same pattern of rumours, accusations and counter-accusations that had become the basis for the truncation of the first military coup in the country. It will be recalled that the January 15, 1966 coup plotters had claimed, without evidence, that the First Republic administration of Tafawa Balewa was planning a jihad, among other things. [3]

Evidence has shown that the major perpetrators of negative propaganda are political demagogues who do not have the people's interests at heart.

What has also been made clear is that freedom fighting is far from their noble intent. In truth, southerners cannot claim not to be as biased and prejudiced as their northern counterpart and vice-versa. The North-South schism becomes even more apparent before, during and after electioneering. Sadly, the prejudiced animosity people have towards a political leader of a particular extraction has become the basis for measuring how well they perform in office or not. There are two handy examples of this notorious situation.

Prejudiced groups moved to ostracise the then vice-president Goodluck Jonathan from taking over the country's affairs during the interregnum (2009-2010) that occurred due to the severe illness of the then president, Umaru Musa Yar'Adua. Prejudice from northern political establishments became so intense that they moved to ensure that a person of northern extraction should succeed Yar'Adua. That was an illogical move that goes against every available doctrine of democracy and constitutional politics, because a sitting vice-president automatically enjoys automatic elevation after the president's demise.

After the death of Yar'Adua, and the assumption of office of President Goodluck Jonathan, Jonathan's tenure was met with hostile antagonisms at every step he took. Northern political demagogues made it clear that they were out to tarnish and destroy his government to secure and control power at all costs. Under Jonathan, Nigeria became a divided country, the worst of its kind and one not witnessed since the civil war. While many of the criticisms against his government were valid, many others were fabricated, untrue and purely meant to destabilise the country to make his administration and person look bad and incompetent. Sadly, their plans worked. Jonathan was harshly criticised for many wrongdoings under his watch, and condemnations and public discontent grew against him. Eventually, President Jonathan lost his re-election bid in the country's 2015 presidential election; a first in the country's 55-year history where an incumbent leader holding the highest position in the land lost a conducted election.

Before I progress further, let me quickly emphasise that the same bricks thrown at Jonathan were similarly thrown at his predecessors and his successor (Buhari). Hostilities under the deceitful umbrella of activism and "opposition" are nothing other than political subterfuge and an attempt to pit citizens against one another on partisan lines. On this, every group in the country are woefully guilty of this uncivilised and destructive show of shame.

A revelation that seems oblivious to politicians of societal Nigeria is that they suffer from the dangerous precedents they stage for others. The playbook used to launch vicious attacks toward Jonathan and his government was copied and documented by those who needed it against the new government. Unknown to the newly elected President Muhammadu Buhari, he had inherited an extremely divided country, a sort of division he was unprepared for. Primarily, some southern citizens viewed him with great suspicion and resentment, especially for his audacity to defeat their "son" in the 2015 presidential election. It is common to witness bad news against Buhari and his government being subtly greeted with "we knew it" responses from those who predicted his government was doomed to fail. Like Jonathan, Buhari's only crime today is not necessarily because he has been a bad leader but because he is of Fulani extraction and a Muslim. Buhari would later find out that he had fallen into the same pit that was dug for his predecessor.

In Nigeria, ethnicity, region and religion are three major yardsticks used in weighing the performance of an incumbent leader rather than logical and unbiased assessment methods. Political leaders such as Jonathan, Buhari and others who occupy political seats of divided entities (federal, states, local government areas or political districts) continue to be met with widespread bias and prejudice. In many cases, it has become obvious that the same people who quickly report the failures of some political administrations are also the chief architects of those same problems. Also, citizens with an established mind of bias readily accept manipulative and sensational news stories without a duty of care to verify and validate. Contrariwise, when positive news items worthy of applause filter to their doorstep, such news is dismissed without readiness to accept it into the comparative scheme of things.

One problem with opposition groups in Nigeria is the sheer sense of impunity and entitlement that they carry along with them. They arrogate a sense of entitlement that things must go their way regardless of the consequences. For them, failure of things to go their way meant the sounding of alarm that society is in ruins and there is a presence of misrule and dictatorship. Therefore, it has become normal to encounter chauvinists who go rogue after losing elections. Electoral loss is an opportunity for them to remind everyone how the electoral process is rigged, how a revolution must take place, and for people to rise and challenge the status quo. That was the case with a notorious self-acclaimed human rights activist and founder of the *Sahara Reporters* online news medium, Omoyele Sowore and his riotous behaviour following the 2019 presidential election. No society should ever tolerate the arrogance of any individual, party or group of people with a paltry percentage score of 0.12% in an election to call for a revolution in a democracy. Sowore might have enjoyed the support of certain people within his circles. He is also free to surround himself with cynical individuals who think the government's arrest and prosecution of his person is a witch-hunt. However, they are mistaken, and most democratic societies would agree that people like Sowore must be made to face the music.

United States authorities did not shy away from arresting and prosecuting the instigators and perpetrators of the January 2021 Capitol Hill attack. Like Sowore and others who tried to undermine our political process, the Capitol Hill attackers had attempted to subvert the polity. They tried to undermine the US electoral process, which granted victory to Joe Biden ahead of the incumbent president, Donald Trump. They were hunted down, in their numbers, across all the states of the US. They faced a new life of reality where most of them pleaded guilty to federal charges against them. If that same scenario were to present itself in Nigeria, political demagogues and shadowy groups would have alarmed the world to "suppression of civil rights" and other alarming bells they so love to ring out that all is not well with the country despite them being the facilitator of some of the country's woes.

As we advance, Nigerians must remain vigilant and wary of those who talk soothingly, in a desperate bid to gain their trust, only to become worse than those they had maligned and uprooted from power. In that regard, precedence exists in our backyard and in foreign territories. The various Nigerian military leaders who came to power through coups faulted their predecessors and hoodwinked the public about how they intended to be corrective regimes. Most failed, not only miserably, but did poorer than those they ousted from office. Outside Nigeria, the world witnessed the development of two-faced monster-leaders who sold a false portrayal of human rights activism to lure themselves into the heart of unsuspecting citizens. Adolf Hitler, Charles Taylor, Mobutu Seseseko, Idi Amin Dada, Pol Pot, Jean-Bedel Bokassa, Robert Mugabe, Jean Kambanda, Augusto Pinochet, and Saddam Hussein are notable examples. Those rulers inflicted pains of unbearable proportion on the very same people they had hoodwinked into believing that they wanted to liberate. Nigeria had seen many such individuals rise to power, many of whom are known to the author and the reader but will not be listed further.

There is empirical evidence to suggest that civil rights groups in Nigeria have consistently sought to propagate divisive messages and biased undertones. There is also a historical and natural angle to the ever-problematic North-South schism. Most notable civil rights groups and media houses are controlled by southerners and largely concentrated in the South.

That is because southerners, who constituted most of the educated elite in the country, established independent media houses and civil rights organisations. Southerners founded those organisations intending to kick against perceived injustice and political misrule. Incidentally, northerners, who held political power for most of the country's political history, administered such misrule. During the period of misrule by leaders of northern extraction, northern-based civil rights groups were inexistent or largely quiet.

Northern-based civil rights groups did not start to gain popularity until the return to democracy in 1999, when a southern Christian took over the country's top political seat of office. I must alert the reader not to mistake civil rights groups for political groups because the latter has always played an active role since the country's formative existence. Nevertheless, the North-South schism became a template for suspicions by northern oligarch and their citizens, and they began to view Southern agitations against misrule as an affront. Rather than northerners seeing human rights activism as a call for national unity against despotism and tyranny, they saw it as a selective call to remove their "sons" from political power. To this day, this pattern has continued to be a major template for negative activism. Northerners instigate animosities against southern political leaders, and southerners continue to spill venoms against northern political leaders. Divisions are not just along geographic North vs. South lines and are not necessarily engaged at the federal level of politics. People of different ethnic, tribal, communal, and religious groups also continue to view one another with so much vileness and resentment, even at regional and communal levels.

A lot has been dedicated to addressing the roles played by political, societal, and economic leaders regarding the disaster that plagues us. Therefore, it must be said again that the author does not intend to shove blame from the doorstep of our various leaders. Regardless, a society that demands and expects good leadership must also create enabling environment for such. For a society to function properly, the principles of good

governance must meet that of good citizenship at a fair point of equilibrium. Anything contrary is equivalent to a broken society, which is what our lovely country has degenerated into.

Regarding opposition and civil rights groups, many groups do not exist to advance human rights in the country. They also do not aim to bring about growth, progress or solutions. Rather, their existence and operations are entirely contingent upon the failure of the Nigerian state. In many cases, some groups are known to exaggerate small faults and to extensively blow the situations out of proportion in a manner capable of causing disruptions, chaos, instability or even bloodshed.

Some individuals and groups are known to match their destructive languages with actions. Some groups are known to carry out acts of sabotage, felony or treason only to turn around and blame the government for punitive actions. In some cases, these groups intentionally orchestrate well-planned activities to ensure that a government loses its popularity and goodwill among the people. As I have said repeatedly, we are the architects of our destruction, leaders and citizens alike. We eagerly damage our country's reputation and image with untrue and misleading stories and then wonder why outsiders view us with scorn and derision.

Certain groups in Nigeria have derived a dangerous culture of expending adequate resources to propagate and spread bad news to paint the country negatively. Although disseminating vital information is crucial and necessary, disseminating misleading "fake news" materials is anti-democratic and damaging to our national growth. It is dangerous for good news and accomplishments to be intentionally shut down and replaced by pessimism and acts of national ridicule.

Agents of schadenfreude mirror the very things they claim to fight. Some carry out such acts unintentionally; for others, it has become their life mission to ruin the country's name home and abroad until whatever they set out to achieve (mostly politically or economically) is met. They operate individually, in groups, or in clustered networks and are scattered all over different areas of the world.

Today, they converge on various social media networks with no other purpose than to announce to the world that the country is next in line to the kingdom of hell. They have well-operated social media groups and pages that mostly carry fake news, brandished to an awaiting set of gullible followers. Good news items about the country and its citizens are not welcomed or tolerated on those social pages and groups, except for bad, damaging and destructive news items. They are unreceptive of patriotic opinions that paint the country in good light. In and within their network, no one dares to disagree with them, and those who disagree with them are considered "sell out", called puppets and other synonymous names in a bid to intimidate such voices. When they instigate unwarranted hostilities, there is a compulsion for everyone else to follow; otherwise, they would unleash a torrential rain of unpatriotic insults on those who engage otherwise. When they gather to protest against a particular policy, action, individual or group, anyone they accost following a different route than theirs is presumed to have been paid or bought over. Such is their level of arrogance, delusion, hypocrisy and e-thuggery.

In addition, it has become a norm to encounter "I told you so" commentators on social media pages or at discourse gatherings. In such situations, people heavily rely on bad news items to exhibit their prophetic dexterity on communal, societal, or national affairs. For such people, they are quick to predict woe on those who disagree with their choice of thoughts, political candidacies, social/political affiliations, economic ideologies, or general opinions. Such people are far from being genuinely concerned about the state of the nation and are far from being the activist that they portray themselves to be. They are vultures with a skilful duty to predict danger and demise, and when it eventually occurs, they feast on it cheerfully. Damaging news materials from agents of schadenfreude sell fast because of the readiness of people to believe how badly damaged their country is, or sometimes how evil and despicable a person or group are, even when such news is obviously manipulated or entirely untrue.

I mentioned earlier how Nigeria is such a complex country that analysing its multifaceted situation could make one look to contradict his own opinions. In this regard, you will recall how I once faulted Nigerians for criticising President Muhammadu Buhari for his honest view that Nigerians are corrupt. I faulted such Nigerians because they expected their president to sell misleading lies on the international arena to a group of experts who have the country's information handy. While it is true that the country's president should be the marketer-in-chief of the country's image, I faulted those who wanted him to sell a lie, as that itself would have done more harm than good. That scenario is entirely different from what some do to intentionally destroy the reputation and image of their own country for their selfish interests.

When Nigerians compare how bad their country is being run to others around the world, they are quickest to use terms like "saner climes". It must be said that no "saner clime" allows anarchy and hostile dissent from citizens in unfathomable proportion like Nigerians do to their own country. No sane clime in the world allows people to intentionally distribute news items that are inciting, misleading or fabricated to stir ethnic tensions that could eventually involve the destruction of lives and property. The Australian Julian Assange and American Edward Snowden learnt that even the sanest climes would not sit idly and allow people to hide under activism to destroy the fabric of their societies. The duo, in unrelated events, concluded that they were acting under cover of activism or freedom of information, among others. However, the US and its Western allies that hold themselves as the epicentres of freedom did not allow such people the kind of freedom they thought they were entitled to. Nevertheless, these are acts that many Nigerians arrogantly commit and expect to be celebrated flamboyantly as human rights crusaders.

Examples noted in this chapter are relevant due to our constant denial of how present-day societies function. Regions of the world where violent dissents and hostilities are rife continue to experience decay, anarchy and chaos rather than the "happily ever after" illusion that activist groups in Nigeria dangerously portray. Still, Nigerians continue to allow themselves to be ridiculed by famous persons whose source of existence is solidly reliant on the chaos and decay of the Nigerian state. For instance, after the overthrow of Malian President Ibrahim Boubacar Keïta in August 2020, Nigeria's former minister and politician, Femi Fani-Kayode, opined on his Twitter account, "25 year old man in Mali led the coup to reclaim their nation. 30 years old in Nigeria watching BBNaija shouting Leycon (sic) my man!."

Obviously, his tweet was not intended to remind Nigerian youths of their apathetic attitude concerning the country's political affairs. His message was to ignite a youth overthrow of the incumbent government, even if it involved violence and bloodletting. Ironically, Femi Fani-Kayode's father, Chief Remi Fani-Kayode, was the deputy premier of the Western Region of Nigeria when equally young Nigerian military officers staged a bloody coup to overthrow the government. The deputy premier was reported to have escaped through luck, although the same fortune was not afforded to many other notable leaders and politicians of that era. Even though the comment from Femi Fani-Kayode amounts to a treasonable felony and an unacceptably immoral one, such opinions typically draw applause from naive and political members of the public desperate for social, political and economic changes. Many people welcome divisive comments, even if made by enemies of the state. I must say, however, that such Nigerians would be foolhardy to think that the desperately desired positive changes will be granted by people whose intentions are motivated purely by selfish interests.

Nonetheless, state and societal enemies are never concerned about the general populace that they so much love to mislead to be fighting for their rights. They thrive on divisions, aggravated dissents and public discontent against legitimate governments. Such hostile activities are well calculated, and they take full advantage of such a situation when it arises; when it does not, they create one. To be very clear, state enemies are fellow citizens who derive

198

joy in seeing the country burn to their advantage, as it allows them to present themselves as "knight in shining armour" who has come to save them from oppression.

Our basis for activism needs to be rigorously checked. We cannot continue to operate a society that depicts the proverbial story of a child who, after killing his parents, begs prosecutors for mercy on the premise that he is now an orphan. That has been the case with criminals, who, for instance, destroy public infrastructures meant to cater for communities on the erroneous and misleading ground that they did it because they were poor. Pity culture in Nigerian societies is why acts of sabotage, theft and crime have been allowed unpunished due to the attachment of emotional influences. We give criminals some "justifiable" excuse to carry out further acts that inflict injuries on us. I must reiterate that we cannot afford to allow people to hide under the umbrella of any invented cover to get away with criminal or treasonable behaviours.

One incident exposed Nigeria's theatre of activism and information manipulation as recently as 2012 during the "Occupy Nigeria" civil unrest that shook the entire country following the government's announcement of the removal of fuel subsidies. The fuel subsidy removal was an intended policy by President Goodluck Jonathan's economic team to curtail the excesses of petroleum marketers and importers involved in highly organised fraudulent practices. By fraudulent practices, we refer to fraud of astronomic proportion that had existed for several decades and is still in place to this very moment. Former finance minister Dr Ngozi Okonjo-Iweala referred to one subsidy fraud incident under the Jonathan administration as "one of the biggest corruption scandals in Nigeria's history".[4]

Behind the curtains of the civil unrest that erupted throughout the country stood an innocent and well-planned attempt to fizzle out economic saboteurs out of the country's petroleum sector. However, something went off that set off the protests. Firstly, President Jonathan made a communication and executive blunder by choosing to announce (through the

PPPRA) the subsidy removal on January 1, 2012. The first day of the year is traditionally a period many Nigerians are stuck in their various hometowns, villages or other places far from their place of residence. It also represents a day of refreshing, a new beginning and a day that symbolises one of hope for many Nigerians. Secondly, according to Dr Okonjo-Iweala, the president had not allowed the economic team to consult with public members before making the announcement fully.[5] According to her, the president had been instigated to make the announcement hurriedly in a manner certain to cause public discontent. It later became evident that some people desperately wanted the failure of the subsidy removal. With these political blunders from the government, enemy forces of the country positioned the Jonathan administration and Nigerians exactly where they wanted.

Immediately after the government announced the fuel subsidy removal, naïve quarters of the media and the machinery wing of the subsidy fraudsters went ballistic. Activists grabbed their ever-ready microphones, and opposition groups clapped elatedly at their opportunity. Nigerians took to the street in utter rejection of the subsidy removal. Political opponents became one of the first beneficiaries as they hijacked the protests and turned them into political rallies of all sorts, especially in states governed by the opposition parties. Social commentators who were clueless on matters relating to the fuel subsidy programme and its removal turned the protests into fanfares of torrential abuses on the Jonathan administration. The fuel subsidy criminals and benefactors of subsidy manipulations had their fair share of recruiting "experts" to tell Nigerians why the subsidies must remain. Entertainers and stage performers took to the podiums at various protest grounds to keep protesters joyous with anti-government songs and chants. In the end, President Jonathan's administration made understandable concessions. The people got what they wanted because the government had been defeated. At least, so they thought. If only they knew that the cost of schadenfreude would be a national loss of colossal proportion to our detriment.

To save the reader's time, I must quickly point out certain events that proved the administration of Jonathan, despite its long list of errors, was right on that occasion, and Nigerians were basically wrong.

- The announcement was made for the total removal of fuel subsidies in 2012 and to peg the price at N142, to which Nigerians reacted negatively. As of 2022, fuel remained fully subsidised, yet the price has skyrocketed to a current price of N165 per litre. Sadly, our negative activism paid for ten years resulted in an outcome of waste, looting, sabotage, mismanagement and financial crimes.

- The role of the chairman of the committee set up by the House of Representatives to investigate allegations of subsidy fraud, Hon. Farouk Lawan is crucially relevant. For years, he had worn an incorruptible face to the public, so clever that it got him the designation of the "Mr Integrity" nomenclature. He was later implicated in a bribery scandal to the tune of $500,000 from oil billionaire and tycoon Femi Otedola. Lawan was eventually convicted for said offence in a matter that made Nigerians question the true merit of their protests in 2012. Obviously, while Nigerians were being misled to protest, their chief protesters were profiting from their chaos and doom.

- Most Nigerians did not know why they protested or the cost implication of their grievances. During the protests in 2012, Nigerians were unaware that subsidies on fuel accounted for 30% of the government's expenditure, 4% of total GDP and 118% of the capital budget.[6] By 2020, subsidies on fuel had doubled that of the entire health budget and also dwarfed the federal budget on education. It also continues to be much higher than budgets appropriated to some other sectors of the economy.

- Nigerians also got to know that a vast number of those who instigated the protests were, and are still, owners of fuel stations and depots. Some are oil marketers and importers themselves. They did not instigate the protests to fight for the rights of the people but to use citizens as a pawn in their bitter game of corruption, theft and economic sabotage of the country.

Ten years after the fuel subsidy protests, Nigerians continue to pay huge amounts for petroleum products, the subsidy remains, and the theft continues. Our economy remains unsustainable, and the county is in debt. With these developments, one could never tell if January 2012 was when the venomous poison of national schadenfreude and negative activism prevented us from getting rid of criminal volcanoes in human form. Sadly, the incumbent president and his cabinet ministers were among those who stirred sentiments against his predecessor and clamoured against fuel subsidy removal. Today, it has become difficult and nearly impossible for them to deal with the menace of fraud and corruption, hidden under the umbrella of "subsidy" for decades.

Generally, Nigerians are not equipped with adequate information on actions and policies against which they agitate. Evidence from previously held protests indicates that most people would welcome any form of dissent that seems to criticise the government without handy information as to the advantages or otherwise of their actions. Nonetheless, Nigerians themselves continue to be the ones who facilitate the financial debt and burden the country has found itself in today. Labour unions are one of the guiltiest groups responsible for dispensing misleading information in the country. An important topic worthy of relevance pertains to the controversial minimum wage paid out to workers in the country.

Contrary to popular opinion, there is absolutely nothing fascinating about approving minimum wage increases in climes like Nigeria, no matter the proportion of increase that administrations purport to have effectuated.

Debates relating to an increase in the minimum wage of workers are a global trend and extremely controversial. The reader should permit me to bring a quick hypothetical situation into this discourse, an illustration of the combined nature of hypocrisy, unintelligence, ineffectiveness, and cynicism of labour and other civil society groups in the country.

After an increase in workers' salaries across the country, labour unions and other civil society groups go to bed and become lazy to effectuate price control mechanisms. They slumber and lag than proactively prevent the usual repercussions that often stem from a wage increase. Some become the actual instigators of price hikes in the country. For instance, the National Union of Road Transport Workers would facilitate the immediate increase in the prices of transport fares, and the TUC would sleep and watch as prices of commodities and market products go up sporadically. Lawyers (without proper guidance by its professional body, the NBA) and real estate practitioners would connive with landlords to effectuate the increment in tenancy fees and related costs. PENGASSAN/NUPENG and their affiliate bodies would immediately use the opportunity to facilitate an increase in the prices of petroleum products. The result is that the currency depreciates, inflation occurs, and the overall economy suffers. Ultimately, the bodies responsible for effecting the minimum wage increase are also responsible for the negative consequences on the overall economy.

Contrary to the fanciful and grandstanding commentaries they run on societal and national issues, many activist-turned-politicians have shown that there is activism and there is capability. They have proven that even the best activists have no clue about leadership and power, at least in our own clime. Adams Oshiomhole was NLC's president for much of Olusegun Obasanjo's civilian administration. Oshiomhole orchestrated mostly unwarranted civil opinions against the new civilian government suffering from severe national losses from brutally corrupt predecessors. The NLC president was a recalcitrant personality who was desperate to be on the good books of the populace. He was in no mood to give the new administration the necessary time to fix a severely damaged country reeling from the injuries of military predecessors. Oshiomhole himself later became a two-term governor of Edo State. After his tenure, Edo remained one of the most impoverished states in the country. He also became the national party chairman of the ruling APC, yet the country could not be said to have fared any better.

Oshiomhole is not the only activist-turned-politician who got to power and failed the people, at least by their own standards. Many former leaders of the much-respected NADECO who got elected to offices failed to live up to the standards they had set for other political and public office holders. Kaduna State Governor Mallam Nasir El-Rufai ceaselessly condemned the Goodluck Jonathan administration for his inability to end insurgency crises threatening the nation. He threw venomous attacks on Jonathan over perceived acts of maladministration, rising corruption cases, and insecurity. El-Rufai gave the Jonathan administration no breathing space and used his social media accounts to launch hostile and near-treasonable attacks. His emergence as Kaduna State governor coincided with the time his political party, the APC, also recorded success at the federal level. Today, the rest is history. By El-Rufai's standard, Kaduna has become worse than he met it, at least in the area of insecurity.

There is an inverse twist as well. Nigerians have become used to elected politicians who failed to turn things around during their time in office, only to become social critics after the end of their term. Former officials have taken up the habit of writing antagonising letters, opinions, commentaries, essays and dissents against incumbent leaders on topics they themselves failed to address while in office. That is because the criticism and condemnation industry is the best tool for public patronage, and such people are often greeted with applause by a large chunk of the quick-to-forget citizenry.

Self-acclaimed activist and former Special Assistant on Media to President Goodluck Jonathan, Reno Omokri, is a typical example of politician-to-activist disingenuous individuals. During his stint as a public officer, he heavily campaigned for citizens' participation in governance and encouraged citizens to build a positive image of the country, home and abroad. Reno Omokri used his office and position to facilitate the growth and acceptance of a public promotional social media page, *"Build up Nigeria"*, to promote the country to a global audience and to set the country's positive image alight. However, it was obvious that politics and its many benefits are the sole motivation for Nigerians entrant into public offices. After the 2015 electoral loss of his boss to the incumbent president, he became the sharp opposite of everything he vehemently championed. Today, he has consistently used the same *"Build up Nigeria"* platform, which in his words, was meant to "share good news only" to stir up venomous hostility, hate, manipulative stories and falsehood against the incumbent government. His supporters are mostly biased and prejudiced persons, who principally followed him due to a shared belief in e-thuggery and e-insurgency, may be quick to defend his actions. However, there is a fine line between activism and e-insurgency; the latter is what people like Reno have chosen.

The media, which portrays itself as the societal torchlight on political and societal activities, ironically became unreceptive of having their activities checked by the general public. Journalists, activists, and media personnel have caught the "overnight riches" infection, just like their contemporaries in other societal areas whose sources of wealth are questionable and largely untraceable. Online news agencies like *Sahara Reporters* constantly peddle falsified information, misleading headlines and overblown news reporting to stir aggravated and disingenuous discontents. Many erroneously believe such news headlines are carried out to expose corruption in government. And while it is true that public officials are devastatingly corrupt, the fraud and corruption in the media erode trust regarding the information that they dispense.

The running of deceptive commentaries, manipulative stories, click-baiting headlines, "fake news" stories and extortive mechanisms to denigrate the country has become common in the media. Relying on deceptive and manipulative mechanisms such as "inside" or "anonymous" sources, media houses and journalists, especially those owned by opposition politicians, enthusiastically run false stories to damage the reputation of targeted political leaders and groups. With so much hysteria, they publish unverified but damaging stories so long as it could give their establishment or paymasters some form of public grace. Hence, the shock culture aspect that should typically follow horrific news stories and rally public discontent towards positive change has become ineffectual. Media bias and sensationalism are heavily responsible for why some criminal suspects and looters of our national treasury get away with their nefarious acts. Sadly, in all of these, truth becomes the ultimate pawn and Nigerians the ultimate casualties.

Nonetheless, biased media agencies are not entirely to be blamed. We could rightly blame citizens' propensity to accept a particular nature of news. Many Nigerians readily believe that their country is damaged beyond repairs. They dangerously hunt for evidential news stories to support such claims. Therefore, positive news stories are intentionally suppressed to pave the way for negative news stories because the latter sells fast. Media houses and modern-day bloggers desperately fish out erroneous comments, gaffes, inciting remarks, flawed commentaries, controversial opinions and other undesirable stories from public figures to sell as headline news to an awaiting audience. The awaiting audience is uninterested in 59 minutes of speech by those they desperately wish to castigate; the 1-minute gaffe is all that matters to them for the individual to be subjected to ridicule. For certain people in certain quarters of bias and prejudice, every avenue to yell mantras such as "Nigeria is doomed", "We have never had it this worse", or "this is the worst administration in this country/state" is one never to be missed.

Of course, there is activism, and there is unadulterated folly. It is incomprehensible to understand why some people lay down their lives for those whose missions are politically or financially motivated. Many violent clashes and bloodletting in our social and political history happened because some people thought they were on the right path and were wrongly assumed to be fighting for a just cause. That applies to those who masquerade under activism to solicit societal support, only to turn around to inflict harm on the same society that embraced them. In most cases, the instigators of violent social and political actions often have recourse programs to escape the repercussions of their actions. However, their often-gullible followers are not always that lucky.

Some examples could be fetched out of activities during the brutal civil war. The then military governor of the Eastern Region and the de facto head of the Biafran government, Colonel Dim Odumegwu Ojukwu, had signalled strong warnings to Biafran soldiers and citizens to ensure a no-compromise situation against the Nigerian government. He had issued a "No retreat, No Surrender" directive and one that he strongly set out to enforce. When Ojukwu spotted plans by some of his top officers and deputies (including his 2-I-C Emmanuel Ifeajuna and Victor Banjo) to negotiate a ceasefire with the Nigerian government, he put them to trial. Some officers were sentenced to death, while others received lengthy prison sentences. However, Ojukwu, who had stubbornly refused to yield to the advice of his subordinates and had allowed a protracted war to consume millions of Igbo soldiers and citizens, could not live up to his dogmatic ideology. When it became clear that victory was unachievable and that federal troops were closing in, Ojukwu abandoned Biafra land and fled the country into the neighbouring Ivory Coast. As it happened, Ojukwu survived, but his lieutenants who followed him into a preventable war and millions of citizens did not survive that war.

Similarly, facts have emerged following the failure of the "Gideon Orkar Coup" in 1990 as regards what transpired during and after that ill-fated chapter of our political history. It has been discovered that the facilitators and chief sponsors of the coup made plans to escape the country in case the coup failed; plans they eventually put into action after the coup's failure. Contrary to the widespread belief that Major Gideon Orkar masterminded the coup, it was masterminded by some officers who used Orkar as a conduit. It later became evident that top officers like Lt. Colonel Anthony Nyiam, Major C.O Obahor, Major Saliba Mukoro, and billionaire businessman Chief Great Ovedje Ogboru, were the major conspirators of the coup plot. Nyiam, Mukoro, and Ogboru (including middle-rank officers like Captain Ben Oziegbe, Captain Sowaribi Tolofori, Lt. Patrick Obasi, and Lt. Sunday Echendu), escaped through a recourse plan they had initiated. However, they left hundreds of military personnel and civilians in the cold to face a military tribunal that found them guilty and summarily executed 69 of them. Years later, the actual plotters were pardoned by new political administrations. A comment attributed to Lt. Sunday Echendu captures the hypocrisy of people who lead gullible citizens to the dungeon on the pretence that they are together when things go wrong. Echendu was quoted as saying:

> We knew if we failed, we would pay the ultimate prize. And I was prepared for that. I was willing to serve up my time. I was also clamouring for the country to take a different direction. I was willing to die for Nigeria.

Ironically, as quoted, the word "we" did not include Echendu, who refused to pay the ultimate price he claimed he was ready to pay. Echendu did not lay down his life as he had vowed but was ready to reap from the fruit of violence and bloodshed that involved others laying theirs. Sadly, as it occurred, those who bought into his words of deceit through indoctrination, manipulation or coercion were not as lucky as Echendu. Echendu took off to his heels and absconded to a new life in the United States.

Nigeria has not been blessed with people who genuinely love the country. Rather, it had to contend with those who seek what they could benefit from through illegal and abjectly corrupt means. Many activists possess dual/multiple passports that enable them to flee the country at the slightest indication of problem or chaos. We have violent instigators whose children and family members are kept safe in foreign climes while they provoke anarchies and hostilities under the guise of revolution, activism, or freedom fighting. For such people, they have a gullible infantry of mostly young people who often buy their "revolutionary" ideologies and violent instigations to cause social unrest.

In general, activism in Nigeria must ensure the unity and progress of the entire country and citizens' true freedom and liberty. Northern groups in the country need to look at their backyard and honestly tell if their societies had the appearance of growth and development, despite having a larger number of representatives in the country's political history. Southern groups should also ask their representatives what they have achieved with the "little" billions at their disposal. Civil society groups that have allowed themselves to be used as tools of manipulation and extortion should not be alarmed when their acts backfire. The segment of citizens that continue to predict and actively orchestrate doom should not also be surprised when the result of their prophecies and actions eventually boomerangs.

Nigeria will begin the process of greatness when we set aside anti-democratic practices that are damaging to the growth of modern societies. We must look at actual problems to draw lasting solutions, rather than being predictors and facilitators of doom and anarchy, as the case has been since our independence.

Inelegant Conclusion

A police officer, who at the time was a DCP, once told me of an incident that led to a bloodbath between rival political factions. According to him, the police, under his command, tried to prevent the two factions from holding rallies on the same day and instituted such a warning to the relevant parties in accordance with the provision of the Public Order Act. However, to his surprise, both parties went ahead to hold rallies at the same location and at the same time. Reportedly, their actions led to the death of several party members and many injuries were recorded from both sides.

According to the officer, some of those who flagrantly disobeyed the Public Order Act and warnings he issued were notable human rights activist groups from both sides who had earlier lamented on every media station how police were trying to deny them their fundamental rights. I put it to him that the police should have been there to offer protection to those people regardless of the obstinate behaviours of the political factions. He responded by saying, and I agree with him, that the best way to protect them was to have followed the police procedural advice. He added that his men barricaded off the areas, but the parties went as far as breaching those barricades to have their way.

Nigerians, as I have come to realise, are aggressively stubborn people who love what they see abroad but will readily disobey all norms relating to sanity right here in Nigeria. Nigerian "activists" do not consider the effect of their activities on the general populace and arrogantly believe that everyone must abide by their set objectives. In their invented world of dogmatism, anyone who disagrees with them has been paid, bought or is the nation's enemy. Some overnight human rights activists would block major roads and highways during protests or civil disobedience under the dogmatic assumption that everybody else is in the struggle with them. During the *End SARS* protests, I lamented how it was grossly irresponsible for highways to be blocked by the protesters. I told them that no country permits a set of people to block major highways because they have grievances (although very valid grievances) against the government.

The two-faced countries of the United States, France, Britain and most recently Canada, who supported the protesters, handled their situations exactly how Nigerian officials responded. They declared a state of emergency even when confronted with situations that were not as bad as the *End SARS* period where police stations were burnt, uniformed men "necklaced," and prisons attacked. As it eventually happened, anarchy broke out. Residents were robbed and attacked in their homes, stores and businesses were looted, and public buildings and infrastructures were burnt. Being that protesters have blocked highways and motorways, it was difficult for law enforcement officials to affect immediate responses.

As regards the "Lekki tollgate massacre", as a private investigator, I find it inappropriate to accept falsified, biased, manipulated, distorted or prejudiced reportage as acceptable pieces of evidence. The military's presence and use of live ammunition to disperse the crowd is condemnable and does not need to be exaggerated for political or selfish reasons. However, the spread of fake news that dozens or even hundreds of people were killed and carted away (without single evidence to prove such) is devilish, to say the least. It is also arrogant and lunatic to blackmail others into believing such an incident occurred while shoving manipulative propaganda down people's throats in a world where criminal pieces of evidence are hard to suppress in such an open environment as the Lekki tollgate.

Such spirit of caution, as I imbibed, is not one that many Nigerians have learnt to adopt, especially concerning the condemnation of their country. It has become an innate behaviour of many Nigerians to use the least available opportunity to yell to the world that their country is in danger. Ironically, the same people who uncontrollably tell the world that their country is burning are expectant to see foreign investments and opportunities in same burning geographical terrain. Jokers!

5: CHALLENGES OF A MUDDLED NATION

Nigeria is a country of many burdens and challenges that prevent real growth and development. With those challenges, the "glory days" Nigerians fervently hope and crave for might forever be elusive. Some persistent socio-economic issues and challenges are unemployment, a non-functional currency exchange system, a shattered education system, bad fiscal policies, terrible economic management, indiscipline, impunity culture, crime and corruption, inadequate social planning, and disadvantageous foreign policies. Some of these issues have been covered adequately in this book and its prequel, others will be covered in the remaining pages, and some will understandably escape attention.

Aside from activities and behaviours that are purely criminal, some sociocultural issues continues to create significant problems for the country in general. The issues are broad, lengthy, multifaceted and strenuous. An extremely complex society like ours continue to defy research that has been carried out or is still being carried out to tackle societal problems across the globe. That is why some of the world's most recommended socio-economic policies introduced to our clime have failed woefully, even as the same policies have recorded significant successes elsewhere.

Many people wonder why the country is grossly underdeveloped (at least by citizens' standards) despite its abundant natural, material and human resources. The country does not lack the resources to reach its development goals. Its resources have been inefficiently utilised. Nigeria's unnecessary burdens are sharply inimical to the growth and development of any progressive-minded society. Every administration in Nigeria, either at federal or regional levels, comes in to meet weighty burdens that no governments in any saner clime should have to accost on their arrival to governance. As you will read, Nigerians always suffer the consequences of allowing those burdens to become part of our national feature.

A Broken Education System

The education system's failure is a microcosm of everything that failed in Nigeria. It is implausible for a nation to progress in other areas of development while its education sector deteriorates. Nigeria's educational problems can be traced to the period during the colonial administration. History recalls that the indirect rule system during colonisation meant that formal education was not compelled on northern indigenes. Also, Christian missionaries, who founded many "mission" schools, were discouraged from extending their activities to Northern areas. The North-South education disparity continued for much of the colonial period until the country set sail for a voyage to independence. Suddenly, northern leaders became aware of the wide disparity between their natives and southerners and immediately acknowledged the role of formal education in the grand scheme of social development. The awareness that education is a compulsive instrument to achieving modern development became a strong political campaign point by politicians. From there, some of the country's problems began.

Before and after independence, politicians used education as a political and electioneering tool. At a point, some political leaders were less concerned with equipping their indigenes with quality education. Rather, they hurried them through the educational ladder to match the competitive challenges of regional politics. Not wanting to be left out of slots in politics, the economy, the civil service and the military, regional leaders manipulated the education system to the demerit of national progress. Although elegantly called education, on the contrary, people wanted to possess a paper (educational certificate) that could get them to work and better their lives only because their politicians told them so. The resultant effect was the awarding of underserving educational certificates to their indigenes.

The aforementioned analysis sufficiently summarises the beginning of the country's certificate syndrome, where institutions churned out unqualified graduates into the society.

The various systems of education introduced in the country, such as the basic form of education administered by the missionaries and the subsequent 6-5-4/6-3-3-4 systems, were fairly in line with universal practice. Nigeria being Nigeria, so many external factors crept in and ensured that the educational sector unpredictably became a curse of its own. One such factor was the maladministration of the education system by a combination of public officials and policymakers who failed to envisage a well-planned future for the country's youths. Another factor was the erroneous misinterpretation citizens had concerning education and its possible benefits. People prepared their children for future white-collar job opportunities without considering the sustenance and growth of other sectors. They enrolled in educational institutions with a very misleading notion created and pushed to citizens that education is an automatic pathway to pull them out of poverty, not necessarily how it could help positively shape their mindset. Prospective graduates became self-centred in their ambitions and were unconcerned with making positive contributions to their immediate society or the nation. People who had enrolled their children in schools had selfish agendas that only intended to benefit their immediate family and no one else. They were reaping from the public purse to fund their education but were unwilling to contribute back to the same society that afforded them such privileges. The country's education system became a farce and was bound to be broken eventually.

Public officials proved unconcerned or largely unprepared to cater for the educational needs of the populace despite the large numbers of people who kept enrolling in institutions. Eventually, administrators could not balance the application and enrolment rates with available resources to cater for the education sector. Applications to various institutions started to overwhelm budgeted funds for the education sector. Citizens, believing in the policy of "free" education promised them by politicians, failed to prepare their children for a well-funded educational system and a better future. As schools, institutions and classrooms became overcrowded, and the education sector generally deteriorated, the private sector became the first profiteers and innocent children of the poor as the first casualties.

Educationists began opening up private schools across the country to address the overpopulation problem in the educational sector. The private schools created class segregation among rich, middle-class and lower-class members of the public. The elites' ability to send their children to private schools did more damage to public schools, which began to suffer systemic abandonment and neglect.

Public officials also began to embezzle funds meant to sustain the educational sector since they had nothing to lose, with none of their children in public schools. School teachers were owed months of salaries or, in some cases, underpaid. School buildings became dilapidated, libraries were short of books and research materials, and school laboratories had more rats than equipment. Mysteriously, dangerous elements surreptitiously sneaked cultism and violent confraternity networks into tertiary institutions. Overall, the entire education sector drifted into ruins. Necessities such as school uniforms, textbooks and other educational materials that the government initially funded became the full responsibility of unprepared parents and guardians. People of means looked away rather than team up to find lasting solutions to the decay in the educational sector. They withdrew their children from public schools and facilitated their transfers to private schools, which kept growing in numbers. More affluent members of the society opted for overseas education.

Today, we cannot pretend that quality education has become the prerogative of the rich. Well-qualified children of people from lesser backgrounds often have their dreams dashed because the children of the elites can always afford to pay their way through, sometimes with lesser qualifications or desire to study. Due to the low admission quotas that are available to most of the country's institutions, commissioners, ministers, permanent secretaries, judges, top military officers, legislators, private millionaires, and billionaires fought their way through to ensure that matriculation slots were afforded to their children, wards or those closely affiliated to them. Where is the sense of justice in all of these when the children of the rich and powerful ridicule children of the poor every day?

The same children whose parents have bought them special privileges are ironically the ones with the loudest voices on social media screaming off about the country's many crises; the same crises they helped propel to their own merits.

The venom of corruption runs from the very top of the country's civil service to its lowest. Unqualified persons became education commissioners, ministers, principals and school heads. Maladministration and incompetence contributed to the lack of supervision and proper management of activities in various learning bodies. Absenteeism, examination malpractice, corruption, money-for-grade, sex-for-grade, sexual harassment and other untellable ills became common in learning institutions by students and officials.

As I have said repeatedly in this book and to serve as a firm reminder, for every time it has been convenient to blame our leaders for the woes that befell the country, the citizens must equally share an equal proportion.

Nigerians, for instance, allowed politicians to get away with the use of deceitful electioneering mantras such as the hammerings on "free" education to solicit their votes. The family is, by nature, the first institution of socialisation and learning but is in complete tatters today. The worsening level of bribery and corruption in our societies today has its roots in the complicity of parents who nurtured their children through the rudiments of bribery and corruption.

My first encounter with the menace of examination malpractice was at a Lagos State Common Entrance Examination I sat for in 1998. I could vividly remember how a tall, dark-skinned man occasionally entered the examination hall to call out a list of examination pupils. He would come in to hand something I later found out to be pre-answered examination papers to the pupils and would depart, only to appear intermittently to repeat the same. Such a practice was strange and incomprehensible at that time to a naïve Johnny JamJam. Nonetheless, it soon became clear to me that it was a ubiquitous practice in Nigeria, where corruption was, and is, conducted as a brazenly open affair. The culture and engagement in examination malpractice did not end at the primary level. Wayward pupils carried the syndrome along with them into secondary and tertiary institutions to the extent that they could not achieve any feat without the involvement of malpractice and corruption. I can convincingly say that at a point, the country's corruption level in the education sector was so high that entrance examinations such as WAEC and JAMB were nothing but a pure façade. Persons not wanting to be left out of the degree-awarding spree - erroneously termed as education - subscribed their children to "special centres" to amplify higher grades, thereby facilitating their chance of acceptance into institutions of their choice. Through that pattern, we have successfully created a pathway for some of the most unqualified persons to secure educational degrees they were never qualified to possess, to the detriment of qualified people from noble backgrounds.

Such people continue to become corrupt public and political office holders who manifest the same behavioural pattern to inflict injuries on us collectively. They are able to get elevated to the top ladder of power and authority thanks to an educational system that taught them the rudiments of fraud, bribery and corruption rather than the opposite.

Examination malpractice at all levels must be frowned upon and abolished from our schools and educational systems. We cannot continue to allow our public and private schools to become breeding grounds for fraud, bribery and corruption. We cannot continue to allow teachers and schools to abandon their primary duties of teaching students for the morally reprehensible behaviour of helping them to engineer malpractices of all kinds. Many schools today have secured for themself a bragging right of having close to perfect examination results in government-conducted examination sittings. That is not because they are necessarily good regarding teaching and general aspects of education, but because they are good at conniving with authorities to cheat and manipulate the system and society.

The dynamic changes that swept the global community in urbanisation, civilisation, science, technology, and other educational growth and development greatly exposed the weakness of our educational system. The changes meant more funding was needed for the country's education sector, which had relied on archaic methods and obsolete structures since independence. Nevertheless, it also indicated that things were about to get worse. Suppose political leaders of the country had the gift of socio-economic telepathy, foresight and vision. In that case, they should have known that the rapid advancement in science and technology meant that governments could no longer singlehandedly fund tertiary institutions and, to some extent, the whole of the education sector.

Education moved from the basic arrangement sharply into one where areas such as computer technology, science, space technology, medical science, military science, criminal science, modern economics and R&D became necessary and compulsive for any society with any hope of moving forward. The modern education system rapidly moved into an age that requires each student to be compulsively armed with learning instruments, comprising laptop computers, the internet, smartphones, well-equipped laboratories, fully updated libraries, updated syllabuses and mechanised backup plans. As the world moved their respective education systems into a new phase, Nigerians obstinately assumed education as one that comprised only books, blackboards, uniforms and sandals; at least, that was the standard up until I graduated from a fairly respected high school (Baptist Academy, Obanikoro, Lagos) in 2004. As I have gathered, that is still the standard up to this very day in 2022.

In most western countries, individuals and non-governmental bodies fund tertiary institutions privately. At best, tuition is assisted through government subsidies, support, grants, and other assistance. In Nigeria, federal and state governments pay little attention to the education sector, with some state governments allocating a disappointing percentage of their budget expenditure to education. Education in Nigeria became so politicised that an entitlement culture among the citizens has allowed it to become forbidden for anyone to talk about its privatisation. It later became obvious that the insistence on free education came at a price that carries the proverbial symbolism of a "penny wise, pound foolish" situation.

Contrary to the popular perception that tertiary education should be free, there is no such thing as free education. No country in the world offers free education, and nothing financially or economically related could be said to be free, at least by simple logic. The debate as to whether the government should fully fund tertiary education or not is one I am not particularly interested in accommodating. The proponents of such a misleading conception that tertiary education should be free are stubbornly unrealistic and rigid in their folly regarding modern societies' practicalities. They are quick to mention tuition-free countries like Germany, Sweden or Norway, yet forget to highlight the contributing factors that made such feats possible in those countries. Those factors are not afforded to even the world's most developed countries, such as the UK, the US, Canada, and France.

To Nigeria's credit, our tertiary education is one of the cheapest in the world. In honesty, however, that conclusion is greatly misleading and paradoxical. Still, it is a true-life statement that could be wholly accepted as factual or thrown into the bin based on its illogicality, depending on who is talking and who is listening. Nigerians may think they benefit from a system that gives them free education, but in reality, it is a system that encourages corruption, hypocrisy, fraud, failure and deceit. The human capital flight (also known as brain drain) that has seen the country lose some of its best brains to foreign countries illustrates this paradoxical scenario. Armed with a certificate from a Nigerian institution that gave them something close to free education, citizens abandon Nigeria post-haste for a better future abroad. They take along with them the cost incurred (through the public purse) in educating them at the expense of those that could have contributed to our nation. The effect of such an ominous trend is that those migrants continue to cheat the Nigerian public purse, which had educated them. Despite getting educated in Nigeria, the country gains nothing in return, except losing them to foreign countries that had no impact on their education. Also, they cheat foreign citizens abroad who had spent hefty amounts to obtain their tertiary education yet are unable to secure jobs because Nigerian migrant workers are preferred for job offers due to their willingness to settle down for relatively lower salaries, among other things.

On funding of tertiary institutions, educational administrators in Nigeria are known to lobby for positions they see as a means of self-enrichment and personal glorification rather than one that enables them to offer distinguished services to the academic community. Universally, the job of an educational administrator is among the toughest and affords no room for sinecure. Some heads of universities and tertiary institutions around the world pride themselves on the amount of money they gather from every possible source. I am inclined to use facts, numbers and figures to drive a solid point in this regard and draw a nexus between funding and educational administration. According to the Council for Advancement and Support of Education (CASE) in the US, a total of $53 billion was given as donations to colleges and universities in the United States for the fiscal year 2021; **two times Nigeria's total expenditure budget for 2021.**

Table showing the total amount donated to tertiary institutions in the US in 2021.[1]

Donors	Percentage of Donation	Amount (USD Billions) est.
Foundations	33.1%	$17.5
Alumni	23.2%	$12.3
Non-Alumni individuals	16.6%	$8.8
Corporations	13.2%	$7.0
Others	13.9%	$7.4

Table showing the endowment funds for some top US, UK, and Canada institutions for 2021.[2]

Institution	State (Country)	Endowment (USD Billions) est.
Harvard University	Massachusetts (US)	$53.2
Yale University	Connecticut (US)	$42.9
Stanford University	California (US)	$37.8
Princeton University	New Jersey (US)	$37.7
University of Cambridge	Cambridge (UK)	$10.0
University of Oxford	Oxford (UK)	$8.5
University of Toronto	Toronto (Canada)	$2.5
University of British Columbia	British Columbia (Canada)	$1.6

The figures above show the willingness of foreign individuals and non-governmental bodies to fund their education sector. As seen above, it is a shame to policymakers in Nigeria that an educational institution like Harvard has an endowment that is twice our country's total expenditure budget. The amount contributed by alums in the US was more than the entire budget for education by Nigeria's federal and state governments for the year 2021. Our failure to hold people accountable for their time in public office is why we are faced with pregnant problems that implode along with the baby and the water. I could strongly contend that members of bodies like ASUU and ASUP are mostly concerned with how much they could milk from public purses and never what they could bring as academicians to their respective institutions and bodies. Respective bodies and organisations are unconcerned with introducing modern policies to achieve educational reforms. Some educational administrators in public institutions are more concerned with their life after retirement and what benefits they could amass than the positive legacies they leave behind.

Poorly trained, inefficient, unruly and incompetent staff at various institutions are why some alumni who could offer financial donations would rather want to be left alone. Most carry animosities of how their institutions had maltreated them. The alum department of some institutions is more interested in extortive mechanisms before they can render any form of support to former students and prospective members. The reader must be warned that he stood a better chance of bypassing the Aso Rock security protocol and meeting with the president than obtaining a transcript from a public tertiary institution in Nigeria.

Learning institutions have been inflicted with the *"la cram la pour"* syndrome. That is a situation where students show absolute disinterest in the learning process other than reading, for the sole purpose of scoring good grades in tests and examinations. Students desperately expend additional resources to abandon the often hostile and unfriendly four-walled buildings we erroneously call educational institutions. That is because tertiary institutions habitually dispense mental torture, stress and fatigue than impart knowledge and proper orientation to students. Gruesome educational calendars, hostile learning environments, and tiresome and unfriendly learning processes are among the few issues facing students at all educational levels.

It has been discovered that teachers across the 6-3-3-4 levels are either unqualified or inexperienced, leading rational minds to question how they intend to give what they do not possess. It has been confirmed that an unacceptable number of primary and secondary school teachers could hardly read or write correctly, at least by teaching standards. Those in tertiary institutions are no better and are notorious for engaging in the bitter waters of school politics for personal gains than the actual practice of teaching and imparting knowledge to students.

In conclusion, our education sector urgently needs a total overhaul involving all tiers of government and well-meaning members of our nation. Tertiary institutions worldwide have become citadels of research and homes to groundbreaking discoveries, especially in economics, medicine, science and technology. We must understand that modern education requires modern-day tools and aides, devices, technological equipment, well-functioning systems, curriculum and proper administration. We can no longer afford to be a society of people that misinterprets a watermarked piece of paper as the hallmark of an educated person when in fact, the holder and bearer of such a paper possess nothing close to the word education.

Our citadels of learning must be purely rinsed of corruption, malpractices, abuse of office, cultism, violence, indiscipline and other ills that are the actual antithesis of education. A broken education system will continue to haunt the general population. A respected American nobleman once said, "An educated citizenry is a vital requisite for our survival as a free people." And if we assumed that we could continue to operate a society that pays little attention to education yet expects miraculous growth, development and stable national security, we are greatly mistaken.

Overpopulation and its Many Problems

The effect of overpopulation as a crushing national burden is primarily underemphasised in Nigeria and Africa. As a topic, it has become taboo in most of our societies and cultures. Throughout my life and time as a researcher, writer, avid reader, private investigator, and most importantly, an African, I can strongly contend that overpopulation is Africa's number one enemy. To avoid doubt and to negate whatever ideological perception the reader might have on the issue of overpopulation, I am inclined to say that this subchapter does not entertain a debate on underpopulation or the general aspect of population. Rather, it intends to focus solely on the disadvantages of "overpopulation". A United Nations publication defined overpopulation as:

> ..the exceeding of certain threshold limits of population density when environmental resources fail to meet the requirements of individual organisms regarding shelter, nutrition and so forth. It gives rise to high rates of mortality and morbidity.[3]

As regards the issue of overpopulation, proponents of uncontrolled population often point to cultural, religious, social, superstitious or other beliefs as to the reason for their intransigence against any form of population control. Nonetheless, a 2015 report by the United Nations aptly opined on the dangers of overpopulation in our world today:

The growth of the world's population over the past 60 years has been unprecedented. World population reached 7.3 billion in 2015, twice the number of people that were on the planet in 1969, reflecting the progress that has been made in combating infectious and childhood diseases and in reducing the burden of premature and avoidable deaths, especially in the poorest countries of the world. Nevertheless, the rapid growth of the world's population, in combination with increasing prosperity, higher standards of living and unsustainable patterns of consumption and production, has led to growing concerns about the impact of human actions on the environment. While the relationship between population size and growth, consumption, technology and the environment is far from simple, lower population growth combined with more responsible patterns of consumption and production would ease pressure on ecosystems to generate food, preserve natural resources and allow the world more time to identify and adopt new technologies...In addition, continued rapid population growth in some countries complicates and exacerbates the challenges associated with delivering basic services and ensuring that no one is left behind. Slower population growth would enable families and Governments to invest more in the health and education of each child, creating a virtuous circle with benefits for the economic, social and environmental dimensions of sustainable development. At the same time, there are a number of countries in which population growth is already very low, or is even starting to decrease, a situation that poses an entirely different set of challenges for achieving sustainable and inclusive growth.[4]

According to WHO, overpopulation is one of the leading causes of the speedy occurrence and emergence of human diseases. Overpopulation worsens numerous environmental and social factors such as pollution, malnutrition, overcrowded living conditions, and lacking health care, which makes poor communities vulnerable to infectious diseases. Diseases such as tuberculosis, malaria, HIV, and dysentery spread faster in overpopulated areas.[5] In this part of the world, it is certain that policymakers, leaders and citizens alike do not have a plan to steady and control the population per the suggestions carefully spelt out by the United Nations (as succinctly quoted above).

The issue of overpopulation and its possible solutions are very complex. Those who ought to have known better had set dangerous precedents. The population issue is systematically used as an avenue for political gains and abetted by the citizens to their detriment. For instance, Nigeria's revenue allocation formulae have ensured that certain regions get revenue allocation based on their total population. As such, politicians from those regions are unconcerned with overpopulation's demerits but continue to see it as a source of revenue. Our electoral system also encourages rigging and fraud since particular regions rely on their overpopulation status to dictate electoral choices over others. Also, the dangerous culture of political grandstanding during electioneering, where unsuspecting electorates are promised "free" government provisions in areas such as education, healthcare and employment, continues to return negative implications. Electorates became unmindful of family planning practices, as they had been hoodwinked into believing their needs would be automatically addressed.

There is also the "Baby Factory" syndrome, where ruthless people benefit from taking advantage of vulnerable women and children for financial purposes. Women and young girls are groomed in carefully selected isolated camps for the sole purpose of childbearing. The children are then displaced all over the country for economic gains, mostly as street beggars in urban areas or as enslaved children, maids and loaned-out workers. Children who are products of baby factories are seen in major metropolitan hubs around the country. They can be found in malls, cinemas, hangout spots, sports facilities, traffic junctions, markets, roads and car parks. While being victims of an organised crime syndicate, the baby factory children are not

226

alone in causing population nightmares on our streets and highways. Nigerian children are abandoned by parents who hardly remember they possess a biological product. Such children eventually develop the habit of fighting for competitive spots in the notorious and horrific sport of begging as their only chance of survival.

Perhaps innocently, many Nigerians underestimate their roles in the societal losses attributed to overpopulation and how it puts them in a prime position to be regarded as part-time architects of our national problems. Older adults who speak glowingly about how organised the society was decades ago are oblivious to the critical and catastrophic effects of their selfish actions on the larger society. One of such Nigerians, a professor of virology, Professor Oyewale Tomori, wept while addressing a group of Nigerians during a televised speech on health security. He had these to say:

> I grew up in the UN, which is Utopia Nigeria. For indeed, at that time, Nigeria was a utopia. It will be an insult to call my father polygamous. He was multigamous. The number of his wives that I know is more than all the excellencies and honourables (sic) who are sitting down here today. I came as number thirty-nine in the list of my father's children. We were being bred as hands for his farm, then we had good governance, just before the colonial masters left. The government of Awolowo introduced free primary education in my region. It was not only free, but it was also compulsory.[6]

As the eminent professor spoke passionately and fondly while recollecting his time growing up in "utopia Nigeria", he was intermittently interrupted with applauses by the "honourables" in attendance who listened to him in agreement and concurrence that the Nigeria of today is in shambles. As expected, the video circulated on social media and everyone acknowledged today's sorry state of the country. However, I am not one to go with the crowd on a road of wrongness, misconception or illogicality. With profound respect to the professor, I feel obliged to highlight the inaccuracies and misleading notions I deduced from his speech.

Firstly, the professor said he grew up in "utopia Nigeria", a period that I presumed coincided with the end of colonial rule, judging from his speech. Therefore, if Nigeria were truly a utopian state, as the professor called it, why did Nigerians decide to leave a utopian state under the leadership of the colonial masters for one of indigenous rule? Is it then safe to say that the professor agreed with my earlier contention that our founding fathers who led us to independence were not ready for the task ahead and had no clue about governance and administration? Secondly, if Nigeria were a utopian state during the period Professor Tomori cited, why were some citizens aggrieved up to the point that their grievances led to several electoral crises, coups and an eventual bloody civil war just a few years after the so-called utopian period? These two questions are outside the bounds of this subchapter's discourse. Still, the condiments of distortion in the professor's speech speak volumes. It also shows how some of our elites have distorted our national history and have also underplayed their own roles in our national woes of today.

The impunity and arrogance with which the professor mentioned the number of his father's children (he was number 39, and one wonders the total number of children his father eventually had) matches the level of societal ignorance on the issue of overpopulation. The professor further highlighted "greedy self-interest" as one of the three killers of "utopia Nigeria".[7] Ironically, the same greed led Professor Tomori's father to give birth to so many children without considering the adverse effects of his actions on the general society. It was only a matter of time before Tomori's father and others realised that the country's "utopian" days were about to be out of luck, all thanks to the population explosion that was never commensurate with developmental growth.

Professor Tomori's father was not alone. Sadly, giving birth to many children is a societal issue that cuts across the Nigerian people throughout the country's entire timeline. Politicians, in their numbers, the elites, the poor, the so-called educated, the uneducated, the mighty, aristocrats, clergies, and everyone else saw human reproduction as an illustrious achievement or some pathway to futuristic greatness. Those who advocate that people can give birth to as many children as they can as long as they have the financial means fail to recognise the changing dynamics of our modern world. Some rich people end up with recalcitrant children who adopt illicit behaviours due to their parent's inability to guide them away from societal vices. Similarly, impoverished persons end up giving birth to social delinquents yet blame the government for its inability to employ such naturally unemployable people.

Like Professor Tomori, another notable Nigerian whose combination of ignorance and arrogance could always be deduced from his words is the former president of the Ijaw Youth Council, Asari-Dokubo. In a video released on his social media page, he had this to say:

> (I have) 21 children, why will I not (have more), my grandfather had 53 children, and I am going to have 106 children. Children are the strength of a man.[8]

The words of Asari-Dokubo, an influential man with a self-acclaimed status as a freedom fighter and activist, are horrific reflections of our backwardness as a people. The notorious influence of such a man is so strong that he garnered enormous support and followership across the Ijaw nation, one that has made him a folk hero in the Niger Delta region. While Asari-Dokubo was constantly at loggerheads with political and societal leaders who refused to do his bidding, he was also building an enormous societal monster called overpopulation behind his backyard. His words, like his actions that preceded him, if taken into practice by his followership, have perilous effects rather than the ability to free them from socio-economic bondage, as he Asari-Dokubo erroneously believed.

Professor Tomori and Asari-Dokubo were not alone. They have cohorts in the field of politics and decision-making. One such person is Nigeria's Majority Leader of the House of Representatives representing Doguwa/Tudun Wada Federal Constituency of Kano State, Alhassan Ado Doguwa. In a bid to remind us of how "powerful" he was at home, he had this to say:

> Mr Speaker, I would like to let you know with me today here are my four respected wives...Mr Speaker, honourable members, I have asked them to rise up to respect the House on behalf of my family and one other reason to let you know that when members call me a powerful man, I am not only powerful on the floor of the house, I am also powerful at home. Mr Speaker, these four wives you have seen have produced 27 kids for me, and I am still counting and counting.[9]

Before I go any further and for relevance, here was the response of the House Speaker, Rt. Hon Femi Gbajabiamila to Honourable Doguwa:

> I must bring to the knowledge of this house a little anecdote what you told me some time ago, you told me...It was getting late..around 7 O'clock, there were many children playing in front of your house in Kano, in your compound and you got worried. You went out and told the children, come on, what are you doing at this time of the day? You people should go to your homes. And one of them said, haha baba, this is my house. So he was one of those 27 children, but unfortunately, I guess the more, the merrier, you get my point.[10]

Rt. Hon Gbajabiamila's response to the Majority Leader is indicative that despite financial capabilities, other crucial necessities of child upbringing and development could still be missing. Other underlying issues that

230

accompanied Hon. Doguwa's words, such as his disgusting display of entitlement behaviour, a privileged culture and misogyny, have been addressed in this book. Coincidentally and oddly, I was writing this paragraph when my security assistant informed me that the House Leader, Alhassan Doguwa, had welcomed his 28th child, indicating his trueness to "continue counting". Hon. Doguwa's mental approach and behaviour are frightening due to the nature of his position.

To be fair, despite the lack of respect for logic shown by the honourable member of the House of Reps, I contend that he could be duly representing his constituents' views and that his behaviours are well in line with the cultural practices of his constituents. After all, Doguwa's father, a politician and member of the Kano State House of Assembly under the defunct Third Republic, reportedly had 40 children before he passed away.[11] While speaking to journalists, Honourable Alhassan Doguwa vehemently defended his position by citing religion and cultural background as his motivating factors while also sending a threat of possible action against potential maligners of his cultural and religious practice. Nonetheless, liberal-minded progressives are beginning to fault Doguwa's position. Former Governor of the CBN and Emir of Kano, HRH Sanusi Lamido Sanusi, is one of such people who have consistently called for social reforms. HRH Sanusi had this to say during a colloquium to mark his 60th birthday:

> Since I am wearing two caps- as an economist and an Islamic scholar, I need to say that at the level of the North and Muslims, we need to look hard at ourselves and questions the choices that we have made...As Emir of Kano, we got scholars to sit for three years. We drafted a Muslim Code of Personal Status that began to address some of these issues. That law was ready in 2019, but it has not been passed. I also sent it to the Chairman of the Northern States Governors' Forum, the Governor of Plateau State, and said, in case any of the governors need it, give it to them. I have not heard

anything. But we keep talking about poverty in the North. We keep talking about Almajirai. These Almajirai did not produce themselves...If you cannot maintain one wife and you marry three; if you cannot maintain three children and you have 17; if you leave those children on the streets without education, without training, you are going to have young men that would be a problem to our society...The youths that you see on drugs, those that are into stealing and kidnapping are all products of that social system. And we need to ask ourselves, is this what Islam said we should have? Are these the children that Islam said we should have?[12]

To move the country forward, Nigerians must decide where to pitch their tents. Deeply progressive and profound messages such as that of the Emir that include calls for proactivity often come back to haunt its preachers. Therefore, it was unsurprising that the state Governor deposed the revered statesman as the Emir. Apparently, Kano citizens did not share the views of their deposed Emir.

Muhammadu Sanusi II is not alone within the spectrum of Nigeria's high and mighty calling for immediate monitoring and control of the country's population. Former President, Chief Olusegun Obasanjo, during an interview with the *BBC HARDtalk* programme, highlighted the menace of overpopulation as Africa's biggest killer of socio-economic growth; he had this to say:

If you ask me what is my greatest worry about Africa, I will say demography. There are other problems, leadership, governance, corruption, lack of adequate infrastructure, but they are either being improved upon, or they are a passing phase, but demography is a ticking bomb.[13]

It might be right to apportion to Chief Obasanjo his share of the Nigerian blame, especially since he held political power longer than any other individual since the country's birth. Nonetheless, when it comes to the issue of overpopulation, it would seem as if citizens themselves should shoulder the blame and gross irresponsibility for their intransigence towards issues that could have made their lives better.

For one, I grew up during the days when the National Orientation Agency and other sister agencies ran heavy adverts, infomercials, and programs on the importance of family planning and other population control mechanisms. During those periods, while the government and its many agencies were advising the masses on the need to embark on family planning practices, citizens simply proved obstinate. However, citizens could be taking notes from their societal, religious and political leaders, many who did not lead by example. A political leader like Alhassan Doguwa is a notable example. For Chief Obasanjo, he noted the roles played by culture and religion in the fight against overpopulation; he was right; he was spot on.

Ironically and quite laughable, when the HARDtalk interviewer, Stephen Sackur, asked the former president how many children he had fathered, the latter used a cultural norm as a resource to dodge the question by saying, "in my own part of the world, we don't count children".[14] When Sackur pressed further by offering to help the veteran political tactician by putting the number at "20 or more", Chief Obasanjo responded by saying "yes". Stephen Sackur, unimpressed, pointed out to the former president that he was part of the overpopulation problem that he had cited. Admirably, the elder statesman yielded and admitted he had told his children and all those who cared to listen not to follow the same faulty route as he had done.[15]

Regarding culture, tradition and religion, several underlying factors are attached to the issue of population control and its many challenges. For instance, modern-day practices that could help control our population (such as same-sex marriage, abortion, birth control medical procedures and family planning) are incidentally frowned upon in most of our societies. I intend to stick to my earlier commitment not to make this book an avenue for ideological arguments. Nonetheless, I strongly contend it is time for us to facilitate a change in thinking in the fight against adverse cultural practices. Cultural, traditional or religious practices that impede our progress and future generations must be abolished or put under rigorous check.

We cannot excuse the culpability of the poor masses, and their ignorance and obdurate behaviours remain indefensible. For instance, it would amount to gross unfairness to hold the patriarch of Yoruba politics, Chief Obafemi Awolowo, entirely complicit for innocuously promising and fulfilling his promises of free basic education, healthcare and housing to the masses, even as the promises returned negative consequences. The erroneous mentality where people carry a superstitious belief in a "better" yet unplanned future must be faulted. These situations could only be explained using real-life illustrations and ones that best describe the nexus between poverty and overpopulation in our nation.

Appropriately, a major chunk of the blame must go to Baba Jinadu, who wrongly thought it was a clever idea to have dozens of children as an insurance and retirement scheme, thereby putting enormous pressure on classrooms, schools and the overall education budget. Similarly, the civil servant, Papa Nnamdi has engaged in a child-breeding spree thereby making a mess of the government's free housing policy. Government housing schemes created to accommodate a family of five now average fifteen occupants. Thanks to people like Baba Jinadu and Papa Nnamdi, most public buildings and infrastructure have become eyesores.

There is also a construction of stagnancy and impoverishment that is not often discussed regarding the issue of overpopulation, yet a ubiquitous trend in most rural and suburban areas. Again, the reader should permit me to continue analysing this trend through the use of factual societal illustrations. Jeju's father is impoverished, but he is the eighth of twelve children. Jeju's father, being poor, unsurprisingly, could not afford to give his children quality education, wealth transfer, inheritances or any such recourse to financial success. For Jeju, any step he takes that gives him an advantage towards a better life is destined to see him hit apparent stagnancy. That is because an entitlement culture encourages his immediate and extended family members to rely on him for daily expenses or to require constant financial assistance. Many Nigerian societies are shamelessly designed like this and habitually meant to ensure that hardworking people like Jeju's quality/standard of life does not get any better. People like Jeju work in futility because the more they earn or get closer to success, the more a large pool of dependence pegs them back. Sadly, there are ominous predictions showing things are not about to change.

A privately conducted interview indicates a predictively devastating future for the Nigerian economy and the nation. Of the 72 Nigerians I interviewed, within the age bracket of 35-50, encompassing both genders and representing different ethnicities and religious backgrounds, I arrived at the following:

- 53 out of the 72 people interviewed have at least a child.
- A confounding 51 out of the 72 respondents are affirmative of their plans to have at least 6 children.
- A more significant number of the respondents still believe in the misogynistic "must be male" construct, leading them to believe in the "as much as possible till I have a male child" theory.
- 33 out of the 72 respondents are either unemployed or have no means of income.
- 31 out of the 39 who earn income make below N50,000 monthly.

The above investigative research indicates a laid down road to eventual and perpetual poverty that Nigerians continue to embark upon by themselves. It also indicates that most Nigerians are willing to labour (probably in vain) all through their entire existence to cater for children they need not bring into an already penurious society. Regrettably, the future looks bleak and prophetically dangerous regardless of present or futuristic economic plans and policies. My private investigation and research also correspond with devastating predictions by the United Nations and other relevant organisations that human population has greatly dwarfed available resources.

Furthermore, my private investigation visits to different camps of Internally Displaced Persons (IDPs) between 2014 and 2016 show a cancerous culture of entitlement. There, IDPs ignore the heavy pressure their status puts on their host by engaging further in uncontrolled child breeding. I witnessed families give birth to as many as four to eight children within the time limit given to them by their host camps and communities. One Garba Mohammed, himself an IDP, told me confidently:

> I have been told several times to leave this place, but I don't have anywhere to go with my four wives and 21 children. I need a job and something from the government monthly to cater for my family and me before I can leave here. I was a transporter before the crisis, and now I am here but nowhere to go. They cannot keep treating me like this harassing me to leave for others to come.

The words of Garba Mohammed and those who think like him are very disturbing. His arrogance and entitlement culture typify the grave dangers of overpopulated families and societies and how they have become a national burden through their obsession with illogical practicality. The entitlement culture that allows Garba to seek compensation for a pandemic he intentionally and ignorantly created must be eradicated. Suppose the book is still in doubt about the absolute demerits and threats of overpopulation of humans. In that case, the below illustration should hopefully put such doubt to eternal rest:

The table below shows the disparity between populations of African countries at independence and now (2020) in comparison with their colonisers.[16] Figures are in millions.

Country	Independence	(2020)	Colonialist	Independence	(2020)
Nigeria	45.14 mil (1960)	206.13 mil	UK	52.4 mil	67.22 mil
Congo DR	15.25 mil (1960)	89.61 mil	Belgium	9.135 mil	11.56 mil
Tanzania	10.35 mil (1961)	59.73 mil	UK	52.8 mil	67.22 mil
South Africa	17.52 mil (1961)	59.31 mil	UK	52.8 mil	67.22 mil
Kenya	8.929 mil (1963)	53.77 mil	UK	53.65 mil	67.22 mil
Uganda	7.216 mil (1962)	45.74 mil	UK	53.25 mil	67.22 mil
Sudan	6.732 mil (1956)	43.85 mil	UK	51.265 mil	67.22 mil
Angola	7.024 mil (1975)	32.87 mil	Portugal	9.093 mil	10.31 mil
Mozambique	10.17 mil (1975)	31.26 mil	Portugal	9.093 mil	10.31 mil
Ghana	6.069 mil (1957)	31.07 mil	UK	51.495 mil	67.22 mil
Madagascar	5.099 mil (1960)	27.69 mil	France	46.62 mil	67.39 mil
Cote d'Ivoire	3.503 mil (1960)	26.38 mil	France	46.62 mil	67.39 mil
Niger	3.206 mil (1958)	24.21 mil	France	44.659 mil	67.39 mil
Burkina Faso	4.699 mil (1958)	20.90 mil	France	44.659 mil	67.39 mil
Mali	5.264 mil (1960)	20.25 mil	France	46.62 mil	67.39 mil
Malawi	4.032 mil (1964)	19.13 mil	UK	54 mil	67.22 mil
Zambia	3.463 mil (1964)	18.38 mil	UK	54 mil	67.22 mil
Senegal	3.038 mil (1958)	16.74 mil	France	44.659 mil	67.39 mil
Chad	3.002 mil (1960)	16.43 mil	France	46.62 mil	67.39 mil

As the above illustration shows, the population explosion in Nigeria and Africa is responsible for a wide range of challenges. The table expressly shows why Africa's enormous population seems to be the causal factor for unattainable progress and why its abundant resources cannot take care of its people. Comparatively, it shows a disappointing disparity between African countries and their former colonies. Another challenge is that, with Nigeria surrounded by extremely impoverished countries, any potential economic victory our country stood to gain is tantamount to setting off a massive immigration crisis and influx of citizens from its poorer neighbours. The ongoing migrant crisis in sub-Saharan Africa is highly delicate and complex as it jeopardises any country's ability to grow steadily, progressively, and uninterruptedly.

Nigerians and Africans need constant reminders about the dangers of overpopulation and the disproportionate breeding of humans into an unplanned world. The issue of overpopulation goes beyond trivial school debates on selected topics for the amusement of others. It is not subject to controversy at the beer parlour or merely for social media commentary. It is a real-life issue with catastrophic and dangerous consequences if not immediately tackled. As noted earlier, high levels of poverty, aggravated rates of criminality, an implosion of crowdedness in urban areas, ever-rising debt and inflation, and depletion of natural resources and social amenities, among others, are the dangers of overpopulation to our societies. Suppose we do not curtail the unrealistic and callous birthing of generations without putting adequate plans to accommodate them. In that case, we are in deep trouble, and Nigeria, prophetically, in the words of Chief Olusegun Obasanjo, is "sitting on a time bomb" and only waiting for an explosion.

Culture of Impunity: "A Very Undisciplined People"

A culture of impunity is the certificate of freedom through which all past, present and mostly repetitive illegal and immoral acts are enabled, primarily because offenders are allowed to go unpunished. The culture of impunity is the blank check people need to spend and purchase whatever they like in the regretful markets of indiscipline, immorality and crime. An impunity culture, aided by political leaders, societal leaders and public officials, is the pivotal encouragement for all forms of immoral, dishonest, and criminal behaviours.

Impunity spreads contagiously and has become a national epidemic across the length and breadth of our country. It is perpetuated through all walks of life, regardless of tribe, ethnicity, religion, affiliation, class, status, age or gender. Impunity culture allows individuals and groups to brazenly effect misconduct without being met with a corresponding level of consequences. It also encourages others to follow in their footsteps. Impunity ensures people have the motivation and urge to perpetuate unpatriotic behaviours. With an impunity culture, people are encouraged to outdo, outmatch and outperform one another in dirty schemes.

At the deep end of our national conscience, valid questions are waiting to be answered. How did we become a country of people with so much disregard for the rule of law? How did we allow Nigeria to become a playground for the most riotous, uncultured and ill-mannered citizens? How did we allow those in power and authority to abuse their privileges on our watch? Despite our country being regarded as one of the most religious countries in the world, could we rightly boast that our attributes match the standard of purity enshrined in the country's two Abrahamic religions? Finally, at what point did it go wrong that we allowed our nation to become a fertile ground for crime and its endorsement?

This book and its prequel have answered some of the relayed questions. At the same time, we may never get the appropriate answers to a few other questions that demand not just answers but national attention and solution. Nigerians are complicated people to study. By morning, they are cantankerously complaining about the devastating influence of indiscipline, corruption and crime; by night, they are seen engaging in the same acts they so want to get rid of. So mysterious is the average religious Nigerian that he could be seen beating the one-way traffic on his way home from a three-day religious programme while accompanying his undisciplined behaviour with a hurl of insults at those who dared to challenge his acts of waywardness. This particular subchapter might be a repetitive colouration of things addressed previously, but that should be forgiven as I am inclined to repeat and emphasise this ugly feature of our national behaviour and culture.

Year after year, Nigerians tend to outdo and outmatch previously held awards that border on ignominy. Our agents of socialisation have become chief architects of decay. The family value is in complete tatters and has become the chief agent of neglect and abandonment rather than moral guidance and proper upbringing of the Nigerian child. We have realised that places typically perceived as the citadels of purity have become defiled by bad behaviours from those who have no respect for no one. Churches, mosques and other sacrilegious institutions have become desecrated. Traditional palaces, educational institutions, and to very daring extents, locations that share vicinities with police and other crime-fighting agencies are not left out of the inflicted pains of anti-social behaviours. Schools and workplaces have become social grounds where the systematic orchestrations of corrupt acts are taught and carried out in significant proportion. Labour unions in the country are avenues for racketeering, anarchy and recruitment grounds for thuggery and cultism.

It was A. P. J. Abdul Kalam who said that "the cost of discipline is always less than the price of regret, so self-discipline is the biggest investment for success in life".[17] Nigerians must borrow a leaf from the book of wisdom of one of India's most respected and reputable leaders of its political history.

Indiscipline and impunity as dangerous features of our society are closely related. As a fact, a rigorous eradication of the latter could drastically reduce or perhaps eliminate the former. While indiscipline is a gateway to immoral and criminal acts, impunity is the motivating factor that keeps it running. Adopting a zero-tolerance approach to indiscipline is very vital, and every step taken individually is a step towards societal and national progress. It is unsurprising to find indiscipline in humans. It is mostly associated with children, adolescents and young adults, and when left unconstrained, could become a characteristic part of full-grown adults. Indiscipline starts from the individual before spreading into the most influential agents of socialisation, where it can finally spread as a regional, national or even global problem. To understand the rebellious nature of most citizens, the reader should permit me to draw real-life examples of life in Nigeria in the best way possible, starting from notorious and unruly practices on our roads and highways.

Let me introduce you to Tade, a commercial bus driver notorious for driving against traffic and disrespecting road signs. Yet, he is the same individual who constantly laments everything wrong with the country. His indiscipline and disregard for the law typify the mindset and everyday behaviour of the average Nigerian. To make fast daily returns, Tade and his passengers meet each other at a point of equilibrium, where indiscipline is customary. Tade picks them up at undesignated spots insofar as it is convenient for both parties. Tade manoeuvres through traffic congestion by bullying other road users off driving lanes and roads. His passengers are his chief accomplices as they keep mute or even applaud him as he trickily drills his ways around; after all, they are the main beneficiaries of his disorderly conduct by getting to their destinations quicker. When authorities try to discharge their duties by arresting Tade for his undisciplined behaviour, as usual, Tade's passengers are ever-ready to rally behind him in solidarity and support. The helplessness of traffic officials to discharge their duties is partly due to their own level of indiscipline and collaboration, mostly through constant demand for inducement and gratification. Tade's illustration is the norm in Nigeria, especially in metropolitan cities like Lagos, where indiscipline has reached its very pinnacle in almost an unmanageable and irreparable manner. People like Tade lament bitterly about traffic congestion, yet are the ones who orchestrate it, dare I say, in uncontrollably animalistic and wildly behaviours.

241

The indiscipline perpetrated by Tade and others is fully supported by the collaboration of elite societal members and law enforcement officers. My findings into the activities of commercial transport operators in Lagos gave me a better understanding of how law enforcement officers have become the actual enforcers and abettors of indiscipline and impunity. I was convinced that law enforcement officers owned 45% of those areas' yellow transport buses (popularly called danfo). I also found out that law enforcement officers and security personnel, mostly of lower cadre, owned 68% of the tricycles and motorcycles in the same area. Top public servants and well-connected private citizens also act as backbones and pillars of support for the undisciplined transporters. Taking these events into account, it shows that the same people authorised by law to enforce orders have become the chief architects of law-breaking, indiscipline and impunity. Therefore, their drivers are not encouraged to obey traffic rules with the knowledge that they will escape accountability for their misconduct. I have taken this particular issue of traffic indiscipline from its root, as practised by lower-middle cadre citizens like Tade and others. Please permit me to illustrate further how our elites orchestrate their acts of indiscipline, impunity and disregard for law and order.

In saner climes, publicly elected officials, VIPs, oligarchs, celebrities, traditional and religious leaders, and military officers, among others, are naturally the most disciplined members of society. Their charisma helps people who look up to them for reverence, respect and admiration to behave the same way as their elites. The opposite is the case in Nigeria, where our elites are at the end of despicable behaviours. They bully other road users and clog our roads with unessential numbers of vehicular convoys while blazing sounds of sirens everywhere. Police personnel accompanying VIPs have become one of the most notorious users of road networks across the country and simultaneously rank as the unruliest bullies of vehicular usage.

Away from the illustrative topic of road indiscipline, we have people like Alhaji Dangbana, who debases the national currency by spraying it at functions to boost his ego. Yet, they are typically the first to complain about the country's inflation rate. People like Alhaji Dangbana speak highly of foreign currencies when encountering them. His memory abandoned him just as his sense of discipline did when he committed the act of defacing the naira. Our national culture of indiscipline and impunity has made condemnable practices such as monies being sprayed at public functions a noble norm. Of the fact I write, it is misleading for anyone to assume that money spraying is traditionally or culturally related to any ethnic groups or regions of the country, as some have speciously opined. If anything, it is related to a culture of sassiness and disrespect, where people's sensitivity is debased, insulted, defaced and devalued just as it is done to the currency. The money sprayers and the money pickers are both symbolic representations of an undisciplined society where impunity and poverty are destructively interwoven. When allowed to go unpunished, consistent behaviours of indiscipline have ways of opening Pandora's box with a destructive cycle of cataclysmic problems.

The acts of spraying money publicly, which Alhaji Dangbana and his likes thought was an innocuous idea, eventually boomeranged and inspired a "get rich or die trying" generation of young people who would stop at nothing to get money and elevate themselves to the top ladder of a sycophantic society. The Hushpuppi and Woodberry saga constantly reminds us of our brazen disrespect for law and logic. You will recall that Hushpuppi had gotten away, or almost did, with fooling himself as a real estate mogul when he was nothing but a notorious fraudster. He had flattered himself as a talented, hardworking luxury shopper and a motivational speaker, among other things; impressions that he was willing to prove at all costs. Even before his arrest, he went about that entire charade despite the underground world acknowledging him as one of the "hottest" internet fraudsters during the peak of his fraud career. In truth, he was a bona fide Nigerian who had seen people get away with acts of criminality: those higher and those lower than him in status or class. In one of his typical videos, which portrayed his grandiose lifestyle backed up by "inspiring" homilies, he determined that Nigerians should hold politicians accountable rather than question him on his source of livelihood. Obviously, Hushpuppi had learned the acts of criminality from the best: the country's political leaders. Sadly, he failed to learn one key lesson, a very key lesson. He failed to learn that the country he resided in (the UAE) and was perpetrating his fraud was nothing like Nigeria. On the premise of that singular mistake, he paid dearly.

Nigerian criminals seemed to have a compulsive obsession with displaying their ill-gotten wealth flamboyantly. A former US federal law enforcement officer who was part of a group that arrested some Nigerian traffickers in the 1990s confided in m, thus:

I am afraid to tell you that Nigerians are an undisciplined people. They were not like the typical narco guys and mafias we have dealt with for several decades. For some reason, we easily identify them by how they lavishly spend money. We did not mean to profile them at all, but there were other rich, industrious and legitimate people we knew from your country that did not spend money with impunity. A simple investigation and background check always turned out that we were right. We always discover that they are politicians who stole their people's funds, drug traffickers, advance-fee fraudsters, or immigration and visa criminals. In law enforcement, crime is sometimes very difficult to solve as we work with tons of daily tips. For Nigerian criminal gangs, their undisciplined and lavish lifestyle from crime proceeds always gives them out.

On the issue of indiscipline, people like Alhaji Dangbana are joined by Iya Rasheed, the fruit seller, who is notorious for being among a pool of citizens contributing to the heaps of refuse that have overtaken our cities and highways. Iya Rasheed and her fellow marketers have many excuses for their undisciplined attitudes, such as blaming the government for not providing adequate amenities for waste disposal. However, it has been proven that they have no intention whatsoever of using waste disposal infrastructures that are put in place by appropriate authorities.

Cities and communities across the country are in a filthy state because discipline on the part of leaders and citizens is culturally absent. Similarly, thoughts of societal development, waste management, management culture, tidiness and cleanliness orientation are not embedded in our social culture. Such is the problematic nature of Nigeria's negligence to areas of neatness and waste management that even places like hospitals, schools, educational environments, government facilities and buildings, and military and police barracks/stations have become some of the dirtiest environments in our society. Recent reports on issues regarding health and sanitisation in the country have been damning. A recent UNICEF report revealed that 23.5% of the Nigerian population engaged in open defecation, placing the country in another inglorious record of 6th among countries with the highest percentage of open defecation.[18]

Evidence has shown that we pay regretfully for acts of indiscipline, far more than we think. For instance, one could be forgiven for assuming that Iya Rasheed is a pious citizen who is genuinely concerned for the country's predicament when she goes on her often-lengthy rant concerning the country's situations. She does not recognise the health hazard and implications of the dirt she litters on the highways during and after market hours on herself, her family and the entire community. Similarly, her greedy practice of adulterating the fruits she sells would later haunt her. Her children who consume the contaminated fruits have been forced to seek treatments in our overpopulated hospitals. Iya Rasheed is about to discover the trueness of the words of A. P. J. Abdul Kalam that the **"cost of discipline is always cheaper than the price of regret."**

On Iya Rasheed's arrival at the hospital, she is met with undisciplined and unruly hospital attendants. Yet to accept blame for her current predicament and out of irritation but within her right, she fiercely engages a nonchalant Nurse Rose in a shouting march. Nurse Rose customarily ought to have resumed by 8 am as stipulated in her terms of employment, but her supervisor's absenteeism has further encouraged her to resume late culturally. Despite Rose's late resumption to work, she still needed time to settle in by sharing the latest entertainment gist and gossip rounds with other understaffed yet undisciplined colleagues. Nurse Rose, despite her lateness, is in no rush to attend to patients and cannot seem to comprehend why she is questioned over her lateness to work. She presumably expects to be applauded rather than condemned, seeing that she is one of the few hospital personnel who deemed it necessary to make it to work in the first place. For Nurse Rose, she should be applauded for making it late, knowing that a large pool of others did not deem it fit to show up to work. Sadly, Nurse Rose is just one out of an enormous pool of private and public officials who disregard appointed opening and closing office hours. In almost every governmental agency, absenteeism, truancy, and late coming of officials to places of their primary assignments have become commonplace.

Nurse Rose is often apoplectic in the discharge of her duties and unconcerned about the conditions of the patients under her care. Her sense of compassion, emotional intelligence and sympathy has been eroded by the lack of adequate financial compensation that should have followed her professional appointment. It should not go unnoticed that her "I don't care" attitude emanated from a defiant build-up of impudence resulting from her employer's complicities. The hospital's Chief Medical Director is an unfit individual with a dishonourable record, and one who maintains such a position due to nepotistic sentiments from "above." Nurse Rose is also aware that her supervisor is a person who only made his way through medical schools via examination malpractices, bribery and corruption. Therefore, she has little regard for the so-called supervisor or the hospital's Chief Medical Director. She is also aware that senior public officials are in the habit of repackaging expired drugs for sale to unsuspecting patients and health customers. The health commissioner or minister overseeing the collective management of the health sector is an undisciplined man with a history of fraud, corruption and abuse of office. As it would seem, everyone within the organisational structure of the health system has become the opposite definition of health and wealth that symbolises that very institution. As demonstrated, people who permit such acts of gross indiscipline and impunity are not ready for growth and development.

Behaviours such as the one from Nurse Rose are why Nigerian MDAs, corporations, businesses and the overall economy have become moribund. Public servants' lacklustre and undisciplined behaviours are a silent staller of our economic growth and progress. Yet, behaviours like this are never discussed as people have been told to blame only one man, the country's president, for the same national chaos they orchestrate daily.

The average Nigerian lives in habitual delusion. He fantasises that he will live in a developed country one day. Still, it never dawned on him that abnormal behaviours such as trading his wares on major roads, building shanties on waterways, ignoring pedestrian and traffic rules, or other immoral behaviours of such kinds are not permitted in saner climes. I may have to beg for early forgiveness if I sound insensitive or unpatriotic by my presumptions that indiscipline and impunity in Nigeria are more of a psychological disorder that needs to be looked into by medical experts and psychologists for a possible cure. There are valid proofs to support this.

On my flight back to the country from Istanbul, Turkey, during the latter period of the COVID-19 pandemic global lockdowns, I witnessed how Nigerian travellers at the Istanbul Airport behaved with so much discipline. They respectfully engaged officials of Egypt Airlines and Turkish immigration. They followed the COVID-19 protocols at the airport screening section obediently, even without being told what to do, as the step-on lines drawn by the officials were quite noticeable to everyone. On disembarking at the Murtala Muhammed International Airport in Lagos, citizens' rowdy, uncivil and disrespectful attitudes came to life. I realised that whatever positive and patriotic mindset most of those passengers might have had was abandoned at the Istanbul Airport or must have departed from them as they disembarked the Egypt Air plane. The same COVID-19 protocols that were respected and followed a few hours prior at a foreign airport were violated with impunity in their home country. It is instructive to understand that there could be no valid excuse for such unpatriotic and undisciplined acts as similar provisions at the Istanbul airport were equally made available to them at the Lagos Airport. Regardless, they thought it upon themselves to disrespect their fellow citizens and treat their nation contemptuously. This is Nigeria, where acts of indiscipline and national ridicule have become embedded in the hearts of the same people who bitterly lament the state of the nation.

As I previously opined, the words "indiscipline" and "impunity" are not inseparable aspects of each other. They encompass a circle of entities that destroy every fabric of decent societies. Indiscipline reached a climax across Nigerian societies to such an extent that people would shut down major streets, roads and highways just to observe personal celebrations. Bribery, corruption, theft, electoral fraud, "419", sexual assault, human trafficking, traffic violations, and even the most violent crimes committed in Nigeria all move freely under the safe umbrella of impunity. Nigerians do not understand the catastrophe of impunity culture. I have observed with keen interest, and with a huge garment of disturbance, the fantastically shambolic opinion of Nigerians as regards petty crimes. For instance, some are of the wrong opinion that authorities expend their resources in pursuing petty thieves and do not do enough to pursue the rich and mighty wrongdoers. It has become common to see condemnation of arrests of petty criminals by some misguided segments of the citizens on social media platforms.

To start with, our elite class of criminals and "big men" crooks did not gain their ignoble status at the top of the criminal food chain overnight. A culture of impunity allowed them to steal, loot and carry out their activities unimpeded. To put it straightforwardly, the man who stole N100 and was allowed to go free is coming back to steal N1,000, after which he would steal N10,000. Unimpeded and unconstrained, he would become impudent and resourced to steal N1 million. Owing to the nature of man to be unsatisfied even amid plenty, he would steal trillions if such an opportunity avails itself.

Today's crop of youths who worship internet fraudsters and other similar individuals are dreadful students of history. Although many erroneously allude to the fact that internet fraudsters are not part of the country's problems and that government should focus solely on those in public/political offices, they are greatly mistaken.

Nigeria did not become what it is today overnight; a culture of impunity that allowed people to commit crimes and get away with it was what got us here. Former slave owners who were not punished but allowed to flourish later became sociopolitical game players during the colonial period and influenced how sociopolitical Nigeria took shape. Violent electoral thugs and ruffians became key architects of sociopolitical Nigeria during the First Republic, and their actions eventually led to the demise of that republican government in 1966. Arms smugglers, economic saboteurs and corrupt thieves were the ones who hijacked the available political spaces in the Second Republic and carried on their penchant for illicit gatherings of funds when they got elected to various offices. The Third and Fourth Republics were besieged by a combination of the previous political establishment and the new entrants comprising of drug barons, advanced-fee fraudsters and other financial criminals.

Therefore, it is foolhardy for anyone to expect that the internet fraudsters they celebrate today would have any good intentions for them in the future. Like those before them, they cannot be expected to find their way into political offices and make lives better. Tears, sorrows and anguishes of people have been their prowess, which is unlikely to change when they enter political or public offices. People who steal and swindle others of their money and inheritances must be arrested and prosecuted to the full extent of the law, no matter how petty their crime might be. Our failure to prosecute such people means that the act of deriving joy from people's tears and sweat will continue when they eventually venture into public and political offices. That, anyway, has been the cycle throughout the country's entire history.

Aided and abetted by foreign countries, mostly Western nations, a culture of impunity is why our political and public office holders continue to travel abroad for things they could rightly have put in place right here on our national soil. They embark on health tourism abroad, enrol into foreign institutions, abandon our tourist destinations for those abroad, and send their children and families to the best institutions and places abroad; they do all of these to the Nigerian people's detriment. For all they care, the country can burn to the ground, knowing fully well that they can always travel at will and escape the engulfing inferno from the same catastrophe they created.

In regard to the curative measures of indiscipline and impunity culture, it is pertinent to ask the price Nigerians are willing to pay to ensure that unacceptable aspects of our national culture are abolished. Many Nigerians who clamour for good governance should be made to understand that with good governance, most houses they had constructed inappropriately or illegally must be demolished to pave the way for the "Dubai" they desperately crave. Illegally acquired wealth must be seized with individuals, parents, families, mentors, celebrities and charismatic leaders being made to pay for the consequences of their actions. People who have lived all their life defrauding or engaging in depraving activities must be relieved of their positions and compelled to live a life of civility. There must be prices to pay for indiscipline even if we, the actors and perpetrators, will be at the receiving end. People who have sexually molested students and co-workers must face the consequences. The normative "do you know who I am" nuisance that has become a causative factor in seeing people escape punishments must be eradicated. Sadly, in all these, a vast majority of Nigerians sit comfortably on the indiscipline and impunity cultures that have become responsible for our broken nation. In truth, we cannot talk about the cure for our numerous national problems without the readiness to face the consequences of our negative activities.

To understand Nigeria's culture of impunity even more clearly, a senator caught on tape assaulting a woman at a sex toy shop was later appointed as a patron of a network of moviemakers under the aegis of the Actors Guild of Nigeria (AGN). Their message was loud and clear; assault, indiscipline and misconduct can be forgiven and overlooked without consequences.

As a people, we must continue to demand better leadership and responsible social responsibility. A culture that encourages indiscipline and allows people to get away with harmful actions without consequences will continue to be behind the rest of the world of civilisation. The child whose parents bribed his way through primary, secondary and tertiary education already knows he can as well get away with every other thing as long as the mechanisms used by his parents are also within his grasp. Rank and file security and law enforcement officers will continue to disobey direct orders from their superiors because the wardrobe of such superior officers' skeletons resides in the lower-ranked officers' homes. We cannot be so thoughtless to expect managers and directors of public and private enterprises to caution employees under them over wrongdoings when such personnel are the foot soldiers of their shady and corrupt engagements.

Rapists and sexual assaulters must be named, shamed and properly documented, and possibly excommunicated from public life till they are readily rehabilitated and disengaged from their reprehensible nature. The criminal database system practised in saner societies must be fully utilised in Nigeria to enable agents of socialisation and the general public to distinguish disreputable citizens from reputable ones. Agents of socialisation, such as churches, schools, the mass media, traditional institutions, and religious bodies, must frown at acts of indiscipline and crime. Additionally, they cannot afford to allow their institutions to be appraising grounds for such acts and their actors.

Nigerians, especially younger generations, must be aware of the consequences of their immoral and illegal actions. Punishments must be meted out without fear or favour to deter would-be offenders. Again, I am inclined to warn that societies that cultivate impunity and allow people to get away with acts of indiscipline and criminality would be foolhardy to expect any level of growth or progress.

Inelegant Conclusion

When many Nigerians talk, they talk so critically of their government and their political leaders. Nevertheless, an inelegant question I would like to put across is if those same set of citizens, in their estimated millions (insurgents, fraudsters, terrorists and their sponsors, kidnappers, economic saboteurs, rogues, cultists, drug smugglers, traffickers, and other reprehensible individuals) believe they deserve good governance.

On the social media platform Facebook, a Senior Advocate of Nigeria was talking critically about the nation's state and how CCTVs should be installed on highways, railways and major roads across the country. I put it out to him that, while I agree those are necessary for crime-fighting, Nigerian vandals, in large numbers and with much impunity, steal and vandalise such properties, as the case has always been. I asked him what country in the world has vandals stealing and destroying every public infrastructure government put in place.

I have realised that many Nigerians pamper their fellow citizens. They believe that citizens do not have a role to play in societal or national building.

Nigerians are people who find it extremely difficult to obey the simplest rules and would flagrantly disobey laid down procedures even in broad daylight. One of the greatest ironies of life in Nigeria is seen on our roads. A mother on her way to drop off her schoolchild could be seen crossing the highways, neglecting the pedestrian bridge over her head. A school bus driver with a vehicle full of schoolchildren could be seen driving with reckless abandonment while beating traffic lights. In both cases, you wonder what kind of education such irresponsible adults pass on to the children, who will eventually grow to see the acts as a norm. Unknown to the undisciplined adults, such misconducts form part of child "education" and are weightier than the ones taught in schools. Also, regarding education, we must be alarmed at the high rates of uneducated children and youths in our societies. They are a disaster waiting to happen. It amounts to self-denial for us to think our children's future is safe and secure with them having to contend with such people.

Most Nigerians who lament the nation's state daily are also the beneficiaries, even in places where they could effect changes. Speaking inelegantly, if you were in a commercial vehicle where the driver flagrantly abuses road signs and laws, and you keep mute without cautioning such a driver. You are no better than the public official who keeps mute while money is stolen. If you were in an office where money is being stolen and kept mute or, even worse, become a participant, you are no better than those who provide intel to Boko Haram terrorists. In their distorted thinking, students who commit exam malpractices but expect free and fair elections are comedians who have not yet discovered their talents. In reality, most Nigerians sit elegantly on the tables I have just broken yet, expect a better, productive, prosperous country.

Many Nigerians think the country is worse today than it was many years or decades ago. That is a contentious debate without any empirical fact to back it up. We wonder how our country has degenerated and sunk so low, but we do not put it right to the faces of the older generations (specifically our parents) on how they let us down. We expect to hold political leaders, pastors, the church, uncles and aunts who do not help, the rich and everyone

253

else accountable but never our parents. Some ideologically discordant people fail to hold their parents accountable yet are found on social media, insulting churches for not offering them "affordable" or even free education. How could Christian schools with barely a thousand entrants give "free" education to you and your dozen siblings in a population of millions? Is that not incomprehensible and directionless entitlement syndrome in action? We need to start holding people accountable, and if such stops at the doorstep of our parents and those around us, so be it!

As regards the standard of education in the country and our exaggerated belief in how superbly intelligent we are, it is relevant to mention that recent developments have proven that we are in serious trouble. Our education standards have fallen. Results from educational bodies such as WAEC, NECO and JAMB are utterly disgraceful. Rather than relevant authorities working on fixing the failing standards, they winked with parents and societal bodies to present a false outlook. Recently, the exam body, JAMB, pegged the minimum cut-off score for admission into the country's universities at 140 from a total score of 400. That followed a trail of previous reductions from 220 to 200, then to 180. That is how far we have sunk. What education system do we claim to operate when we deem it fit to offer entry to students with a paltry score of 35% in admission examinations? The fact that parents, bodies, institutions and general members of the society saw it as a welcome development is even more horrific to digest. But that is unsurprising in a country where mediocrity is often applauded and welcomed by the general populace.

As recent as the 1960s and 1970s, when citizens of American and European countries were building their nations, our parents were busy in "the other room", as one president called it. During those same periods, skyscrapers were being built abroad, industries were founded, and businesses, discoveries and inventions were made. Nevertheless, our previous generations engaged in the mass production of innocent children rather than the mass production of goods, services, inventions, infrastructures and other areas of development. Along with their African counterparts, it was as if they had so much time on their hands and were busy producing children while the rest of the world was creating a better future for their generations.

Many Nigerians need to understand that today's world is faced with daunting challenges. Baba Abdul, who gave birth to neglected dozens of children some years back, should know that those children have become terrorists, insurgents and bandits today. Baba Osas, who gave birth to dozens of children while feeding them only food and moral teaching, should be informed that his offspring have neglected his ideals and have become drug smugglers, prostitutes, bandits and kidnappers today. I am raising an alarm that things are about to get worse. On our watch, those who give birth to dozens of children today, aided and unconstrained by dogmatic beliefs and excuses; their children are coming to cause us grievous harm tomorrow. Our usual "this is the worst president in history" slogan is one that we might have to save for use in the very very bleak future.

6: ILLUSIONS AND MISCONCEPTIONS

Nigeria is a land of several illusions and delusions where people perambulate the country with an arrogance of how superior their beliefs are over others. As a fresh reminder, the title of this book was not accidental. It was careful preferred to ensure that no Nigerian escapes culpability from our chaotic state. Our warped mindset and parochial attitude to life realities have made us see ourselves and those we share an affinity with as being blameless in the negative and destructive situation of things.

Although the book's title has been carefully worded with the word "destroy" against the word "destroyed" with the hope that we can still salvage the country from the ongoing inferno that plagues us, some believe that the country is destroyed, far beyond repair. Suppose we are to believe in such a doomed statement. Then the valid question should be, who destroyed Nigeria? One thing is clear, no Nigerian I have met or spoken to is ready to accept culpability. Some blame the British colonialists; the Igbo blame the Hausa-Fulani group, the Yoruba blame the Igbo, the Hausa-Fulani blame southern elites, and the young blame the "old politicians". Christian groups are adamant that Islamist fundamentalists are the country's major problem, and some even think religion is the country's major problem. Nigeria's book of blames, accusations and counter-accusations is endless. One thing is clear, in an extremely prejudiced nation such as Nigeria, any attempt to pin even the most judicious blame on any group is bound to cause further chaos than any intended solution.

Individuals and groups of Nigeria carry the audacious arrogance that they are blameless and pious. Groups and societies of Nigeria are stubborn of the opinion that they are the best thing to ever happen to the entire nation and that their absence in the scheme of our togetherness will surely doom the others. They carry the dirty illusion that other people and groups are doomed without them. They canonise individuals of their extraction even when such individuals carry behaviours that guarantee them a sit at the devil's vineyard. Such is the level of our prejudiced mindset, even as we lie that we are out to save the nation from its misery.

The country's problems today can be traced back to its pre-independence historical roots, where people have been told that other groups are out to eliminate them. Such filthy manipulation and propaganda have come to form the basis for suspicions up to this day. Yoruba historians and writers will tell you that Obafemi Awolowo was the best thing to ever happen to the country and that his failure to become the country's leader has gotten us to this situation. Their Igbo counterparts carry the same apocryphal nonsense that other groups ganged up against Nnamdi Azikiwe from becoming president. They believe the country would have been a "mini-America" if he had been voted the country's leader. We are divided, biased, and prejudiced, but one thing is clear: we should stop pretending to be better than the rest. Our biased and prejudiced mindset is the problem of the country. They have become cultured and metamorphosed as hate, bitterness and violent instigation against others.

Growing up in conservative communities in Nigeria, I was fooled into believing that Nigerians were the most cultured group in the world. Like many others, all we were ever told was that our political leaders were the country's problems. We were told how other nationalities, especially Westerners, are culturally doomed and that they were moral degenerates. Little did we know then that older males in communities were defying many younger girls, and as reported, some by their family members. Little did we know that most adults were bribe seekers, takers and givers. It was not

257

shown to us that most of the people we hero-worship in our communities were criminals, villains and the most morally reprehensible citizens responsible for our impoverishment. We were not informed that most of the cultural practices we thought were beautiful were detrimental to our existence and were inimical to modern growth and development. We did not know that the beautiful existence of religion in the heart of society has been fabricated to enslave us and pit us against one another. As we grew up, at least personally speaking, everything that was sold to us as the reality of life became a farce. In the grand scheme of things, our failure to prepare for the world we find ourselves in today, like many others, has created confounding problems for us.

With the advent of social media, news reports continue to emerge that sharply contradicts the farce of pious livings that have been sold to us. As displayed on social media, the life of Nigerians carries the actuality of who they are. Nigerians on social media join the rest of the global community not in areas of global discussion that aim to solve global problems but in areas that sharply contradict their self-embellished status. Nudity, slurs, e-thuggery, pull-them-down syndrome, hate, blackmail, schadenfreude and their urge to see others go down are common among Nigerian youths on social media. Behind their gathering and discourse on national, social and trendy topics lay actual intents that are far from noble.

Nigerian citizens, from all corners of the country, cutting across all segments, have been found wanting in areas of purity and civilisation. Although it is furthest from my intention to question people's personal interests and life choices, it is instructive to understand that we cannot claim to be one thing when in actuality, we are at the extreme of the things we claim to frown upon. We claim to be deeply religious, but a recent statistic shows that we are the country with the highest viewership of pornography. We are home to one of the most alcoholics in the world. Drugs, prostitution, cultism, gangsters, racketeering, financial crimes, fast-money culture, gender-based violence, paternity fraud, and tons of unfathomable vices have been discovered to find a foothold in geographical Nigeria. Sadly, some of the mentioned human behaviours are lower in the pecking order of globally frowned upon behaviours, at least compared to what torments us, such as terrorism, insurgency, banditry and unwarranted killings.

Where and how did we have the audacity to speak of beautiful cultures every time we engage each other in conversations, and how dare we profess to be religious and pious when facts and figures greatly contradict the fruitless lies that we sell?

Our presence in foreign countries is no longer welcomed. Nigerian immigrants, who so love to blame their political leaders for everything wrong but found themselves in saner climes, carry the same dirty attitudes to such climes. Many countries have put in place stringent conditions for intending Nigerian travellers. In fact, the Nigerian passport is, to put it inelegantly, one of the most useless in the world and treated with utmost disdain by foreign authorities. Recently, the United Arab Emirates, one of the only countries in the world that allow us something close to free access to their destination, has put stringent conditions in place for Nigerian travellers. That was due to the behaviour of Nigerian fraudsters and cultists in their country, not to mention those who overstayed their visa duration. A sad revelation from that chapter of the event is that we are not among the top 10 foreign nationals in their country, yet we are the ones who top their most notorious list.

Growing up, they told us that Nigerian athletes were the most talented group globally, even as results and logic contradict our claim. That has become unsurprising to me today. Through patriotism and love for the game and our fellow citizens, we gather to wish them well and support them. However, our support and patriotism might just be a waste of time, energy and emotional strength. While others prepare arduously years ahead of sports tournaments and events, our athletes are let down by sports authorities and administrators who erroneously believe in wonders and mystical interventions to win matches and tournaments. It might be true that bad leaderships are responsible for our bad outings at sporting events, but that may be taking assumptions too far. Where Nigeria and its citizens failed, some countries of the world that have been reported to be more corrupt and under brutal dictators score higher performances in outings and events. Where and why do we then carry the false notion that we are the most talented people in the world? Are we being patriotic, wholly conned or intentionally blind to the facts before us?

A critical look at life in present-day Nigeria today makes it clear that mendacity and hogwash storytelling somehow became an inexplicable sad part of our culture and existence. As bitter of a pill it might be to swallow and unfathomable as it may be to let sink in, we must admit that those we call heroes today and those whose statues and symbols are displayed right to our faces are the opposites of the applauses that have been given to them.

Our history is filled with prejudiced accounts of storytelling. They often show the Nigerian people's deadly bifurcation and the extent to which writers and storytellers are willing to defend people of their extractions despite glaring evidence to condemn the activities of such people.

The January 15, 1966 coup plotters were nothing other than cold-blooded murderers. They were not revolutionaries or ideologists as they saw themselves or arrogantly called themselves. They were people who carried out murders of democratically elected people who, even if they disagreed with them, should have allowed the course of social changes to make the necessary corrections. Some of the coup plotters, such as Major Ademola Ademoyega and Captain Ben Gbulie, have written accounts of historical events leading up to the coup. They inadvertently proved that their actions were fabricated from rumours, hearsays and suspicions rather than genuine or factual pieces of evidence. It is shameful for any individual or group to attempt to justify the January 1960 coup. They toppled a very young independent, democratic government and became the chief architects of our problems today. When one of the coup plotters, Captain Ben Gbulie

260

appeared at the Oputa Panel, his words and demeanours proved that he was an unrepentant and prejudiced bigot. It is even more disappointing when people of Igbo extraction try to justify or condone the activities of the January 1960 plotters as anything close to revolutionary. Their actions, even if not ethnic, gave credence to the fact that they were out on an unholy mission.

The coincidences that trail the coup itself equal the same suspicions that initially fuelled the plotters' actions. Up to this day, it is hard to sell that the coup was not ethnically motivated, being that people of Igbo extractions primarily carried it out, with the majority of the victims being Northerners. Further fuelling such suspicions was that the principal Igbo political leader at the time, Dr Nnamdi Azikiwe was out of the country during the coup. It did not help matters much that, by coincidence, the "beneficiary" of the coup happened to be an Igbo officer, who ironically was the most senior Igbo officer. In Nigeria, where most people base their judgements upon historical distortions sold to them by prejudiced historians and account writers of their extractions, it is relevant for us to put things the way they are. If the January 1966 coup were not ethnically motivated, it carried the hallmark of suspicions that went farther than the ones the plotters had of the politicians they ousted. Sadly, those mere suspicions became the basis for their actions, and no credible piece of evidence was enough to justify their actions. To this day, suspicions and fears are part of our national culture, and we have not progressed further by inflaming them.

The July 1966 counter-coup plotters proved even worse than their January counterparts. Judging by historical analysis of events, it was certain the January plotters acted with the main motive of securing power, although will forever be unclear if they had any motive for ethnic cleansing. The same could not be said for the July counterplotters. Evidently, they set out to seize power, gain their "revenge" for the January aggression, and kill as many Igbos and southern collaborators as possible. Shamefully, some were rewarded for their murderous activities rather than face condemnation. If history were truly kind, or if we were a country with honesty as a prime mover in our political culture, none of the architects of the July 1966 coup plot should be celebrated as national heroes. They could have gotten away with seizing political power and eventually becoming powerful military generals, with some becoming heads of state. However, with the country becoming a democracy, it is disgraceful to morality and piety to have the faces and images of some of the most corrupt and evil-minded monsters engraved into our memory and, even worse, celebrated as heroes.

As a Nigerian, having studied the accounts of events between July 1966 and 1971, I frown upon having a man like Murtala Muhammed celebrated as a national icon. It must be said that, although he was regarded as a disciplined officer, his role in the murders of Igbo officers in July 1966 and his alleged use of brute force with full intention to commit genocide against Igbos during the Nigerian Civil War do not qualify him to be embellished as a national hero. Suppose we are to be fair and prudent in our analysis. In that case, it is equally unimaginable that people of Igbo extraction idolise Chukwuemeka Odumegwu Ojukwu to the extent that he enjoys a godlike status in Igboland. As I wrote earlier in this book's prequel, Ojukwu's position on matters that led to the brutal civil war was understandable. However, his demeanour and dogmatic insistence on a war that led to the death of millions of his people is not worthy of heroic status.

Today, the Igbos blame everybody for the results of the war. Most of their storytellers, historians and political analysts have written disparaging and untrue stories about the involvement of other groups. They blame the Yoruba, the Hausa, and the Fulani for their "roles" and also include the Niger Deltans in the blame trade as well. It is even common to see them blame the British, the Americans and other foreign groups. Sadly, they never see a reason to blame Ojukwu or members of their fellow extraction whose activities directly led to war and the killings of their people. When the respected Igbo elder statesman, Dr Nnamdi Azikiwe, reminisced on the events leading to the war and lamented the roles of Igbo sons in prolonging the war longer than necessary, he was shouted down, harassed and insulted by the recalcitrant Igbo community who obviously had declared war on not just fellow Nigerians but on matters of truth.

It must be noted that the prejudiced mindset of the Igbo people as regards matters of the civil war, or truth in general, is not just a behaviour solely attributed to them as a people; the entire people of the Nigerian region are equally guilty of such a flawed and prejudiced mentality and approach to national issues.

Still on the 1966 coups and the aftermaths, Generals Ibrahim Babangida and Sani Abacha were alleged to be active participants during the 1966 killings. Suppose those activities had no genuine links to them. In that case, the activities that took place under their direct watch as military heads of state cannot be rewarded with applause. For Babangida, under his watch, Nigeria became a country synonymous with anarchy. State-sponsored blood and violence became part of the polity under both heads of state. Up to this very moment, some of the funds stolen under General Sani Abacha are being repatriated back into the country. Nevertheless, it insults the sensibilities of most Nigerians that such a hooligan in uniform and a bloodthirsty murderer has a stadium and major highways named after him.

A popular Yoruba saying has it - in translation - that "a person we see and shed tears (for perceived ignominy) but erroneously adjudges such as an applause (is one living in delusion)" best describes the Nigerian situation. We expect to be taken seriously by the global community when they see us as an embodiment of mockery due to activities in our sociopolitical terrains. I am afraid to say such activities mock logic and common sense. Suppose superstition is to be taken so seriously the way we do in this part of the world. In that case, our national currency will surely be doomed when we decide to have faces of people with questionable character on them.

Proponents of the idea that religion has been a destabilising force in Nigeria are not delusional. There are historical activities that suggest they might be right. Fulani Jihadists at the start of the 19th century carried out the first notable incidents of large-scale religious intolerance and fundamentalism on Nigerian soil. Although, like every other revolution, they carried the excuse and notion that they were out to cleanse society of impure practices and injustices. However, the murders they committed showed indifference, if not worse, to what they claimed they disliked. At the helm of the Jihadist movements was an Islamic scholar, Usman Dan Fodio. Today, history books are replete with the historical "achievements" of Dan Fodio as an ideal revolutionary and fanciful remarks are accompanied when talking about his role in activities that shaped Nigeria, when in fact, his imprint of fundamentalism, extremism, insurgency and dare I say terrorism have traceable roots to his person.

Religious intolerance and fundamentalism in Nigeria as a bane of national existence should be unsurprising when students are taught at schools to see a man like Dan Fodio as a hero rather than the usurper and murderous individual he and his so-called revolutionaries were. A country that hopes to achieve peace must be truthful to its younger generations and not paint issues the way they are not. Sadly, there is reality, and there is the colouration of issues, and the latter is what has become our culture, perhaps in a way not to exacerbate extremely divisive issues.

One of the inexplicable features of Nigerian citizens is their apocryphal belief in things that ought to be or should have been, rather than the true reality before them. Many Nigerians have no genuine reason to regard Murtala Muhammed as a hero other than that he was assassinated and had his history cemented with emotional guidance. They had so fancifully believed in tales of his disciplined nature that they quickly forgave him of all his sins and confined his status to heroism following his assassination. The same could be said for others, such as the late President Umaru Musa Yar'Adua, whose death gave him a heroic status, as he did not live enough for them to judge his tenure in office. As I noted earlier, every group in the country had individuals of their extraction they embellished as heroes and so fancifully believe would have made the country a better place if they were allowed to become its leader. We believe the country is doomed when other groups reject people of our extraction or affiliation in social or political matters. Such is our flawed state of mind even under the fraudulent canopy of activism, love or patriotism.

Chief MKO Abiola was one individual Nigerians have regarded as a "president we never had" (as some fancifully called him). It is incomprehensible to see Nigerians, especially people of Yoruba extraction, canonise Abiola the way they do. If historical analyses are anything to go by, I do not regard Abiola as a potential national saviour. It must also be noted that he was not a man whose historical activities show the blamelessness sold to Nigerians for far too long to the extent that a federal holiday was declared to honour him.

Incidentally, Chief MKO Abiola was a close ally of the military. He became a multi-billionaire through the connections and network of military leaders, one that spanned twenty years before the 1993 election. His network and familiarity with the military hierarchy got him so rich that it irked the person of human rights activist and legendary music icon Fela Anikulapo Kuti who dedicated an entire album to criticising MKO and his financial firm, ITT.[19]

Nigerians generally agree that massive corruption, theft and embezzlement took place and that our national wealth had been siphoned since independence. Curiously, they simultaneously seem to absolve people of corrupt practices, especially when they share ethnic or religious affiliations with devious individuals. That MKO Abiola profited enormously during a period when our national wealth got plundered, siphoned and notoriously embezzled was enough to question the legitimacy of his wealth and his intention for the Nigerian state. Clearly, Abiola was a beneficiary of an ill-broken sociopolitical system, and he profiteered from a political subterfuge system that Babangida and cohorts probably designed to fail. After all, it is on record that Abiola played a vital role in the politicisation of the military and the militarisation of politics throughout a critical period in the country's history. There are credible reports that linked Abiola to the 1983 coup, which ended the civilian administration of Shagari.[20] Abiola was also reported as one of the financiers of the 1985 coup against the anti-capitalist administration of Buhari.[21] As a financier and coup monger, Abiola used his press outfits to deride state establishments and individuals who refused to dance to his tune. Babangida admitted that those were necessary tools in turning public opinion against the government and an essential tool that enabled his government to come to power.[22]

Many Nigerians had (and still have) notoriously misleading perceptions regarding Abiola and the June 12 saga. One such is the wrongful assertion that Abiola was without blemish regarding the pillage and theft of our national wealth because he was never a politician. Little did they know the catastrophic roles played by private citizens as collaborations in the thefts and embezzlement of our resources, much of which the reader will read in this book's sequel. Also, Abiola miscalculated the ambitions of those he relied on to give him his due mandate. After Babangida's resignation, Abiola sought Abacha's help to declare the ING as an illegitimate body, reinstate him as the rightful winner of the June 12 election, and have him declared president-elect. Abacha was the then Minister of Defence and seemed to have such power as promulgated in the decree that brought the ING to political life. Little did Abiola know at the time that Abacha and others were the actual orchestrators of the whole shenanigans? Abiola was a presidential candidate who lacked an accurate understanding of the individuals, political society and nation he wanted to govern.

This book and its prequel have not featured the personal lives of key actors and players of political Nigeria. However, judging by how Abiola had been so revered as a man destined to turn the tide of things around, it might help the reader to understand that Abiola was a man whose personal life

266

does not tally with the reverence bestowed on him as a possible messiah. He was extremely polygamous to the extent that it was reported that he had 19 concubines and an estimated 50 children, according to inside sources who verified publicly available information. After his death, his entire business legacy collapsed. The reader will recall that I earlier noted this trend as one of the individual factors responsible for the impoverishment of generations in Nigeria.

Any attempt to attach ugliness to people held in high esteem by Nigerians is quickly rebuffed and shouted down by not just the masses but a quarter of educated personalities who ought to know better. It is fully my intention to unapologetically write distastefully but truthfully about those who led Nigeria to its current state. We will continue to run in circles unless we let generations after generations know the truth about our reality. The failure of people of northern extraction to see Usman dan Fodio as a bloodthirsty usurper has given birth to mentees like him who currently terrorise them today in the name of jihadism and Islamic fundamentalism. The failure of the Igbos to hold Ojukwu responsible for the murders of the Igbos is what has given birth to terror groups who blindly follow an unstable personality like Nnamdi Kanu and his cohorts to terrorise Igboland under the canopy of freedom fighting. The Yoruba failure to caution Awolowo and the AG/UPN political gang lords is partly why the region is home to its challenges of thuggery and chaos. The list of our mistakes is endless. We have made villains as heroes, and we have made heroes as villains.

Religious and traditional custodians are no more than people who have allowed themselves to get dirty and drown in the country's muddled water of partisan politics despite the false pretence that they care about the populace. The military were not the only ones who infested their authority on us as a people. Tertiary institutions, roads, highways and national monuments are named after individuals with corruption and gross misconduct records. Many of those charged for gross misconduct after the 1983 toppling of the abjectly corrupt Second Republic later had their names engraved in various regions of the country. They are today idolised and immortalised by the same people whose resources they have stolen.

Our country is in trouble. Morals are fast going into extinction. Money worshipping and glory hunting are fast replacing every available moral virtue that there is out there. Some of the most celebrated lawyers, bankers, engineers, accountants, auditors and private contractors in the country today are also the chief architects of ensuring that criminals, wrongdoers, looters, terrorists, kleptocrats and other nefarious individuals enjoy haven.

Most of the people mentioned in this book and those who escaped scrutiny have one thing in common. None of them, or those close to them, ever accepted culpability for their actions. Despite all of Abacha's glaring atrocities, his wife and children have publicly defended him in interviews and on social media platforms. His former Chief Security Officer, Hamza Al-Mustapha, proved to be his protector while he was alive and did the same after his death. Long after Abacha's death, Al-Mustapha has engaged in firefights through media interviews and press briefings to dismiss allegations against his erstwhile boss. Abacha's longtime friend General Jeremiah Useni and other inner circle members have granted various interviews to exonerate the late dictator of accusations levelled against him. Professor Omo Omoruyi rigorously defended General Ibrahim Babangida, especially regarding the June 12 election fiasco. The former wrote a voluminous book detailing events that aimed to vindicate the elder statesman from the events that ended the Third Republic. The children of convicted armed robbers such as Anini, Samuel Oredein and the rest have come out to deny their parents' involvement in the accusations that were levelled against them. The late kleptocrat Diepreye Alamieyeseigha's brother spoke so elegantly about him shortly after his death. Nigerian youths who claim they want to see socio-economic changes also have parents and family members who occupy positions of authority. Those positions are the fountain of the happy and flamboyant life they enjoy, one that denies millions their fundamental entitlements. Some of the country's most devastatingly corrupt personalities have written fanciful and embellished accounts of "things that happened" (aka their "truth"), leaving one to ask again; who are the architects of Nigeria's engulfing flame?

Inelegant Conclusion

Speaking inelegantly, I could say vehemently that we do not know the colour of our problems, as commonly used in street parlance. Everything about us that relates to piety and rich cultural assemblage is nothing but a farce and a lie. In Nigeria, a music icon was also a drug addict whose influence on Nigerian youths is linked to the prevalence of drug abuse, just like the impact of his music. A particular "human rights lawyer" whom I investigated was so notorious to such an extent that he has been able to secure the acquittals or dismissals of more than 32 individual cases against high-profile Nigerians. Separately, the individuals were charged for financially-related crimes in the amount of not less than a billion naira each; that list could be endless if we lowered the amount other clients were alleged to have stolen below the one billion naira range of study. Sadly, he is one among a pool of his colleagues who sell embellishments to Nigerians but are aiders and abettors of crime and national sabotage.

As we try our best to rid our society of tribalism, hate, prejudice, and other archaic beliefs and practices that are detrimental to the development of modern societies carried on by previous generations, today's generation proved they are not any better or even worse. Today's generations of mostly youths have imbibed unholy practices that are equally detrimental to social and national development, such as drug abuse and cultism. Sex enhancement sales and usages, addiction to gambling, skin bleaching, sexualisation, and neo-prostitution are just a few out of an inglorious list of activities that modern-day youths actively engage in, to their detriment and that of our collective moral culture.

It has become our national culture for us not to take responsibility for our disdainful behaviours and to suppress ugliness at all costs, even if it will liberate us from our current shame. We hate responsibilities, and we detest accountability. We know the group whose daughters are mostly into prostitution and child trafficking in the country. We know the group whose children are mostly into financial fraud, aka *Yahoo Yahoo*, in the country. A particular segment of this country has been afflicted with the scourge of cultism to such an extent that I discovered that 6 out of 10 of their sons between 18 and 40 have been initiated into one deadly cult group or the other. We cannot pretend that a particular group are not primarily responsible for watching as their sons engage in drug trafficking, counterfeiting, piracy and other financial crimes. A particular group in this country is more renowned for violence and extremism than any other positive influence they offer. Sadly, when people are called upon to fix their homegrown problems by people of other extractions across the pond, they get riled up and resort to the use of slurs and attacks. They only want to look elsewhere for whom to blame for national problems, even when their roof has an engulfing fire currently plaguing it. We are pretenders, and the whole world knows this.

Suppose we all claim to be innocent of the Nigerian problem and continue to absolve ourselves of the blame for how things went wrong. In that case, the multibillion-naira question is, WHO IS RESPONSIBLE FOR NIGERIA'S WOES?

7: CONCLUSION - NIGERIA AND OTHER STORIES

April 30, 2022, was the date that I decided to send the final manuscript of this blessed book for final publishing. Ongoing events during this period have proven that the problems facing us are huge and byzantine. Presently, these problems seem impossible to solve. There are currently insecurity crises in all the country's geopolitical zones. Secessionist groups have become louder than ever, terrorism and insurgency are rising, and kidnappers and bandits have gained more audacity to launch attacks at will. Unemployment, illiteracy, food insecurity, crime, corruption, badly depreciated naira, rising national debt, and a damaged economy, among other things, are problems that demand urgent and simultaneous surgeries. Any future administrator has the likelihood of falling into an unfair climatic trap. That is because impatience and intolerance have become phenomena features of citizens who have become the bitter enemies of life realities. For those citizens, urgent solutions are needed from newer administrators from their first day in office; the reader is free to use such urgent solutions as synonyms for miracles and wonders.

I must also repeat that this book is a sequel to an earlier book, _"How We Destroy Nigeria: Precedence of Doom"_, which detailed how we got to this present mess. The roles played by past and present leaders of the country, the violence, the insecurity and the build-up of our anarchical situation have been documented in this book's prequel.

Most of the problems facing the country today are artificial problems that should never be part of our existence in the first place, much more subject to reparations or solutions. Sadly, the problems are here, and we are left to deal with their devastating effects. Today, the multi-trillion-dollar question on everyone's lips is, how do we solve these problems? It is also relevant to ask ourselves how we got to this current quandary, where the curatives to our problems have become even more cataclysmic than the actual problems. Solving Nigeria's problems is an exorbitantly challenging task, especially when the most incompetent individuals remain in charge of our societal and national affairs. To call them incompetent is being economical with words; they could be argued as the actual problems.

As things stand, no problem seems to outweigh the other, and all problems must be tackled synchronously. We cannot tackle the problem of crime and corruption without tackling the problem of unemployment and vice-versa. We cannot fight unemployment and leave the issue of insecurity and terrorism unattended. The government cannot pay security officials stipends and expect them to deliver on the promise they took during their pledge of allegiance to the nation. The problems of unemployment, poverty and insecurity are far from being solved if our population continues to increase disproportionately. Economic woes will continue as long as our geographical space creates a hospitable environment for economic sabotage, insecurity, violence and terrorism.

Present-day realities have shown that reputation has become a key global asset of civilised nations, far more than we think. A country with a reputation for anarchy and anti-social ills should not expect socio-economic progress anytime soon. In today's rapidly changing world, financial investors have ample reasons to abandon climes that pose any threat to their economic interests. In truth, today's Nigeria poses many threats to potential investors.

Nigeria is a very complicated nation. It is so complicated that I could be reprimanded by a large segment of those who believe we are not a nation but a country. The discourse surrounding the country's existence becomes even

272

more convoluted and nauseating, sometimes leading to bitter confrontations when matters of ethnicity and religion come into play. So aggressive are issues of national discourse that it triggered one of the country's nationalists, Chief Obafemi Awolowo, to declare our beloved country as "a mere geographical expression". As noted in this book, it is instructive to set the record straight since events have proven his opinion incorrect. Up till this day, ideologically intransigent politicians who continue to influence their filthy will on their constituents fabricate most of the divisions that many allude to. Several historical and contemporary examples underpin this opinion.

Nigeria is a land of people with an ideological inconsistency. Such inconsistencies are aggravated in public discourse by influential figures for no reason other than self-interest or power acquisition. There is nothing true or believable about the fact that Nigerians are not one or should never be one. Such ideological fallacy and misconstrued absurdity are fabricated by charlatans who quickly change tunes when they get to power to steal and loot "their own turn" at the national level. Those who propagate the belief that we cannot live together should be reminded that Nigerians cohabit all over the world in foreign climes with people they share no nationality, ethnicity or affiliation. It is then a misleading narrative for an Igbo to question why a competent Hausa person governs him or for a Hausa to question why a Yoruba is at the helm of affairs. Likewise, why should the religion of anyone matter in Nigeria when the state religion of those in climes they travel to or send their children for education is irrelevant to the same persons? Why does a Yoruba man have a problem with Enugu being more developed than Oyo when he has no such problem that Dubai is by all comparison better than Oyo or any other state in the country? Why are Nigerians willing and able to travel to foreign societies and countries but unable to do the same to regions within their own country? It would seem as if there is a presence of envy than any other logic to the issues that we have to contend with. Unwarranted suspicion, envy and fear of domination among Nigerians are responsible for why intolerance and prejudice exist in our various societies.

Much has been said about restructuring and regional governance. The British practised the regional governance system using indirect rule for almost a century. It recorded relative success compared to how it and other systems have failed woefully in the hands of indigenous leaders after independence. I firmly believe that the country is in dire need of restructuring. It is long overdue and must be discussed and allowed as urgent as possible, if not for anything but to calm down aggressions from aggrieved segments of the populace. Nonetheless, I am worried about the relevance of restructuring and what difference it would make from what has been ongoing for decades.

One could be easily forgiven for assuming that the translation of regional government as regards the economic and financial impact to be "give me a piece of what we have stolen, let me go feast of it", "This stolen property is mine to keep", or "This property is mine to steal". A critical look at how regions, states and areas have fared under their kinsmen at the helm of affairs affirms that theft of resources does not exclude any individual or group. Theft of resources has become national cancer that has had people from every geographical corner of the country participating in it unapologetically.

It is far from my intention to malign the positive roles played by our founding fathers. However, contrary to popular perception, Nigeria gained its independence more because of the willingness of the British to give up their hold on their colonies around the world and not necessarily due to the brilliance or resistance of the country's founders. The negative consequences that followed the crude power play and political activities administered by the nationalists immediately after independence demonstrated that they were not ready for proper governance. That was unsurprising, after all, the news of impending independence came as a rude shock to emerging politicians of the North, and they made their displeasure known that they were not ready for independence. Today, the same Britain that granted us independence is being swamped by today's generation of Nigerians due to the dangerous precedence of bitterness, hatred, prejudice and ethnic bias that the founders had set.

In sociopolitical Nigeria, it is common for personal interests to come in the way of people's political ideologies. That is a major reason I have never been inclined to believe that a particular region or group of people should be held solely responsible for the country's woes. The same political leaders who mislead the population using divisive propaganda also deviously orchestrate plans to remove their "sons" when they stop benefiting selfishly from the share of their national cake.

The misconception that people of a particular extraction should be held responsible for domination and political marginalisation in this country is incorrect. It has been alleged that several southern leaders actively connived to deny the late Chief MKO Abiola his "June 12" electoral mandate. The said southerners were aristocrats, traditional rulers and elected governors of Chief MKO's SDP party. Notable business people and influential figures from Chief MKO's home state of Ogun were also identified as his underground adversaries. Similarly, previous primary and general elections that had taken place in the country have shown how political stalwarts of people from the same ethnic groups or geopolitical zone in the country made rigorous attempts to sabotage their fellow "brothers" from emerging victorious for personal or politically motivated reasons.

Regarding the country's many challenges, most Nigerians only want to be told that the country's problems are solely the handwork of politicians and leaders. The attendant problems that have been scrutinised in this book, which point to the direction of citizens, are in most cases dismissed by people who erroneously believe that "if the head is rotten, the body follows". Blames that should be transported to the doorstep of citizens to engineer sociopolitical or economic solutions are wrongly attributed to political leaders. Society supports the unemployed man with 10 children to hold the leaders accountable for his misconceptions. When he eventually gets a job that earns him a monthly sum of N1million monthly, he decides to give birth to an additional 12 children, thereby adding more burdens on himself, society and the nation at large. Sadly, most Nigerian families typify this pattern of behaviour. Individual behaviours that impede individual and national growth must be addressed and not left for the government to micromanage.

Generally, as citizens, we must accept the blame for the sorry state of our nation. Past and present occurrences have proven that the blame game machine should be dished and made irrelevant unless we decide to engineer its use in an unbiased and balanced fashion. People from all the major groups, religions and regions have ruled the country, yet none could be said to have fared sufficiently well. The country has practised both the unitary and federal political governance systems; both failed woefully. Similarly, contrary to popular perception, the country has had many educated and bright men in positions of power. Professors, doctors, economists, astute military officers, teachers, renowned bankers, famed writers, historians, legal luminaries, and rights activists, among others, yet their failures were as astounding as the reputation that preceded them. Different economic and social programs have been deployed to tackle the country's many challenges. Yet, we are faced with colossal losses that emanate from the effects of such policies and programs.

In truth, we are in trouble. We are in very deep trouble. We have allowed problems that should have been tamed right from the very start to implode right in our faces. Our economy is on life support and needs urgent social and economic surgeries. If no one else is bold enough to admit it, I Johnny JamJam will. In recent decades, the country has only been supported by two major sources of revenue. The first is the official and formal oil and gas sector, which accounts for most of the country's total revenue. The second is the unofficial and informal street fraud sector, which accounts for a massive chunk of direct revenue for most citizens. My usage of the term "street fraud" was intentional to encompass every aspect of financial crime in the country. Suppose economic predictions are anything to go by. In that case, Nigeria's oil and gas sector might be heading towards a moribund state as global purchasers and consumers look for alternate sources of energy and consumption. Similarly, if high-tech and cyber security predictions were anything to go by, the days of internet fraudsters in the country are numbered.

Most of the country's group of wealthy people have become stupendously rich as far as illegalities and immoral amassment of wealth permits them. Some Nigerians whose parents, or themselves, engaged in economically debased activities are ironically the ones with the loudest voice when it comes to condemnations of the sorry state of our economy. Real estate investors continue to amass massive lands for the sole purpose of selling at ridiculously higher prices. Yet, the same people wonder why many people are homeless today. The real estate market in Nigeria is one that systematically contributes to poverty, inflation, neglect and economic disadvantages. There are credible reports that some people who import electric generators into the country are partly responsible for power sabotage. I once got a report of an estate manager who was caught bribing electric distribution managers to deny his residents power supply in order to profiteer from diesel supply to the same residents. When I put the topic out on a public platform, I found out it was not a singular behaviour as many others reported they had discovered such a trend among some unscrupulous individuals. Obviously, many Nigerians, by themselves, contribute daily quota to the perceptible agony that has become a national component.

As critical as the issue of unemployment is to societies and nations of the world, it is one that I felt reluctant to discuss in this book for reasons I hope the reader understands. My reluctance is connected to the fact that most of the problems discussed so far in this book are contributory factors to unemployment. It would therefore amount to tautological and overdraw analysis to hammer on those same factors. Nevertheless, outside the normal economic factors that give rise to unemployment in saner climes, Nigerians by themselves continue to ensure that the rates of unemployment remain on the high side. By those acts, we constantly contrived to create conditions that give rise to unemployment in the country.

In Nigeria, the noticeable causes of unemployment are poor and inconsistent economic policies, absence of entrepreneurship and investment support, insecurity, political instability, population explosion, economic sabotage, corruption, excessive dependence on the oil and gas industry, economic monopoly, digitalisation and automation, illiteracy and inadequacy/lack of skills, lack of infrastructure and unfavourable social and economic climate.

Another contributing cause of unemployment in the country is the problem of overpopulation. It could be argued as the most worrisome cause of unemployment due to the unmanageability of voluminous human figures even after other factors have been properly put under relative control. Having highlighted overpopulation's devastating consequences on societal Nigeria in earlier pages, I carefully reserved its impact on unemployment for this chapter. Nigeria's problems started with our inability to predict the future rightfully and to also cater for the futuristic needs of unborn generations. It has been said that the best way to kill a venomous snake is by cutting off its head. In that regard, I strongly contend that the country needs to address the issue of unemployment by tackling the monstrous culture of insensitive human overproduction. A nation that hopes to achieve a sustainable pinnacle cannot do so with a population of employable persons that grows ten times the estimated level of available jobs. Even worse is Nigeria's situation, where eventual population growth often surpasses projections while eventual job creations become far less than projected estimates. A compulsive fraternity with outdated beliefs is why penurious persons notoriously give birth uncontrollably to children they cannot cater for. They cannot provide such children with adequate education or offer them any form of apprenticeship. Still, such people expect a miraculous source of intervention to grant the children a viable livelihood. That has become a major reason political demagogues use underprivileged people to achieve inglorious feats. Politicians see the donation of brooms, wheelbarrows, grinders and other meagre infrastructural items as empowerment tools, much to the delight of recipients.

Societies prone to violence at every given opportunity scare away investors and are a bad omen for financial growth and investments. The prevalence of violence, riotous clashes and other forms of civil disruptions have affected employment opportunities in many ways. Many communities have seen businesses burn to the ground at every slight provocation. The burning of businesses, shops, factories, stores, and other economic buildings only removes more people from the labour market. We cannot continue to lament unemployment in the country during the day and exacerbate activities that lead to it at night.

Another bad omen for investment opportunities and job creation is bribery and corruption. Public officials have become a bane in people's conduction of business activities. Investors frequently lament inappropriate demands for bribes by public officials before they could be granted permission or given adequate necessities to conduct their business. The multiplicity of government agencies and task force members also creates hostile business environments, as these agencies only serve to extort businesses, especially foreign and naïve investors. It has been widely reported how traditional and community leaders demand heavy bribes from potential individuals with plans to invest in their communities. Some leaders put rigorous bottlenecks and scare tactics in place, to extort plausible investors. Habits like these continue to see communities that should have developed and become a hub of commercial activities eventually turn into a den of criminal activities.

We are no longer in the era where investors were short of geographical locations to invest. Today, Nigeria suffers from certain setbacks regarding investment opportunities on its national soil. New developmental factors such as science, technology, research and development and other similar innovations have enabled investors to carry out massive functions from fewer geographic locations. Also, as peace and stability returned to some regions of the world, it puts countries where violence is rife at much greater economic and investment risk.

Some people have claimed that the high unemployment rate is the reason for financial fraud and crimes in the country. That is a mystifying two-way lane that needs careful examination. Firstly, what investor would want to invest in a society that openly welcomes financial fraud and criminality? Businesses have closed partly due to fraudulent activities by employees who used every tactic to defraud their employers. Secondly, perpetrators of crimes are fanatically obsessed with getting rich overnight. They have become afflicted with the "get rich quickly" syndrome and are not in a hurry to join the labour market of hardworking citizens. Therefore, it is unsurprising that such people are the most notorious saboteurs of legitimate businesses, as we have numerously witnessed. There may be some bad news in the future. As long as crime and corruption are openly tolerated and welcomed, jobs and investment opportunities are not coming.

The excuse mill for fraud, corruption and other forms of criminality must be destroyed and burnt to the ground. Foreign individuals, businesses and nations have become lesser inclined to do business with crooked people. Likewise, people who make excuses for misconduct create a haven for criminals and also encourage them to engage in more similar activities. There is always an excuse for those who use one-way traffic routes, and there will always be an excuse for those who steal our electric power cables. Wayward students who engage in examination malpractices equally have their bucket-fill of excuses. Those who steal from their employers have reasons for their actions when caught. *Yahoo Yahoo* boys have an enormous pool of resource-filled excuses to use as the reason for engaging in their fraudulent behaviours. It is up to us to forge a functional moral code for the progress of our nation or to continue to see unacceptable wrongdoings as norms.

As unpatriotic as it may seem and perhaps an unacceptable admission at that, it is not further from the truth if we opine that crime, corruption and indiscipline have become an innate characteristic of the average citizen. This opinion is further reinforced by the atrocities committed by a disgraceful proportion of citizens abroad. Abroad, Nigerian embassies and their personnel carry out intolerable acts in the climes they are designated to serve foreign residents. Similarly, Nigerians abroad have been known to engage in street fighting, cultism, organised fraud, crime and other nefarious activities.

Recently, the UAE, South Africa, and Malaysia have red-flagged Nigerian travellers due to violent clashes attributed to Nigerians living in those countries. Such behaviours by Nigerians indicate that excuses for committing acts of violence and financial fraud in Nigeria are untenable, as the same platforms for excuses are largely unavailable abroad where they constituted their misconduct. I am worried that political demagogues and their apparatuses in every corner of the country will continue to have abundant mercenaries who wish to see the country burn to their delight. Unenterprising citizens, criminal minds, social misfits and their siblings will continue to see the country as the "worst country on earth", thanks to political demagogues who see it as such and who use such excuses as a pawn to lure them into burning down the country at will. Some Nigerians have sold our names positively and have become good ambassadors of our dear nation to the global community. Still, I am inclined to continue hammering on the largely unacceptable proportion of those dragging us in the mud. How true is it that Nigerians, in general, excel abroad and are the reports of Nigerians who excel abroad worth celebrating? I doubt so, at least not on a comparative basis, especially if we were to judge by the country's large population, which makes it unsurprising to see the reflection of Nigerians everywhere in the world.

For every Chimamanda Adichie, whose brilliance as an author and female rights activist needs no reminder, there is an uneven

proportion of hundreds of Nigerian money-worshipping females who sell their bodies in various parts of Europe and the rest of the world. For every David "Davido" Adeleke whose music exports have seen him win numerous international awards and become arguably the country's biggest exponent to the world in recent times, there is a shameful portion of foreign citizens like Hushpuppi. Their activities have been highlighted in this book.

I am deeply concerned by the increasing use of false reporting (fake news), dirty propaganda, the malicious spread of information, blackmail, schadenfreude syndrome, and violent instigation of ethnic groups against each other, especially through the use of social media. Unscrupulous internet combatants and debauchedly motivated social media handlers have become primary "authorities" for information. Vulnerable users erroneously construe inciteful messages of hate and disunity as authoritative facts. These patterns have very disturbing impacts on democratic processes and could be used to instigate hostilities, cause havoc, and provoke unjust conflicts that, if not carefully managed, could explode into full-blown wars.

I am deeply concerned that while foreign countries are planning for a world that would accommodate their citizens and inhabitants for centuries to come, even as leaders of such societies will not be around for that long, our leaders and citizens continue to deteriorate an already decayed society for their future generations. I am deeply troubled that our leaders, policymakers, and elites continue to steal resources they will not be around to spend in future decades. Some incongruously say they do what they do (steal) for their children and generations. However, what kind of monsters rewards their children by stealing the collective wealth of millions of other children? What kind of morally debauched people steals massive wealth for children who might not live to enjoy such wealth due to the chaos and disasters that their parents had created?

Environmental degradation is taking place in most of our regions. Our natural resources are getting depleted, just as our population has been on an uncontrollable increase. We are in trouble. Our soil, water, land, air, homes, and communities have all been polluted. On the physical side, they have been polluted by gas flaring activities, deforestation, oil spillage, illegal bunkering, theft of historical antiques, aquatic pollution, and threat to mangrove habitats, among others. On the social side, we have been polluted by corruption, greed, bitterness, hostility, fraud, indiscipline, corruption, prejudice, mental enslavement, debauched cultural practices, and religious fraud, among others. Environmental and civil rights activists are sending strong warnings and signals, but we are paying no attention to them.

As Nigerians, we should be troubled that our country has become a dumping ground for some of the world's morally reprehensible behaviours. The presence of warmongering foreign media houses and other misleading agents of socialisation is responsible for why Nigerians continue to go for each other's throats for frivolous reasons that are substantiated only by prejudice. I am troubled that we have allowed our nation to be used as a pawn of engagement by foreign entities that continue to use the country to their advantage. Foreign media houses, economic and financial institutions, monetary and regulatory organisations, and other regional bodies have used our country as a pawn to facilitate their selfish interests. The activities of foreign organisations - with CNN and Amnesty International being the guiltiest culprits - must be scrutinised, as they cannot be allowed to use Nigeria to their advantage the way they have done with several war-torn regions. I strongly believe these organisations do not mean well for us, or any other country for that matter. Rather, they feed on hostilities, divisions and warmongering to sell breaking news headlines to their global audience.

I am troubled at how we do not hold people accountable enough for their actions and allow them to trample on our rights, especially if they share affiliations with us. Our so-called frowns against crime and corruption are biased and flawed. We must develop a culture of holding societal, economic and political leaders accountable for their actions or inaction during their time in office. We must say, "Mr President, you have failed us" or "Mr Governor, you have let us down" whenever we accost them at anytime and anywhere. Such defiance must be in the spirit of genuineness and sincerity and not one of bias, prejudice, or the typical castigation of blames on the basis that they do not share the same ethnicity, region, or religion as ours. We must extend the same to ministers, special advisers, commissioners, local government chairpersons, council members, Vice-Chancellors, heads of MDAs, and other public and political office holders.

Also, we must be ready to acknowledge our faults along crossed lines of general misdeeds to turn the country around for the better. We must eradicate and expunge activities that have allowed some to refer to the country as a failed state. Joseph Conrad once said, "The belief in a supernatural source of evil is not necessary; men alone are quite capable of every wickedness." That is the case with our fellow citizens who believe that the "blood money" phenomenon only applies to human killings to evoke a spiritual connection to obtain financial, material or political success as depicted by Nollywood or television actors. Their father, who took a road construction contract and used the money to send them through school and live a life of comfort at the expense of innocent souls, is enough proof that blood money exists. As depicted by Nollywood, the "village witch" is not the only killer of dreams. A woman who denies qualified persons their rightful admission to an educational institution and replaces them with her unqualified children of cronies is the real-life killer of dreams. All these must change for the better. The country must continue to move forward, with corrective measures occurring right from individuals to our homes, streets, the community, nation and everywhere we find ourselves.

I am deeply concerned that Nigerians are in captivity all over the world. I am worried that many Nigerians are mentally enslaved by forces that should typically serve as a guide to freedom and liberty. For reasons bordering on religion, culture, tradition, circumstances, or outright crime, Nigerians are in one form of bondage or the other. I am worried about the high rate of our citizens languishing in jails across the world, many of whom I have gathered could be innocent but unable to get fair trials. I am concerned about the large population of those remanded in our prison centres across the country's geographical corners, 70% of whom are said to be awaiting trial for several years.

Finally, as we all should, I am worried about the alarming rate of disunity among us as a people. I am deeply troubled by the fact that we have allowed the intrinsic and unavoidable phenomenon of human disagreements to be treated as one that must result in violence and bloodshed. I am troubled that we now wake up from our beds to bear unwarranted hate and bitterness against fellow brothers and sisters with whom we do not share an association. We do this based on inciteful messages that had been pierced into their hearts by extremely wicked and divisive elements. The rising cases of violence of all kinds and other reprehensible crimes against man and God in our various societies are intolerable and inexcusable. I am worried that these situations will continue to set our nation back; even worrisome is that no nation on earth can progress when inhabitants take up arms against one another, especially based on untrue perceptions and misleading beliefs.

In truth, as humans, we will inevitably disagree, especially in a multicultural nation like ours. Where we disagree, we must learn to disagree courteously and in the most civilised and responsible manner. Constructive disagreements mean reshaping ourselves, looking outwards and responding to the crises surrounding us with the love of God and the peace and unity that we can achieve. We must disagree with the sole purpose of agreeing and helping each other to identify the common goal of progress, even if we cannot achieve conformity. Also, I do strongly believe that we can achieve peace and progress by not allowing elements of darkness to lead us into doom. Contrariwise, we cannot expect peace and progress by allowing bloodthirsty, selfish, greedy and depraved souls to speak on our behalf at the table of peace and progress.

There are massive challenges before us in a world where egoism, compulsive atomisation and anti-pluralistic ideologies are becoming bigger threats to our collective existence. I implore us to continue ensuring that differences in ideals are not interpreted as threats. Disagreements with other groups must not be perceived as affronts to our identity or existence. Through our shared, inspired, and genuine attempt to foster a spirit of national reconciliation, we will be able to understand that the image of God can be seen in every tongue and society. We will also understand that differences in tongue and creed are insufficient and invalid to be the basis for unwarranted animosity and bloodshed anywhere in our nation, or this world for that matter.

As I noted earlier, some of our problems are universal; and others are unique to climes like ours. Today, some saner climes are confronted with problems that have replaced those currently experienced by us. Sadly, those problems faced by civilised nations are not captured in this book or its prequel, as we are decades behind the sort of civilisation that should warrant such problems be matters of conversation in contemporary Nigeria. Despite being blessed with enormous human and natural resources, we have been greatly affected by problems other climes have dealt with and moved past and beyond. That is all we need to conclude that, collectively, we are far behind progress and decades behind civilisation.

INDEX

BIBLIOGRAPHY

Adetunji-Adeoye, John Walker, How We Destroy Nigeria: Precedence of Doom, Ascology Ltd, (2022).

Ellis, Stephen, This Present Darkness: A History of Nigerian Organised Crime, Oxford University Press. Kindle Edition.

Maier, Karl, This House Has Fallen: Nigerian in Crisis. Penguin Books, (2000).

Okonjo-Iweala, Ngozi, Fighting Corruption Is Dangerous: The Story Behind the Headlines, The MIT Press, (2020).

Akinola, Bolaji, Authority Stealing: How Greedy Politicians and Corporate Executives Loot the World'S Most Populous Black Nation. AuthorHouse (2012).

APNEWS, MICHELLE FAUL, Failure of BCCI Seen as Plot Against Third World With AM-BCCI, (August 1, 1991).

PMNEWS, Joe Abah, Ghost worker scam: Why people are fighting BVN-linked IPPIS, (May, 19 2020).

Institute For War & Peace Reporting, Joe Agbro, Nigeria's Romance with Marijuana (January 20, 2015).

ALJAZEERA, Philip Obaji Jr, Survivors of Nigeria's 'baby factories' share their stories (May 3, 2020)

UNODC, Trafficking in Persons and Smuggling of Migrants, Prevention of human trafficking. https://unodc.org/nigeria/en/prevention-of-human-trafficking.html

Historical Association, The Voice of History, Steven Pierce, Legacies of the Cement Armada, (August 20, 2021).

The Africa Report, Olivier Holmey, A SCANDALOUS TALE Mozambique's $2bn scandal with shipping company Privinvest and Credit Suisse (April 20, 2021).

Apex News Exclusive, Metamorphosis Of Ills In Our Society – A Historical Excursion At The Time, (March 27, 2021).

Anyanwu, J. C, & Uwatt, U. B. BANKING FOR THE POOR: THE CASE OF THE PEOPLE's BANK OF NIGERIA. African Review of Money Finance and Banking, 1, 87–103. (1993)

Nwosu, N. I, THE POLITICS OF OIL SUBSIDY IN NIGERIA. Africa: Rivista Trimestrale Di Studi e Documentazione Dell'Istituto Italiano per l'Africa e l'Oriente, 51(1), 80–94. (1996)

The Guardian, Samson Ezea, Prevalence of internet fraud among Nigerian youths, (January 28, 2017)

Ukaegbu, C. C, Indiscipline in Nigeria: Causes, Patterns, Interventions and Implications for National Development. Issue: A Journal of Opinion, 25(1), 63–67, (1997).

Ebohon, S. I, STATE AND RENTIER CAPITALISM IN NIGERIA: THE POLITICAL ECONOMY OF HYDROCARBON NATIONALISM AND DEPENDENCE REPRODUCTION. Journal of Third World Studies, 30(1), 209–234. (2013).

A Publication of Human and Environmental Development Agenda, A COMPENDIUM OF 100 HIGH PROFILE CORRUPTION CASES IN NIGERIA, 3rd Edition, (November 22, 2019)

News Sources:

BBC News

BBC News Pidgin

Businessday NG

Champion Newspapers

Channels Television

Daily Champion

Daily Trust

EFCC Media & Publicity

Nigerian Tribune:

PM NEWS

Premium Times

Punchng.com

Reuters

The Cable

The Guardian Nigeria:

The Nation

The New York Times

The Sun Nigeria

The Washington Post

TIME

US Department of Justice, Office of Public Affairs

Vanguard

Corruption Cases Database - https://corruptioncases.ng

NOTES

CHAPTER 1: HOW WE SABOTAGE NIGERIA'S ECONOMY

[1] Ellis, p. 295
[2] http://www.nigeriahc.org.uk/economy
[3] YouTube: Kemi Adeosun was speaking at "The Platform" organised by the Covenant Christian Centre
[4] Ibid
[5] https://nairametrics.com/2021/01/19/nigeria-spends-n29-trillion-on-recurrent-non-debt-expenditure-in-last-10-years/
[6] BBC News, November 24, 2003
[7] Information from General Authority for Statistics, Kingdom of Saudi Arabia
[8] Information from https://www.india.gov.in/nsso-reports-publications
[9] The Sun Nigeria, January 25, 2017
[10] The Cable, May 3, 2016
[11] https://twitter.com/renoomokri/status/727554019397361664
[12] https://nhcarnival.org/ and https://nationaltoday.com/notting-hill-carnival/
[13] https://tfconsultancy.co.uk/reports/nottinghillcarnival.pdf and https://www.london.gov.uk/decisions/md2425-notting-hill-carnival-2019-2020-and-2021
[14] The Financial Times, The money and politics behind the Notting Hill Carnival, August 24, 2018
[15] The World Bank Data: Agricultural raw materials exports (% of merchandise exports) - Nigeria
[16] UN Department of Economic and Social Affair New York: Review of Economic Activity In Africa 1950 To 1954, Supplement to World Economic Report, 1953-54
[17] PricewaterhouseCoopers, Unlocking Nigeria's Agricultural Exports, 2019

[18] Former Finance Minister, Audu Ogbeh in an interview with The Guardian Nigeria Newspaper on December 31, 2018

[19] In quick succession, Econet, MTEL and MTN were the first three private companies to be granted a license the Global System for Communication (GSM) operations in the country. Globacom and Etisalat soon followed.

[20] GGFR, World Bank Reports: Global Gas Flaring, Tracker Report (APRIL 2021)

[21] Information from https://gasflaretracker.ng

[22] NBC New York, September 27, 2012

[23] The Guardian Nigeria, May 8, 2021

[24] The Guardian, October 26, 2020
   Businessday NG, November 8, 2020

[25] Information from the Debt Management Office Nigeria and the World Bank Report

[26] Mr Brian Sedgemore was speaking at the UK House of Commons on 8th November 1985.

[27] Ibid

[28] YouTube: Babangida's interview with the BBC - https://www.youtube.com/wacatch?v=erQXfphTsfQ

[29] Vanguard, July 31, 2021

[30] Guardian UK, February 9, 2005

[31] Ibid

[32] Statistics from the World Bank are used and can be found using the below access links:
   https://data.worldbank.org/indicator/IT.MLT.MAIN?locations=US
   https://data.worldbank.org/indicator/IT.MLT.MAIN?locations=NG
   https://data.worldbank.org/indicator/IT.MLT.MAIN?locations=FR
   https://data.worldbank.org/indicator/IT.MLT.MAIN?locations=ZA

CHAPTER 2: FINANCIAL CRIMES AND CORRUPTION

[1] Oxford Advanced Leaner's Dictionary, International Student Edition

[2] Oxford Advanced Leaner's Dictionary, International Student Edition

[3] Dow Jones, Risk & Compliance Glossary, https://www.dowjones.com/professional/risk/glossary/financial-crime/

[4] Shang-Jin Wei, Corruption in Economic Development: Beneficial Grease, Minor Annoyance, or Major Obstacle?, (November 1999)

[5] Stanislav Andreski, The African Predicament: A Study in the Pathology of Modernisation, (London, 1968), p. 120

[6] NBCNews.com, November 18, 2015
Qz.com, November 26, 2015

[7] Ibid

[8] Terisa Turner, "Commercial Capitalism and the 1975 Coup", in Panter-Brick (ed.), Soldiers and Oil, pp. 166–97

[9] The Los Angeles Times, September 22, 1985
https://www.theyworkforyou.com/debates/?id=1985-11-08a.255.0

[10] APNews, August 1, 1991

[11] Ellis, p. 290

[12] A mathematical sum of $2 million per day was calculated, an astronomical figure in 1975.

[13] Nigerian Tribune, October 10, 2018

[14] Okonjo-Iweala, p. 95

[15] Vanguard, February 28, 2016

[16] The Premium Times, December 27, 2016

[17] Vanguard, January 2, 2021

[18] Okonjo-Iweala, p. 91

[19] Ibid

[20] The Financial Times, July 11, 2020

[21] Akinsola, p. 155

[22] Okonjo-Iweala, p. 100

[23] Ibid

[24] The Premium Times, November 5, 2019

[25] Okonjo-Iweala, p. 83

[26] The Africa Report, April 20, 2021

[27] Ibid

[28] Okonjo-Iweala, p. 88

[29] https://ndic.gov.ng/failure-resolution/closed-financial-institutions

[30] https://www.worldbank.org/en/publication/gfdr/gfdr-2016/background/banking-crisis

[31] Lagos State's budget (the highest budgetary expenditure in the country) had a N405 billion budget allocation for 2009

[32] Facts and figures used here are contained in the 2015 and 2020 annual reports released by the Nigeria Deposit Insurance Corporation (NDIC)

[33] Ibid

[34] FTC.Gov, Federal Trade Commission, $586 million Western Union settlement: Be careful about the company your company keeps (January 19, 2017)

US Department of Justice, Office of Public Affairs press release, January 19, 2017

[35] The Washington Post, November 8, 2018

http://moneygramremission.com/case-documents.aspx

[36] Obtained from a lecture delivered by UNODC Executive Director, Antonio Maria Costa titled; Anti-Corruption Climate Change: it started in Nigeria. 6th National Seminar on Economic Crime, Abuja, (November 13, 2007)

[37] Okonjo-Iweala, p. 35

[38] BBC News, March 15, 2016

[39] Okonjo-Iweala, p. 50

[40] Okonjo-Iweala, p. 51

[41] The Cable, July 13, 2020

Channels Television, July 17, 2020,
https://www.youtube.com/watch?v=Ty_VX1jeznA

[42] U.S. Securities and Exchange Commission, December 11, 2008, 2008-293

[43] Ibid

[44] https://legalpediaonline.com/corruption-in-criminal-justice-administration-in-nigeria/#_ftnref253

[45] Ibid

[46] A Publication of Human and Environmental Development Agenda, A Compendium Of 100 High Profile Corruption Cases in Nigeria.

[47] Investopedia.com, Enron Scandal: The Fall of a Wall Street Darling, (November 26, 2021)

[48] Ibid

[49] BBC News, August 3, 2021

CNBC, Ten Years Later, Some Press a Different View of Enron, (December 2, 2011)

[50] Vanguard, March 8, 2022

CHAPTER 3: FINANCIAL CRIMES AND CORRUPTION II

[1] Ellis, p. 40
[2] Ibid
[3] Ellis, p. 17
[4] Colonial Reports, LAGOS No. 321, GENERAL REPORT FOR 1899, p. 26
[5] Interview granted to The Sun by Major Mustapha Jokolo
[6] BBC News, November 25, 2011
[7] United Nations Office on Drugs and Crime: As assessed on https://www.unodc.org/unodc/en/human-trafficking/human-trafficking.html
[8] Ellis, pp 52-54
[9] Colonial Reports, Nigeria No. 1710, GENERAL REPORT FOR 1934, p. 82
[10] Adetunji-Adeoye, p. 12
[11] The Royal Institute of International Affairs: Nigeria-Related Financial Crime and Its Links with Britain, An Africa Programme Report by Michael Peel, (November 2006), p. 14
[12] Ibid
[13] Channels Television, February 1, 2022, https://www.youtube.com/watch?v=VAaaYR51rEs
[14] Nollywood Comedian Babatunde "Baba Suwe" Omidina, popularised the term in a movie titled Ogede Didun.
[15] https://www.wired.com/2004/01/netherlands-nabs-nigeria-scammers/
[16] The Royal Institute of International Affairs, Nigeria-Related Financial Crime and Its Links With Britain, An Africa Programme Report by Michael Peel, (November 2006)
MailOnline UK, November 19, 2006
[17] The Guardian UK, July 22, 2005
[18] MailOnline UK, November 19, 2006
https://www.wired.com/2004/01/netherlands-nabs-nigeria-scammers/
[19] Ibid
[20] BBC News, April 17, 2012
[21] Ibid

22 Africanews.com, June 19, 2020
23 US Department of Justice, U.S. Attorney's Office press release, June 18, 2020
24 https://www.emirates247.com/crime/local/operation-fox-hunt-2-dubai-police-take-down-hushpuppi-woodberry-ten-international-cybercriminals-2020-06-28-1.695146
25 US Department of Justice, U.S. Attorney's Office press release, July 28, 2021
26 The Premium Times, March 2, 2017
27 The Guardian Nigeria, September 14, 2021
28 The Guardian UK, Buhari agrees Nigeria is corrupt, but how is he tackling it? (May 11, 2016)
29 US Department of Justice, U.S. Attorney's Office of Public Affairs, June 28, 2012
30 The New York Times, October 14, 2015
31 The Guardian Nigeria, February 5, 2017
32 https://www.voanews.com/amp/a-13-2007-04-30-voa5-66712357/559902.html
33 YouTube: https://www.youtube.com/watch?v=HzEyfAmAzOk
    Facebook:
https://www.facebook.com/bbcnewsyoruba/videos/2218739368264675
34 BBC News Pidgin, May 13, 2018

CHAPTER 4: SCHADENFREUDE AND DESTRUCTIVE ACTIVISM

1 Vanguard, September 30, 2010
2 Okonjo-Iweala, p. 17
3 Adetunji-Adeoye, p. 67, 187
4 Okonjo-Iweala, p. 27
5 Ibid
6 Brookings Opinion-Ed, Nelipher Moyo and Vera Songwe, Removal of Fuel Subsidies in Nigeria: An Economic Necessity and a Political Dilemma (Tuesday, January 10, 2012)

CHAPTER 5: CHALLENGES OF MUDDLED NATION

[1] Council for Advancement and Support of Education, Giving to U.S. Higher Education Rose Nearly 7% to $52.9 Billion, (February 16, 2022) Forbes.com: Philanthropy for U.S. Colleges Up 6.9% In 2021; Tops $52 Billion (February 17, 2022)

[2] Information used here was accessed from https://www.nacubo.org/Research/2021/Public-NTSE-Tables

[3] https://stats.oecd.org/glossary/detail.asp?ID=1978

[4] UN Department of Economic and Social Affairs: Integrating population issues into sustainable development, including the post-2015 development agenda. P. 39

[5] https://eartheclipse.com/environment/problems-of-overpopulation.html

[6] Channels Television, https://www.youtube.com/watch?v=EgkZRFaaQ8I

[7] Ibid

[8] Facebook, https://fb.watch/aLStliv60X/

[9] Channels Television, January 29, 2020
YouTube: https://www.youtube.com/watch?v=RG_ybSn5Mh4

[10] Ibid

[11] Punch: February 10, 2020

[12] Muhammad Sanusi II was speaking at the Inaugural Annual Colloquium during his 60th birthday celebration on August 15, 2021

[13] BBC Sounds, Former president, Chief Olusegun Obasanjo, was talking with BBC's Stephen Sackur. https://www.bbc.co.uk/sounds/play/w3csty5d

[14] Ibid

[15] ibid

[16] Statistics from World Bank, United Nations and Statista were used in the compilation of these figures and stats.

[17] The Shillong Times, A CULTURE OF INDISCIPLINE, April 21, 2021

[18] https://www.unicef.org/nigeria/water-sanitation-and-hygiene

[19] The ITT (International Thief Thief) album by Fela was intentional vilification of Chief MKO Abiola and the telecoms company, Internal Telephone & Telegraph. Abiola was the company's Chief Executive Officer in Nigeria.

[20] Maier, p. 60
[21] Ibid
[22] YouTube: Babangida's interview with the BBC -
https://www.youtube.com/wacatch?v=erQXfphTsfQ